Non-dualism in Eckhart, Julian of Norwich and Traherne

Non-dualism in Eckhart, Julian of Norwich and Traherne

A Theopoetic Reflection

James Charlton

BLOOMSBURY

NEW YORK · LONDON · NEW DELHI · SYDNEY

Bloomsbury Academic
An imprint of Bloomsbury Publishing Inc

1385 Broadway	50 Bedford Square
New York	London
NY 10018	WC1B 3DP
USA	UK

www.bloomsbury.com

Bloomsbury is a registered trade mark of Bloomsbury Publishing Plc

First published 2013
Paperback edition first published 2014

Selections from Meister Eckhart: The Essential Sermons, Commentaries, Treatises and
Defense, E. Colledge & B. McGinn (trans.), Paulist Press, New York, 1981,
used by permission of Paulist Press.

Selections from Julian of Norwich: Showings, E. Colledge & J. Walsh (trans.),
Paulist Press, Mahwah, NJ, 1978, used by permission of Paulist Press.
Selections from Meister Eckhart: Teacher and Preacher, B. McGinn (ed.), with F. Tobin &
E. Borgstadt, Paulist Press, New York, 1986, used by permission of Paulist Press.
Selections from Thomas Traherne: Centuries, Poems, and Thanksgivings,
2 volumes, H.M. Margoliouth (ed.), Oxford University Press, London, 1958,
used by permission of Oxford University Press.

Selections from Thomas Traherne: Poems, Centuries and Three Thanksgivings, A. Ridler, Oxford
University Press, London, 1966, used by permission of Oxford University Press.

Library of Congress Cataloging-in-Publication Data
Charlton, James, 1947-
Non-dualism in Eckhart, Julian of Norwich, and Traherne: a theopoetic reflection/James Charlton.
p. cm.
Includes bibliographical references (p.) and index.
ISBN 978-1-4411-5263-3 (hardcover: alk. paper) 1. Dualism. 2. Hinduism–Relations–
Christianity. 3. Christianity and other religions–Hinduism. 4. Eckhart, Meister, d. 1327.
5. Julian, of Norwich, b. 1343. 6. Traherne, Thomas, d. 1674. I. Title.
B812.C49 2012
147′.3–dc23
2012020951

ISBN: HB: 978-1-4411-5263-3
PB: 978-1-6289-2133-5

Typeset by Newgen Imaging Systems Pvt Ltd, Chennai, India

Contents

Acknowledgements

These reflections are indebted to Wayne Hudson, Lucy Tatman and Anna Alomes. Their dynamic, relational world views have nurtured me spiritually and intellectually. I am also thankful to Gerard Hall and Veronica Brady for their insights and suggestions. I thank Antony Bellette for sharing his expertise on Traherne and for allowing unrestrained access to a private collection of manuscripts and books. And I thank Sonja Vanderaa, whose clarity and active compassion unveils the inner power of others.

I gratefully acknowledge the generosity of many authors and publishers in allowing me to quote from their books. Particular thanks is due to Paulist Press and to Oxford University Press for providing primary source material. Wherever I have tried and failed to contact authors or their estates, I ask forgiveness. I am also grateful to the people at Bloomsbury Publishing, New York, for their support of this project and for their careful attention to detail. In particular, I wish to thank Haaris Naqvi and Ally Jane Grossan. In addition, for skilful and efficient copyediting and indexing, I thank Srikanth Srinivas and Justin Heinzekehr, respectively.

There are many references to various scriptures in this book. I offer these texts for their perspectival integrity, not as 'the proof' of anything.

Abbreviations

BgG (or Gītā):	Bhagavad Gītā
Gk:	Greek
KJV:	King James Version
L:	Latin
LT:	Julian's Long Text
MHG:	Middle High German
NJB:	New Jerusalem Bible
NT:	New Testament
NRSV:	New Revised Standard Version
REB:	Revised English Bible
Skt:	Sanskrit
ST:	Julian's Short Text
Up:	Upanishad

Introduction

The great religions are the ships;
poets are the lifeboats.
Every person I know has jumped overboard.

— Hafiz (Daniel Ladinsky, trans.)

The metaphorical process of poetry is the natural predecessor and the continuing ally of theology. At its best, theology has always probed ultimate questions with an awareness of its own dependence on metaphor. Sensing the role of imaginative intuition, good theologies are rightly chary of putting forward absolute certitudes. Aware of the necessity of creativity in theologizing, Stanley R. Hopper writes as follows:

> When language fails to function at the metaphorical or symbolic levels, the imagination goes deeper, soliciting the carrying power of archetype, translating the archetype from spent symbolic system into fresh embodiments.[1]

Theopoetic writing consciously includes the attempts of the imagination, rather than of logic or of analytical reason, to express the Inexpressible. The current return to theopoetics was famously foregrounded by Emerson who asserted that theology and philosophy would one day be taught by poets. Within its hybridized, sometimes unorthodox, ways of attempting the impossible, theopoetic readings of texts may be presented, represented, interpreted against the apparent grain and laced with titbits of personal experience. Relevant nouns include the following: 'intersection', 'interpellation' 'connection' and 'reconnection'.[2]

This book responds to the neglect of what could be termed 'spiritual non-dualism' in the Western heritage. Whatever the reasons for this, it is not my intention to address any damage caused by excessively dualistic patterns. Rather, I intend to bring to the fore the non-dual tone of Thomas Traherne, Meister Eckhart and Mother Julian of Norwich. They share what might be described as qualified or moderate non-dualism. They also share a concern for unitive spiritual experience, expressed in their attempts to balance an absolute level of truth with a conventional level of truth. On their view, the *conditio sine qua non* of 'being human' is participation in the divine.

For present purposes, the term 'non-dual' implies bringing the subject (e.g. the Source or the One) and the object (e.g. a worshipper of the Source) more closely together.[3]

Although aware of the usefulness of dualism, and of the subject/object distinction in particular, these reflections should be viewed as a countervailing perspective. Traherne's type of non-dualism could be nominated as 'experiential non-dualism' in partial distinction from the more 'conceptual non-dualism' of Eckhart and perhaps Julian. But labelling of this kind is less than satisfactory. Neither writer defines the sense (or senses) in which they favour non-dualism. They are unlikely to share an identical non-dual stance, and their individual views might oscillate between various meanings.[4] Their intention is to awaken their hearers and readers, not to a conceptual understanding of non-dualism, but to what they understand as Christocentric non-dual experience.[5]

The focus of Chapter 1 is on Traherne. Chapter 2 goes backward in time to focus on the work of Eckhart. Chapter 3 moves slightly forward in time to concentrate on Julian. Chapter 4 develops the understanding that a non-dual approach to life involves *kenosis*, the practice of self-reduction in order to allow space and time for the care of 'the other'. The fifth and final chapter offers 'awakening' as an implied theme of the previous four chapters. My own poetry is deployed, where it might interweave the work of Traherne, Eckhart and Julian, or otherwise advance the recovery of non-dual vision and non-dual action within bodily spiritual life.

Distinctively, Traherne begins with recreations of a child's sense of non-duality. He keeps imaginative truth in tension with conceptual truth; he keeps experiential truth in tension with both. Accordingly his poetry moves between a claimed experience of 'oneness' with the divine and an experience of 'otherness' from the divine. The experience of 'not twoness' might be said to equate with a kind of inner resurrection or ongoing process of identification with the Source. All of my chosen writers share the implicit notion that as we 'resurrect' from a sense of 'twoness', we are more likely to respond with inclusive love. I picture them as re-weaving 'feeling' with 'thought' and as re-weaving spirituality with theology. The divine and the human are understood to share something fundamental: Both are constituted by relationship. Here I aspire to be faithful to theology as practical philosophy. I also desire to be true to an understanding of *perichoresis*,[6] the 'inter-permeating' life of the divine, as signalled by the Christian theopoem of the Trinity. The enactment of *kenosis* leads into a *perichoretic* life. Both are linked to the imaginative openness and acceptance associated with authentic lived experience.[7]

Traherne was active in the Commonwealth era of English history and in the Restoration period (Charles the Second). His origins remain obscure; it is known that he attended Brasenose College in Oxford. The records of the college imply that he was probably born in 1637. He graduated BA in 1656 and MA in 1661. Documents of the Church of England state that he was appointed to the parish of Credinhill, in the county of Hereford in 1657 although he was not ordained as a priest until about 3 years later. Traherne left his rural parish in 1669, having been appointed as a private chaplain to one of the king's functionaries in London, the Lord Keeper of the Seal (Sir Orlando Bridgeman). The last years of his life were spent with the Bridgeman family in their home in Teddington (then a village on the outskirts of London). He died in 1674 and was buried within the local church.

The literary era in which Traherne lived was dominated by the names of Milton, Dryden and Marvell. Compared with these writers, he is idiosyncratic. His style and diction set him apart; his enthusiasm is unrestrained. And yet his vitality is curiously fused with abstraction; it would seem that his poetry is laced with theology, both heterodox and orthodox.[8] He employs various modes and covers diverse subjects, but seldom raises contemporary issues. As far as the poems are concerned, he gives us little clue as to the upheavals of seventeenth-century European history.

Eckhart was born in the village of Hochheim in Germany in about 1260. He became a friar of the Dominican Order, later graduating in theology/philosophy from the University of Paris. This entitled Eckhart to be known by the academic title of Meister. He quickly became popular as a preacher, lecturer and debater, in Paris and in large areas of Germany. The year and place of his death is uncertain; leading Eckhartian scholars suggest 1328. He is thought, at an early age, to have been influenced by the scholarship of Albert the Great and by a group of broad-minded Dominicans who gathered around Albert in Germany. They were appreciative, not only of Neoplatonism, but of Jewish and Islamic philosophy, as well. Eckhart probably represents the closest Western analogue to the *Advaita Vedānta* of Ramana Maharshi (1879–1950). I wish to advance the idea that Ramana, Eckhart, Julian and Traherne share an emphasis on unitive reality or unitive consciousness. Further, I suggest that they share an 'internalist' emphasis on inner transformation. Their view is that every person can enter a life of participation with the divine. We are all invited to join the life which is boundless, formless and characterized by limitless Awareness.[9] Such is the human *raison d'être*.

Julian's now famous book is accepted as one of the first European prose works written by a woman. Born in 1342 (about 13 years after the death of Eckhart), Julian died between 1416 and 1420. She wrote *Showings* (or *Revelations of Divine Love*) while living as an anchoress in a cell attached to St Julian's Church, in the city of Norwich in the English county of Norfolk. The book consists of reflections on what she describes as 16 visions of the Passion. She states that she experienced these visions during severe illness in 1373. The intended readers of Julian's *Showings*, in both its short and long versions, were 'God's faithful lovers'. This is made clear in a brief but anonymous introduction to her fourteenth-century manuscript. Until last century, the number of the book's readers, whether faithful lovers of God or not, was modest.

As inferred earlier, Chapter 4 elaborates my readings of Traherne, Eckhart and Julian to the effect that non-dual experience leads to a self-abandoning (*kenotic*) life. These writers are interested in 'a true identity' emerging from 'a false identity'.[10] I intend to make use of the concepts of true and false self. Although this particular dualism might find its analogy in Eastern traditions, the intention will not be comparative. Different texts rely on different conceptions; comparison is not appropriate.[11] There are, admittedly, pitfalls to any discussion about a true and a false self, especially if one's imaginings are confined to a hypothetical, 'inner reserve' of separateness from the world.[12] And it would be rash to declare that the non-dualism of Traherne, Eckhart and Julian parallels the dominant non-dualism of 'the East'. But a *congruency of sympathy* is evident, although the metaphysical presuppositions differ. I suggest conjunctions between the work of the three Europeans and some of the teachings of

Ramana Maharshi. He was not a traditional *Advaitin*. He did not feel bound by cultural accretions or 'externalist' practices. But he brought to *Advaita Vedānta* a universalist tone, while retaining a classical view of the non-dual, supreme Self (capital 'S') and of spiritual awakening.

It is well known that religious writers within various Asian traditions conduct their work, strategically, at the absolute truth-level as well as at the conventional truth-level. Traherne, Eckhart and Julian do the same. This is not surprising. Since its early centuries, Christianity has made use of the concept of two truths. It has also made use of non-dualism. Evidence for this can be found in the Gospel accounts.[13] Jesus is represented as teaching in a way that was considered transgressive by the power brokers of his day. He provided an alternative to the traditional dualistic approaches.

Traherne attempts to bridge the concepts of immanence and transcendence, where 'transcendence' refers to a form of existence which is 'other' than humankind. Immanence refers to the ongoing embodiment of transcendence. That is to say, immanence implies the earthly and day-to-day 'arrival' of whatever is meant by transcendence. Paradoxically, Traherne would seem to regard the transcendent as participating *within* immanence. He appears, with Julian and Eckhart, to assume that the divine exists both outside the world and inside it. The divine remains transcendent and yet can be encountered within the world of nature and culture.

All three writers naturally attempt to find a balance between transcendence and immanence. Their God is the One Source, who is non-totalitarian and not abstracted from embodied life.[14] Humanity is deemed to find its integrity, its true self, in bodily relation to the One Source, conceived as both transcendent and immanent. Hence transcendence is manifest in immanent ways, including solidarity with all humanity.[15] A demanding 'activity' from humanity's perspective, practical transcendence is understood to be within life rather than beyond it. A feature, therefore, of the theopoetic work of Traherne, Eckhart and Julian, is their tempering of the abstract with the quotidian; indeed, with the bodily and the instinctual. They evince a pastoral intention which is based on the view that humanity, to be true to itself, must participate in three dimensions: reason, emotion and faith. They recognize that the eye of faith can degenerate into delusion or illusion, when severed from reason and emotion.

A 'metaphysics of participation' is of vital importance today, in my view. It would appear to be relevant, even in versions of theology which are regarded as post-metaphysical. Participation is basic to theopoetics. And theopoems are a natural dancing floor, so to speak, for the tender gyrations between transcendence and immanence. The dancing is experienced as an embodied way of being, and then, as an incarnational way of *seeing*. As theopoetics becomes more widely 'named' as such (for its attempt to say the unsayable, and then to unsay it),[16] differing perspectives will continue to emerge. An expansive theopoem which takes a *perichoretic* approach to 'construing God' will place communion within the divine heart. The word *perichoresis* is from the Greek '*chorus*' (which literally means 'dance') and '*peri*' (which means 'around'). For Christians *perichoresis* came to mean the interpenetration of the three 'persons' who are imagined as comprising the Source of All.[17] The word can also evoke the interpenetration of all creation by the Source, which is said to coinhere in all things.[18] The *perichoretic* notion points, therefore, to relationality in God and to a divine passion for relationship with all creation.[19]

Richard Kearney pictures *perichoresis* as 'God-play'. He writes of '. . . a circular movement where Father, Son, and Spirit gave place to each other in a gesture of reciprocal dispossession rather than fusing into a single substance'.[20] A well-known visual expression of 'God-play' is the icon *The Holy Trinity*, painted by Andrei Rublev (d.1430). To spend time with this icon is to see three figures which are distinct, yet not separate. Even as they sit together, they defer to each other. The atmosphere is calm, yet there is interaction or interplay; indeed, a calm but vibrant, circulatory exchange of energy. I will return to Rublev's visual theopoem in Chapter 4.

Traherne, Eckhart and Julian share the Rublevian concern with communion. If spiritual life is a movement towards (re)union with the Source, it implies a 'dynamic wholeness' which is prefigured within this world. The life of Jesus can thus be viewed as a mirror of the life of each person. In a mysterious, non-dual way, human beings are understood to be participants in the life, death and renewed life of Jesus. This is the primary theopoem of Christian tradition; it is not located elsewhere, but is grounded in life's perpetual 'now-ness'. Based in participatory consciousness, it is a theopoem with a unifying and transformative vision.

A claim of grace-given incorporation within the Source has long been recognized in Eckhart. But the non-dual tone of Traherne and Julian has either been insufficiently recognized or overlooked. A burgeoning popular literature on Julian highlights her refreshing emphasis on feminine images for the divine. This is sometimes held to be her greatest contribution. Julian's non-dual aspect and her resonance with her near-contemporary Eckhart (and much later with Traherne) tends to be set to one side. Her work does not seem to have been known by Traherne, but given that he could read Greek, Latin, Italian and French, it is probable that he had access to the Latin works of Eckhart.

Expressions within Christianity of the mystery of 'not twoness' are as old as the statements attributed to Jesus which have a non-dual tone. Reconstructed in the four Gospels, these statements are the poetic, epigrammatic and parabolic legacy of Jesus and imply a reversal of contemporary dualisms. Various situations are reversed; people do not receive their just deserts; the official guests at a wedding are marginalized; homeless people are embraced; the established economic order becomes unworkable. People listening to Jesus are invited to place themselves within the 'is-ness' of the moment. They are stimulated to view life as an opening out of relationships. The Source of all relationality is construed as true and just, but not according to the standards of the dualistic, contingent and impermanent world.[21]

A moderate non-dualism does not carry with it a complete and definitive code of belief or behaviour. It perhaps implies that any final appeal to external authority holds the risk of becoming untenable. Within such a frame, there is less emphasis on the attainment of supposedly higher moral standards, and more emphasis on expressions of the unitive mystery. Efforts to inculcate higher standards, as if by decree, are seen as moralism; moralism, in turn, is seen as an exclusion of reciprocity and, therefore, communion.[22]

Traherne expresses a hunger for 'co-union' with the Source. He comes close to claiming that you and I can be incorporated within the Source. This amounts to an assertion of mystical knowledge, even when allowance is made for the imprecision of the word 'mystical'. Many of us might be uncomfortable with such an assertion. We are indebted to Kant and are sceptical concerning ancient writers who might credulously assume 'a God's eye view of the world'. The question might largely be one of perceptual experience; Traherne, Eckhart and Julian hint at a particular kind of awareness. It is an awareness that emerges from a non-dual tendency and includes a concern that humanity's lived experience should be one of true and just relations. A spiritual quality obviously interweaves a concern for relationality. In Traherne, Eckhart and Julian this moves beyond 'relationship' and heads in the direction of 'identity'. Therefore, within their varied conceptions, my chosen theopoets favour a move beyond a 'relationship' with Jesus the Christ, towards 'identity' with him. If they do not use the word 'identity', this is my reading of their implication. On this interpretation, Christianity is less a reiteration of 'belief' than a communication of *being* Christ to the other, who is also 'Christ'.[23]

Traherne differs from Eckhart and Julian, who in turn differ from each other. But all three base their lives and their writings upon a sense of divine presence. They view human life as a process of returning to the Infinite One who creates consciousness. Either through an epiphanic occurrence or, more typically, through a gradual surrendering of the false self, these writers desire that we should divest ourselves of what today might be called ego-centredness. In more traditional words, they desire that we should 'Realize' (that is to say, in affective, lived experience) our grounding in non-dual or unitive consciousness. Their shared viewpoint is that by submersion in the One Spirit, within and without, we can cease to think, feel and act from a sense of separation.[24]

1

Thomas Traherne

Traherne's vision is uncommonly expansive. He resists labels and categories. He elevates the senses and sensuality; he praises embodiment. The joy-filled condition of 'felicity' (his theme-word) can be found through an active embrace of the temporal 'within' the divine and the divine 'within' the temporal. Forgetting the conventional distance between the human and the divine, Traherne loses himself in a personal blend of matter and spirit. A second theme-word will suggest itself: 'interpenetration'.

As with his predecessors Eckhart and Julian, this quirky poet-theologian sees more with the eye of the heart than with the mind of doctrine. But I hasten to add: Together with his predecessors, Traherne knows that without a doctrine, spiritual life can be reduced to the appreciation of art. Traherne venerates the given, natural world, as do the multitude of his godchildren (such as Thoreau, et al.). But he employs a deeper theopoem than many of his descendants would care for. This deeper strand might be called Christ-centredness. To Traherne, the divine is relational and therefore accessible in mutual reciprocity. Paradox of course will always attend a non-dualism which is coupled with some version of theistic transcendence.

As appears to have been the case with Eckhart and Julian, Traherne was born into a top-heavy world. That is to say, top-heavy with beliefs about divine transcendence. He seems to rediscover a joyful awareness of inherent value. Accordingly, it might clumsily be said that he finds Earth-centredness within his cosmically configured Christ-centredness. I have already implied that the tone of Traherne anticipates that of later writers, whereby the randomness of the contingent world is appreciated on its own terms. My own poem, below, owes its sensibility to Traherne, via aspects of Romanticism.

Yellow-tailed Black Cockatoos

Random as rags whooshed off a truck,
    they indolently amble on the air. This caterwaul:
      wee-la. Yes, there,

husky, high. It seems an idle sortie,
    a lope of meander-flight, a frittering in the eye
      of foul weather.

Gale winds begin to split and peel
  a suburb of weather-board husks, but the flock
    keeps following its memory-grid

to grubs in weakened trees. (Birds like these
  saw dinosaurs plod through dust.)
    They prise, rip,

rasher the acacia bark, and change trees,
  wheeling and veering like black Venetian blinds
    collapsed at one end.

Then they dip, curious,
  to an English willow;
    shimmy down bare verticals on hinge-claws;

whir out
  on a glissade of whoops:
    concertina-tailed, splay-winged, wailing.

Although Thomas Traherne is a spontaneous, vigorous poet, his work carries a consistent, theopoetic argument: All things in the universe are interconnected and inherently valuable. Ahead of his time, Traherne writes of a universal partnership. He asks his readers: 'Can you see the way things *are*? Do you not experience things as *inseparable*?' References to the natural world are frequent in Traherne, yet attenuated. His readers can provide their own contexts. Today, theopoets who lose themselves in a blend of matter and spirit will usually add more detail. In the poem above, I attempt a Trahernian openness that is both exultant and meditative.

As already hinted, Traherne does not treat the words 'God' and 'world' as denoting two completely extrinsic realities. The divine is transcendent, but not in the sense of 'floating entirely free' of this world. It is within our immanent and significant world that divine and human transcendence work together.[1] Traherne has a vision of the reciprocity of 'all Things'. It is *here* that we are able, or unable, to transcend that which defeats us. Ordinary, potentially 'Joyfull' life is where transcendence is manifested. A mushroom, an ant, a stone has inherent value. This value resides within the entities themselves; it is not merely 'endorsed' by an extrinsic God.

For most of humanity's literate history, poetry's purpose has been to contemplate the divine. In Traherne's England, this purpose included the consideration of *all life* as linked to the divine. Within such a view, each finite thing can reveal infinitude. In modernist terms, a poet might speak of 'Reality' as a stand-in for the divine and describe it as a web of singularities, none of which is completely separate, and all of which seem to be 'in process' in different ways. But Traherne (together with Eckhart and Julian)[2] uses patristic language. This includes a vision of infinite goodness; it also takes account of humanity's desire to 'find itself' within that goodness. The God of Traherne and predecessors is One, and yet triadic in manifestation. In my understanding, this means that God is held, simultaneously, to be the giver of goodness, the gift of goodness itself and the 'process of goodness-giving'. The Infinite One is 'all-ways relating'.

A devout humanist

Traherne trusts his own sensations. But this trust is not separate from trust in the divine. All five senses are part of God's way of manifestation. In the poem *My Spirit*, he regards his spirit as inseparable from the senses that pertain to that spirit. He acknowledges no ultimate separation between spirit and intellect. Both are parts of the whole; they inform each other continually. *My Spirit* appeals to me as Traherne's most overtly non-dual piece of writing. I will progressively quote most of it and venture some brief comments. Below is the opening verse and part of the closing:

> My Naked Simple Life was I.
>> That Act so Strongly Shind
> Upon the Earth, the Sea, the Skie,
> It was the Substance of my Mind.
>> The Sence of self was I.
> I felt no Dross nor Matter in my Soul,
> No Brims nor Borders, such as in a Bowl
> We see, My Essence was Capacitie.
>> That felt all Things,
>> The Thought that Springs
> Therfrom's it self. It hath no other Wings
> To Spread abroad, nor Eys to see,
> Nor Hands Distinct to feel,
>> Nor Knees to Kneel:
> But being Simple like the Deitie
>> In its own Centre is a Sphere
>> Not shut up here, but evry Where.
>
>>> O Wondrous Self! O Sphere of Light,
>>>> O Sphere of Joy most fair;
>>> O Act, O Power infinit;
>>> O Subtile, and unbounded Air!
>>>> O Living Orb of Sight!
>> Thou which within me art, yet Me! Thou Ey,
>> And Temple of his Whole Infinitie!
>> O what a World art Thou! A World within![3]

The opening line 'My Naked Simple Life was I' appears to equate Traherne's self with Life itself. The non-dual confidence of the first verse is overt. Antony Bellette[4] states that the poet identifies the phenomenal with the spiritual. That is to say, the subject matter of the poem, that which concerns 'my spirit', is inseparable from *the senses* of that spirit. Bellette continues: '. . . the poem establishes in its opening lines the almost godlike indivisibility of the person'.[5] To me, this is part of Traherne's attractiveness; he cannot separate his participation in a spiritual life from his enjoyment of the world of phenomena.

In the first verse of *My Spirit* the poet risks identifying himself with '. . . a Sphere / Not shut up here, but evry Where'. The second verse (below) speaks of the necessary action which is the outward manifestation of the 'Sphere'. The 'Centre' of the 'Sphere' now manifests as the principal 'Act'.

> Whatever it doth do,
> It doth not by another Engine work,
> But by it self; which in the Act doth lurk.
> Its Essence is Transformed into a true
>   And perfect Act.
>   And so Exact
> Hath God appeared in this Mysterious Fact,
>   That tis all Ey, all Act, all Sight, ...[6]

The third verse maintains the focus on a non-dual interaction between mind and matter. Does the reality of the world reside within the poet's mind or within the matter of the world? The question does not concern Traherne. The natural world '. . . Was all at once within me'. All natural things '. . . Were my Immediat and Internal Pleasures'. These are phrases which occur in the third verse of *My Spirit*:

> Her Store
> Was all at once within me; all her Treasures
> Were my Immediat and Internal Pleasures,
> Substantial Joys, which did inform my Mind.
>   With all she wrought,
>   My Soul was fraught,
> And evry Object in my Soul a Thought
>   Begot, or was; I could not tell,
>   Whether the Things did there
>   Themselvs appear,
> Which in my Spirit *truly* seemd to dwell;
>   Or whether my conforming Mind
>   Were not even all that therin shind.[7]

The non-dual purport is well-perceived by Bellette[8] when he says: 'In the third stanza the act of perceiving objects in the world is virtually equated with the realization of them in the mind (or soul, or spirit, the words seem interchangeable), with the result that material reality and mental act are no longer separable'. *My Spirit* exults in the reality of the material world; the poet is grateful for his 'Capacitie' to feel 'all Things' (verse one); he understands them all as originating with God's inner rationality.[9]

A few lines further on, Traherne blatantly declares that his soul is '. . . Simple like the Deitie'. Here again is a remarkable non-duality. Distinctions are blurred, as between the feeling subject and the felt object. Traherne is a participant with the divine; he shares in God's habitation within (as it were) '. . . a Sphere / Not shut up here, but evry Where'. Perhaps these risky words hint at literal translocation. The trope is repeated in the fourth verse, below. Traherne projects his happiness; he can play happily with capitalization. He now writes the words 'Evry where' instead of 'evry Where'.

> . . . my Mind was wholy Evry where
> What ere it saw, twas ever wholy there;
> The Sun ten thousand Legions off, was nigh:
> > The utmost Star,
> > Tho seen from far,
> Was present in the Apple of my Eye.
> > There was my Sight, my Life, my Sence,
> > My Substance and my Mind
> > My Spirit Shind
> Even there, not by a Transeunt Influence.
> > The Act was Immanent, yet there.
> > The Thing remote, yet felt even here.[10]

In the first two lines of this verse, Traherne puns with the word 'wholy'. His mind is not separate from whatever it is engaging with. It is a 'holy' engagement; and the wholeness or holiness is inherent to both parties engaged in the communication. The word 'twas', near the beginning of the lines just quoted, refers ambiguously to the poet's mind and to the item or object or value that his mind is connecting with. He also puns with 'Eye' (sometimes spelt as 'Ey') and 'I'. The poet claims a *seeing* and a *loving* self. His self, the 'I', sees things and then loves the things that it sees.

Here is the fifth verse of *My Spirit*.

> > O Joy! O Wonder, and Delight!
> > O Sacred Mysterie!
> > My Soul a Spirit infinit!
> > An Image of the Deitie!
> > > A pure Substantiall Light!
> That Being Greatest which doth Nothing seem!
> Why, twas my All, I nothing did esteem
> But that alone. A Strange Mysterious Sphere!
> > > A Deep Abyss
> > > That sees and is
> The only Proper Place or Bower of Bliss.
> > > To its Creator tis so near
> > > > In Lov and Excellence
> > > > > In Life and Sence,
> In Greatness Worth and Nature; And so Dear;
> > > In it, without Hyperbole,
> > > The Son and friend of God we see.[11]

Traherne writes of a soul which refuses to be intimidated by the doctrine concerning original sin. It is a prelapsarian or Edenic vision; Traherne seems unlikely to have taken a literal view on 'the Fall'. Arthur Clements praises Traherne's acceptance of both an essential self and an inherent beauty. But in a concession to an older tradition, Clements cites D. H. Lawrence to endorse the apparent viewpoint of Traherne that '. . . the isolated ego (is) a fiction, an illusion, a lesser reality – the glitter of the sun on the surface of the waters'.[12]

Non-dual lines which are less explicit than *My Spirit* are numerous, such as: 'His Name is NOW, his Nature is forever. / None Can his Creatures from their Maker Sever' (*The Anticipation*, lines 26–27).[13] When he writes 'His Name is NOW' the poet is saying, on my construal, that one side does not eclipse the other. Experiential truth and conceptual truth are brought together in a vision of transformation. The poet is attempting the apprehension of reality in the Now . . . in the Here. He writes: 'By an Act of the Understanding therefore be present now / with all the Creatures among which you live. . . . / You are never what you ought till you go out of yourself / and walk among them'.[14]

Traherne's poems can achieve the kind of testamental exuberance that theology eventually must rely on, if actual lives are to be transformed. It seems reasonable to suppose that, whatever the religion, human need will tend to gravitate towards the testimony of the transformed. Hence the debate about Western 'spiritual' non-dualism will continue. Those who believe that they can bear witness will ensure it. Traherne was an enthusiast for subjectivity, in a world becoming noisy with the claims of the new sciences. If his colleagues ever looked closely at his poetry (which seems doubtful), they would have found his non-dualism unsettling.

If Traherne is influenced in some respects by several kinds of Neoplatonism, there is no 'upward' movement of the senses towards the realm of the Idea. Rather, he views all creation as infused with a divine energy. This draws all things 'upwards', but not to an abstract Idea. Traherne believes in the aspiration of all things to recover union with God, as understood in biblically personal terms. Within himself, the poet finds no ultimate separation between intellect and spirit. Bellette[15] states that 'Reality for Traherne is not divisible in this way'. There is, instead, an adherence to a '. . . law of mutuality which unites God and man and harmonizes all imagined opposites'.[16] This outlook can be viewed as non-dual Christian materialism.[17] It lies behind my poem below.

Moments

The mind by its nature is a singulare tantum.
I should say: the overall number of minds is just one.
- Erwin Schrödinger

Back-lit by low sun,
a magpie flicks mulch aside,
brings death to a millipede,
life to a fledgling.

Nothing seems separate:
neither magpie, soil, millipede,
nor eucalypt leaves
that sweep the sky.

Such moments are antithetical
to ecstasy. Perhaps they represent
transcendence in a curious way,
by highlighting the oneness

of terrestrial history.
A myriad-formed presence,
not fully translatable
to sense,

draws me back
to animal unity.
It returns me
to the moment,

to all that any creature
ever has.

The words 'nothing separate' and 'animal unity' (above) do not imply mysticism. The intention is to reduce the gap, fostered by various religious perspectives, between 'the world' and 'the beyond'. Similarly, Traherne's trope of 'intermutual Joys' (from *Ease*, but implied throughout his work) is not inherently mystical, as popularly understood. If the term is taken to imply an interest in the ethereal, then Traherne is scarcely a mystic. His concerns lie with the sensuous beauty of the material world, as seen from a spiritual and non-dual point of view. Following Traherne, the poem of mine below tries to 'harmonize' things which might initially be considered opposites.

Bluebottle Jellyfish at Manly

A maze of withered blue balloons
and hard-to-see spaghetti
strewn on sand: something to note
but not to touch. Each bluebottle,
four creatures in one
or one in four; their birth
and fusion obscure. No-one's sure
why half their population glides
west around the seas,
the others struggling east.

> But if we ever saw
> the way things are,
> we'd know ourselves inseparable
> from bags of gas, from tentacles:
> the paralysis they promise,
> the release.

For Traherne, the word 'spiritual' does not necessarily imply the more modern sense of psychological well-being or 'soulful' potential. By 'spiritual life', Traherne tends to mean the 'pneumatic life' of experiential knowledge of oneness with divine Spirit. This becomes clearer with prolonged exposure to the poems. By 'pneumatic' I mean that he takes the Greek word *pneuma* as having found its equivalence in Christian thought as 'spirit', as distinct from *psyche* or 'soul'. And so, in a context of elevated entreaties and expostulations, Traherne attempts to recapture the unselfconscious happiness of a safe, healthy childhood. But specific details about his own life are not his main concern. Especially in *Centuries*, which consists of both prose and poetry, and in works that conform to a more regular poetic, Traherne writes for the spiritual nourishment of the reader.

Bellette observes that Traherne's eclectic work has a 'unifying direction'. This unifier is '. . . the passionate desire to experience God, world and self as one, and to embody this experience in the most effective and appropriate literary form'.[18] In accord with this desire, Traherne's work carries forward a theme '. . . of the transforming recognition of all that lies about'.[19] This is encapsulated in Traherne's use of the word 'News'. The poet desires to receive 'News' rather than, for example, mere information which might have emanated from a supposed authority.

On News

> News from a forrein Country came,
> As if my Treasure and my Wealth lay there:
> So much it did my Heart Enflame!
> Twas wont to call my Soul into mine Ear.
> Which thither went to Meet
> The Approaching Sweet:
> And on the Threshhold stood,
> To entertain the Unknown Good.
> It Hoverd there,
> As if twould leav mine Ear.
> And was so Eager to Embrace
> The Joyfull Tidings as they came,
> Twould almost leav its Dwelling Place,
> To Entertain the Same.[20]

The 'News', for Traherne, is true knowledge of the nature of things. He claims that 'Nothing is so Easy as to teach the Truth becaus the Nature of the Thing confirms the

Doctrine'.[21] But if there is false 'News' or incorrect information, then '. . . the Nature of the Thing contradicts your Words'.[22] The mind which can appreciate the nature of things is closely aligned, in Traherne's thinking, with the Mind which created those things.

Traherne's unifying direction, mentioned by Bellette, is shared by Eckhart and Julian. The three also share a meditative tradition which commonly found expression in a theme of spiritual travelling. The metaphor of spiritual life as 'a journey' was not always the cliché that it might be today. John Bunyan's *The Pilgrim's Progress* did not reach wide acclaim until the late seventeenth century. The 'travelling' in Eckhart and the others was primarily *a return* to conscious union with the divine. It is an analogue of the Self-realization (*Ātmā siddhi*) of classical *Vedānta*, wherein 'the Self' (capital 'S') or limitless Awareness is the only 'subject', within which everything else appears as an outpoured 'object'. Traherne shares with Eckhart and Julian a *Vedāntin*-like concern for the *re-cognition* and *re-animation* of God's image in humanity. This image is more than a reflective image, for when the false self reverts to primordial Realization, the true nature of humanity has (re-)emerged. Self-realization (*Atmā siddhi*) is basic to classical *Vedānta*. The origin of the term is no doubt complex; different epochs are likely to have produced different understandings. But the meaning might be summarized in a working definition as follows: An experiential knowledge of the identity of the inner and outer worlds; the identity of subject and object. In Christian terms, the emergence of humanity's true nature can imply a reversion to humanity's prelapsarian nature. On this view, 'Self-realization' might be viewed as a parallel to the 'God-likeness' attributed to the primordial couple in Eden. Within both perspectives, there is *participation* in divine activity, within all of one's *temporal* relationships. Within the NT this is summarized in 2 Pet. 1:4, wherein Christ's followers are reminded that they '. . . share in the very being of God' (REB).

I wish to underscore my view that Traherne, Eckhart and Julian share a concern to move beyond 'relationship' with Christ, towards 'identity' with Christ. On this view, Christian life is more the communication of *being* Christ, as distinct from mere belief in Christ. The paradox is that Christians are also understood to be in the process of transformation into Christ. If there is a sense I am *already* Christ, then obviously Christ is yet to be wholly *manifested*. The incarnation story remains incomplete. If I claim to be 'Christian', this will include an expectation that my body/soul is being transformed into the 'true me' which is 'Christ'. I am to relate to 'the other' as Christ relates, indeed, I am to see 'the other', and ultimately all 'others', as Christ. America's most recognizable poet, Walt Whitman (d.1892) declared that he was not a Christian. Nonetheless, he is popularly regarded as having viewed the 'others' as though they were Christ himself. The following poem of mine recalls Whitman's lived experience (during the American Civil War) of non-separation.

Letter to Walt Whitman re: Iraq

If you were there now,
you'd lie down with those
who struggle on the ground

like half-squashed worms,
down with the maimed,
misused, disowned.

If you were there now,
you'd kneel, importunate,
give yourself to silence, mutely
cradle the stomach-blown
villager.

Traherne appears to believe that the entire created order is endowed with the Eckhartian 'spark'.[23] All things participate, in measure, in the divine light. Therefore Traherne assumes that a theology of nature, in its own right, is required. In this, he moves well beyond his immediate tradition, which might be taken to assume that nature merely provides the context for humanity. Traherne assumes that a divine energy is immanent in the world of oysters, snails, badgers, fungi, herbs; even stones. If there was a traditional view of 'top down' divine condescension, Traherne wishes to balance it with the 'upward' aspiration of all things. My own theology of nature, as implied in *Sister Spider* (below) and other poems, might be more reserved on the 'upward' movement. But I hope that it shares Traherne's grounded, this-worldly emphasis. Distinctively, for the seventeenth century, his love for the world tilts his theology away from the traditional motif of 'divine descent'. He counsels:

By an Act of the Understanding therfore be present now
with all the Creatures among which you live:
and hear them in their Beings and Operations Praising GOD
in an Heavenly Maner. Som of them Vocaly,
others in their Ministery, all of them Naturaly and Continualy.[24]

In the following poem I aspire to adhere to Traherne's advice.

Sister Spider

This large, sedentary spider
        which shares our bathroom,

spending hours wiping droplets
        from her leg hair,

has a dusting of animated poppy seeds
        on her back.

Greetings, spiders, with whom we inhabit
        common space;

and potoroo and magpie, also having a part
        in us, and we with you.

Greetings to everyday epiphanies;
        not forgetting you insects,

in bodiliness our brothers;
        and you, the unseen forms

which might infect, or assist,
        being heirs with us and all the other creatures

which walk, crawl, fly, slide, multiply,
        divide or stay put;

joint heirs of such molecular inheritance
        that where our skin stops,

our bodies do not stop,
        greetings.

Traherne sees divine energy everywhere. This is not merely a poetic posture; he grounds his thinking, first, in his senses, and second, in a robust reading of scripture. By the latter, I mean that Traherne eschews quietism and any clichéd notion of humility. After his own fashioning, he might be seen as a Christian materialist; in many ways and in many lines he immerses himself in matter.[25]

It might also be said that he was a seventeenth-century naturalist and humanist, in his own manner. He has an inclination to fill a blank book with 'Profitable Wonders', as we see below.

An Empty Book is like an Infants Soul, in which any Thing
may be Written. It is Capable of all Things, but containeth Nothing.
I hav a Mind to fill this with Profitable Wonders.
And since Love made you put it into my Hands
I will fill it with those Truths you Love, without Knowing them:
and with those Things which, if it be Possible, shall shew my Lov;
To you, in Communicating most *Enriching Truths*;
to Truth, in Exalting Her Beauties in such a Soul.[26]

Traherne infers that he has been given a blank book, probably by a patron. It is the late 1650s or early 1660s. On one level, he describes in the book his own joy-filled childhood. But it is clear that Traherne has little interest in autobiography. From the start, he intends to write about the realization of spiritual potential. But his 'Profitable Wonders' include the notation of earthly 'Things'; these figure prominently in Traherne and are understood as gifts. Without material gifts, there will be none of his famous felicity. This is because all things bear the divine imprint; the poet's 'Empty Book' (and elsewhere, the image of a mirror) must receive and record (or reflect) the literal matter to hand, in order that the senses can branch outwards to perceive the connectedness of all other things.[27] The head of all things, to Traherne, is Jesus the Christ. This is the Pauline Christ, the head of 'things in heaven and things on earth'.[28]

Traherne writes in so-called Plain Style. He also seems to write within an established meditative tradition, the origin of which is disputed. Some critics have traced it to continental Europe before the Reformation, at a time when Renaissance writers were revered.[29] English 'Plain Style' superseded the elaborate figurative language, or dense metaphoric style, of, for example, John Donne (d.1631). The transition is evident in the poetry of George Herbert (d.1633) and perhaps in the work of Richard Crashaw (d.1649), even though Crashaw developed a penchant for a sensuous and convoluted imagery, as befitting his penchant for Baroque Catholicism. Other English poets who evinced Plain Style included Robert Herrick (d.1674), Andrew Marvell (d.1678) and Henry Vaughan (d.1695).

Traherne's diction seems to aim at a minimum of ornamentation and allusion. Despite the regular use of abstract words and concepts, Traherne favours a relatively transparent mode, which might be called a prelapsarian or 'pure' way with words. It is strangely hypnotic in its overall poetic effect. For example:

> All appeared New, and Strange at first, inexpressibly rare, and Delightfull,
> and Beautifull. I was a little Stranger which at my Enterance into the World
> was Saluted and Surrounded with innumerable Joys. My Knowledg was Divine.
> I knew by Intuition . . . .[30]

In claiming the use of intuition, Traherne joins Eckhart and Julian. Traherne's report of intuitional knowledge is later followed by a qualification, when he observes that he can recall his early experiences by means of 'Highest Reason'. Traherne purports to be unaware of any contradiction here. It emerges that 'Highest Reason' equates with 'intuition' in his thinking. Eckhart and Julian also believe in a kind of 'high reason' as well as the use of intuition. More than Traherne, however, Eckhart and Julian speak of revelation from God. They imply that their grasp of the content of that revelation is by means of intuition.

Imagination as a liberating power

The opening two lines of *Centuries* 3:3, below, are well known. The corn was 'orient' or brilliant; the wheat was 'immortal'.

> The Corn was Orient and Immortal Wheat, which never should be reaped, nor was ever sown. I thought it had stood from everlasting to everlasting.

Is it 'matter' that has prevented humanity's greater access to wisdom and compassion? Not according to Traherne. As these lines indicate, he has an acute experience of matter as animated by spirit. His Edenic, prelapsarian vision proceeds with specificity: dust, stones, gold, green trees. Traherne partly sees himself as delivering a spiritualized tour of childhood, with less metaphor than we might expect. But there is unity, for in the second line (above) Traherne unites things with the singular pronoun 'it'. In the lines below, the distinctiveness of the objects which are named is also more apparent than real:

> The Dust and Stones of the Street were as Precious as GOLD.
> The Gates were at first the End of the World, The Green Trees when I saw
> them first through one of the Gates Transported and Ravished me;
> their Sweetness and unusual Beauty made my Heart to leap,
> and almost mad with Extasie, they were such strange and Wonderfull Thing:
> The Men! O what Venerable and Reverend Creatures did the Aged seem!
> Immortal Cherubims! And yong Men Glittering and Sparkling Angels
> and Maids strange Seraphick Pieces of Life and Beauty!

The singular word 'Thing' is a synecdoche. It gathers up the two plurals of 'Trees' and 'Men' and includes all the things and values which the meditation has named to that point. Traherne is non-dualistic here; distinctions have, and are, breaking down. He uses four successive exclamation marks, by way of underlining that all are encompassed by the timelessness which is a 'quality' of God. Verbs drop away. Again, this serves to emphasize that the temporal world participates 'in' time-free infinity. These lines chime with lines in *Wonder*: 'I nothing in the World did knowe, / But 'twas Divine'. They also resonate with the closing lines of verse six of *The Salutation*: 'Into this Eden so Divine and fair, / So Wide and Bright, I com (God's) Son and Heir', Traherne continues:

> Boys and Girles Tumbling in the Street, and Playing, were moving Jewels.
> I knew not that they were Born or should Die. But all things abided Eternaly
> as they were in their Proper Places. Eternity was Manifest in the Light
> of the Day, and som thing infinit Behind evry thing appeared:
> which talked with my Expectation and moved my Desire.
> The Citie seemed to stand in Eden, or to be Built in Heaven.
> The Streets were mine, the Temple was mine, the People
> were mine, their Clothes and Gold and Silver was mine,
> as much as their Sparkling Eys Fair Skins and ruddy faces.
> The Skies were mine, and so were the Sun and Moon and Stars,
> and all the World was mine, and I the only Spectator and Enjoyer of it.[31]

He 'knew not that they were Born or should Die'. Since the divine is capable of 'exploding' from within all entities, and since all people latently occupy timeless reality and possess infinite sight, Traherne does not see the children as trapped within the temporal round of birth and death. The poet claims to have been spoken to by the 'infinit'. To return to the possibility of Neoplatonic influence, and to risk ruining Traherne by means of classification, it might be said that he regards the body/soul as carrying God's original Ideal (or the original thoughts of the primal universe).[32]

Obviously conscious of attempting to say the unsayable, Traherne knows that 'the Light of the Day' (lines 3 & 4, above) has brightly spoken; therefore he will not deny his experience and will arrange his nouns, abstract concepts and relatively unadorned style to serve a numinous (and unorthodox) vision. Diction is heightened to achieve a heightened sense of non-dualism. But a handful of pages later, his apparent recollection of childhood is less enthusiastic. The numinous experience now includes a shadier side. But Traherne quickly wishes to re-establish a tone of equanimous expectation.

> Another time, in a Lowering and sad Evening,
> being alone in the field, when all things were dead and quiet,
> a certain Want and Horror fell upon me, beyond imagination.
> The unprofitableness and Silence of the Place dissatisfied me,
> its Wideness terrified me, from the utmost Ends of the Earth
> fears surrounded me. How did I know but Dangers
> might suddainly arise from the East, and invade me
> from unknown Regions beyond the Seas?
> I was a Weak and little child,
> and had forgotten there was a man alive in the Earth.
> Yet som thing also of Hope and Expectation
> comforted me from every Border.[33]

The first detailed consideration of Traherne's work as mystical did not appear until almost 300 years after his death. I have in mind the book by Clements, quoted earlier, who makes reference to non-dualism in Traherne. Most surprisingly, Clements[34] believes that the *Vedāntin* assertion *Tat tvam asi* (Skt, literally *That thou art*)[35] has resonance with Traherne. As far as we know, Traherne had no knowledge of *Vedānta*. Yet Clements' imaginative courage leads him to the view that *Tat tvam asi* is, in effect, 'vital and basic' to Traherne.

I want to agree with Clements, despite the lack of evidence that Traherne's influences were sub-continental. Clements sees that Traherne was intent on experiential Christianity, in an age of so-called objective statements. The poet's personal vision impels him to invite the reader to go deeper than 'the isolated . . . role-playing ego'.[36] By means of an astute understanding of mystically weighted Christianity, Clements assesses Traherne's hope of 'transcending mere individuality' and attaining 'inner unity or, paradoxically, our truest individuality'.[37] The poet's childhood is presented to us as intuitively knowledgeable regarding the things of God. These things include the 'all Things' of the cosmos. Inclined by nature towards the mystical, the child soon absorbs the adult world of distancing and conceptualizing. The child then '. . . divides this from that, Thou from that, and distinguishes as other what in actuality is non-dual, indivisible, inextricably interrelated and interdependent'.[38]

Clements makes a direct comparison between Traherne and Eckhart, based on the poem *The Preparative*. The second verse is below.

> Then was my Soul my only All to me,
>   A Living Endless Ey,
>   Far wider than the Skie
> Whose Power, whose Act, whose Essence was to see.
>   I was an Inward *Sphere of Light*,

Or an Interminable Orb of *Sight*,
     An Endless and a Living Day,
A *vital Sun* that round about did *ray*
     All Life and Sence,
A Naked Simple Pure *Intelligence.*[39]

According to Clements, both Traherne and Eckhart express a comparable 'state of being'.[40] By this phrase, Clements means a comparable 'condition of the soul'. He has in mind the occasion and the 'place' of the Eckhartian birth of God in the soul. The comparison might gain by quoting from the sixth and penultimate verse of *The Preparative*. Here, Traherne is writing of a child's mystical experience. We know from a range of Traherne's work, and its contexts, that the childhood is his own. He has reimagined it; we might say he has reimaged it. And if his childhood eyes were clear-sighted, the focus of the mature is mainly on a clear, *intuitive* sight.

     Divine Impressions when they came,
Did quickly enter and my Soul inflame.
     Tis not the Object, but the Light
That maketh Heaven; Tis a Purer Sight.
     Felicitie
Appears to none but them that purely see.[41]

There is consonance between Trahernian light/sight and my poems *One Light, Many Lamps* and *To Your Fully Open Eyes*.[42] But in lines preceding the ones above, Traherne writes of a child's receptive state.

     I was as free
As if there were nor Sin, nor Miserie.
Pure Empty Powers that did nothing loath,
     Did like the fairest Glass,
     Or Spotless polisht Brass,
Themselvs soon in their Objects Image cloath.[43]

As in Eckhart, there is the image of a mirror: Either glass or polished brass. Like a mirror, the child receives 'Divine Impressions' and may reflect (and alter? or recreate?) what he or she receives. Traherne feels that, at the time of writing, he has been granted the adult sensibility to recover his childhood vision of non-duality. He can re-find the divine 'in the eternal Now-moment'.[44] As an adult, he has acquired some knowledge and a degree of wisdom, as distinct from a child's intuitive wisdom. He can therefore find the divine again; Traherne becomes didactic at the close of the poem, asking the reader to 'Get free, and so thou shalt even all Admire'.[45]

We do not know if Traherne was a dancer; did he accompany his patron Susanna Hopton to balls in Herefordshire? Whether or not he did, he is aware of the reciprocity of the dance, the cosmic dance. He chooses to be aware, centuries before eco-concern, of interconnectedness. He pays attention to the reciprocity of all things with everything else. And God, to Traherne, is within and without; behind and before; below and above. I have mentioned his tendency to use abstract language. In my view this is a studied use; it is intended to lure the reader into an awareness of the concrete and the particular.[46] He is a poet of full participation; he also sees the sacred everywhere, and desires to awaken me to 'the now-moment' of my interconnection with the divine. In the poem *The Anticipation*, Traherne announces: 'His Name is NOW'.[47] Subject and object come together again, to disclose 'the single reality which is life, the deity'.[48]

As one of the very few Trahernian scholars ever to mention non-dualism, Clements is able to interpret the poet's outlook as follows: 'Our finite minds, our conventionalizing eye and conceptualizing psyche, perceive disordered plurality, but the timeless and spaceless Spirit seizes all things in their unity; in God's mind everything is eternally now'.[49] This is not necessarily to equate God with 'Life'. Clements sees Traherne as putting forward a Neoplatonic view of 'Thought' or 'Intelligence' which functions as the substratum (or the site?) of unitive mystical experience.[50]

There might be a parallel, here, with Eckhart's attempts to write from God's point of view. From such a standpoint, all things might constitute a singular reality. In the second verse of *The Preparative*, quoted above, we saw that Traherne declares himself to have been '. . . A Naked Simple Pure *Intelligence*'. And in the poem *Thoughts III* he states, near its beginning, that 'All Wisdom in a Thought doth Shine, / By Thoughts alone the Soul is made Divine'.[51] He is not suggesting that through cognitive acts humanity can literally become God. His concern here and elsewhere is more enticing. Since enlightened human 'Thoughts' are reflections of 'Thoughts' within God, this God is figured as interconnecting Living Spirit. The word 'within' occurs often in the poems. But when he advocates 'inwardness' he is not thinking of introspection, as we might conceive of it today, but something akin to 'going inward' in order to recognize the One within.[52] Thus Traherne would encourage us to experience what could be called an aware, holistic life. His own special word for this is 'Felicity'. He is preoccupied with Felicity: the remembrance of it in infancy, and the continuation, or rather, the regaining of it. Felicity is regained by means of the senses. Direct experience is supported, in due time, by the study of theology and philosophy and via literary composition.

Traherne regards himself as a participant in God's creation. He identifies his 'soul', and sometimes his 'Mind', as participating in the activity of God. He does not claim identity with the 'uncreated being' or with 'the essence', so to say, of the traditional God. But he does claim a unity with the divine act of 'releasing' words which prove to be creative. One such word, prominent in Traherne, is 'Sphere'. He can describe both God and the soul in terms of an endless sphere. The soul can be viewed as endless, everywhere; even as infinite. Traherne can describe the soul as infinite inasmuch as it lies within God's infinity. His language is markedly non-dual.

> . . . my Soul is an Infinit Sphere in a Centre. By this may you know
> that you are infinitly Beloved: GOD hath made your Spirit a Centre
> in Eternity Comprehending all: and filled all about you
> in an Endless maner with infinit Riches: Which shine before you
> and surround you with Divine and Heavenly Enjoyments.[53]

He also can claim a unity with the divine act of seeing and loving. The mind of God and the mind of Traherne are described by the poet as being, at this point, *one*. God's is the original love and Traherne's is the created love. The seeing and the loving is reciprocal. In the following poem, I attempt to honour the wisdom of marsupials. Their clan-structures seem to be informed by an inner archive of creature-consciousness. Within each discrete group, the individuals appear to behave according to guiding principles. Yet they seemingly welcome me into their world, to the extent that I am detached from any sense of superiority.

So Much Light

I long for the ceiling
to yawn,
the roof to break open.
I long to step
from my clothes,
face real weather:
sky, rain
and sun full-on.
Bare feet on clay,
rough soles
conversant with soil.
I'll re-learn
a moist vocabulary,
lose myself in mute
languages: smell, taste,
sight and touch.

Stepping out,
there's broad moonlight,
enough to read
a large-print text.
Twitchy noses arrive
to read a different script;
four-legged seers shuffle
through the fence
to munch.

I am one with the in-
and exhale of all.
I crouch before things
of which my head
knows nothing
but my heart
senses
to be here.

The sub-text of poems such as this is the interdependence of matter and spirit, or the possible interconnection between macrocosm and microcosm. As I mentioned above, Traherne conceives of the divine as interconnecting living Spirit. This Spirit is not separate from me; we are not two. But neither are we one, in the sense of numerically one. The corollary of this is that I am not separate from twitchy-nosed wallabies. I am also not separate from those people whom society might designate as 'evil'. We are not two; neither are we one. Traherne is interested in the recognition or recovery of union with the divine. Eckhart and Julian precede him with a parallel interest. Their non-dual reflections, especially in Eckhart's case, have proved inconvenient for religious potentates who might resist the living spirit's democratic dispensation. But such reflections have an extensive, if often concealed, history within Christianity. The ninth-century Irish-born philosopher John Scottus Eriugena, influenced by neo-Platonism, could write:

> . . . . we ought not to understand God and the creatures as two things
> distinct from one another, but as one and the same. For both the creature,
> by subsisting, is in God, and God, by manifesting himself,
> in a marvelous and ineffable manner creates himself in creatures.[54]

Such a viewpoint might be dismissed as pantheism. A more accurate characterization would be panentheism. The catch-phrase 'everything is connected' has a long history, both of support and of opposition. It might still be opposed by some theologians whose work fits crudely into the term 'classically metaphysical'. On the other hand, many others are attracted to some form of panentheism.[55] Generally speaking, this view asserts that the divine works in and through a fully connected, unitary physical universe, yet is not limited thereby. My next poem plays with creature-consciousness (and interconnecting Spirit).

The Paradise Here

They ease me out of my head, these wild creatures;
they link me with real things. It's only five o'clock,
and already three macropods are resting their bottoms
on the courtyard tiles, deciding where to dash next.

I'd been reading about macaws,
how they understand essentials.
Flying from scattered points,
they'll reach a distant fruiting
vine together. Their thoughts
hold true alignment; when afraid,
their fear matches reality
and doesn't run ahead, like mine.

Wild creatures know more than they can say,
more than I can hear. They instruct me,
close to the roots of being, where every creature
is inhabited by joy, where all our days loop beyond calendars,
morph into space, combine and divide without limit.

As with *Sister Spider*, quoted earlier, I hope this poem holds some resonation with Traherne's *Thoughts IV*. Unusually, for a poem of his, *Thoughts IV* allows for particularities.

Fowls Fishes Beasts, Trees Herbs and precious flowers,
Seeds Spices Gums and Aromatick Bowers,
Wherwith we are enclos'd and servd, each day
By his Appointment do their Tributes pay,
And offer up themselves as Gifts of Love . . . .[56]

Overall, the poem *Thoughts IV* is pervaded by a theme of mutuality. The implicit subject is that of the highest good: The mutual giving and receiving of communion. We are rightfully stimulated by that which we see.

An essay by James Balakier (2007) has related Traherne's work to modern phenomenology. Balakier writes of Traherne as prefiguring the work of Edmund Husserl (d.1938). Distinctively, Husserl appears to have believed that a transcendental self is accessible by means of reflection, first, on one's own consciousness and, second, on one's temporal relationships. Balakier contends that Traherne alludes to a holistic state of consciousness. It is a state of 'restful alertness'.[57] In my understanding, such a fourth state would parallel that of the Upanishadic *turīya*, the fourth and 'super-conscious' state of the *Ātman*.[58] Believing that Traherne entered a natural transcendental consciousness, a 'threshold experience',[59] Balakier maintains that it was marked by '. . . an essential joy, not directly associated with reading scripture or participating in a religious ceremony, but simply present within his mind itself'.[60] Traherne speaks of himself as simultaneously 'Ravished and Transported' and 'Doting with Delight and Ecstasy' yet settled in 'Repose and Perfect Rest'. These are Trahernian phrases cited by Balakier.[61] They bring to mind the 'Secret Power', mentioned in the poem *Thoughts I*. This 'Power' is represented as a phenomenon that underlies thought.[62] It is able to bring the perpetual motion of thought into a restful order. Balakier's understanding of Traherne's theme of felicity is developed in a full-length study which makes use of rediscovered texts (2010). Placing Traherne in the early modern history of a science of cognition, Balakier suggests that the poet ultimately regards felicity, not as an emotion, but as cognitively grounded.

If a religion, in general, tends to regard 'matter' as completely different from 'spirit', the Christian story of incarnation highlights their interrelation. The failure of the church to protect the interrelation eventually led to accusations by Nietzsche, and later Dewey, to the effect that Christianity de-energizes people from actually *doing* something about (for example) injustice. But this need not be the case. If Traherne was alive today, he might be imagined as adhering to an Earth-centred model of divine Spirit. He might be imagined as regarding Spirit as the enfleshment of the divine within a vulnerable, teetering biosphere. Within such an Earth-centred model, the universal yields to the particular. Spirit is regarded as indwelling actual situations, actual people, in a time called Now.

This is not to conflate or confuse the One Spirit, the Divine Mind, with matter, but to highlight their interrelation. They are inseparable, although not identical. The natural world and Spirit co-inhere. Practically, the presence of Spirit in the world is the presence of gifts and graces for the benefit of others. In Christian terms, Spirit is not only humanity's 'ground of being' but humanity's ground of love. This love nurtures the daily energy which constitutes humanity's life. The elaborated Patristic tradition tends to assert that you and I are, in truth, the activity of Spirit living its life *as us*. Earlier, I quoted at length from *My Spirit*, in which Traherne's diction, including his non-dual language, is markedly elevated. Here again are the opening lines of the fifth verse:

> O Joy! O Wonder, and Delight!
> O Sacred Mysterie!
> My Soul a Spirit infinit!
> An Image of the Deitie!
> A pure Substantiall Light![63]

Margaret Miles links such delight with the vision of what Plotinus called 'the unity'. It is, of course, a vision of interconnectedness. Approaching the end of an essay with the title 'Happiness in Motion: Desire and Delight', Miles writes:

> If, as I have claimed, happiness depends on intimate knowledge
> and experience of the consanguinity of living beings,
> then happiness is an art of perception, the vision of an eye that can,
> and must, be cultivated. Not a vision of the heavenly city;
> nor that of an imagined utopia. But now. Here. Bodied and social.
> Happiness as desire and delight, delight and desire, in motion,
> *active* in the world.[64]

But Miles emphasizes that happiness does not just happen, but depends on vision and the experience of connectedness. I imagine that Traherne would agree. He might also say that happiness lies within the happy person, but needs to be accessed (he everywhere implies) through acts of thought (especially those of remembering) and through the discipline of writing. After lengthy preparation, which involves suffering, '. . . a Man must like a GOD, bring Light out of Darkness, and Order out of Confusion. Which we are taught to do by His Wisdom, that Ruleth in the midst of Storms and Tempests'.[65]

The reader is informed that she faces an ambiguous blend of difficulty and easiness. 'To be satisfied in God is the Highest Difficulty in the whole World And yet most easy to be don. . . . the Best of all Possible Things must be wrought in God, or els we shall remain Dissatisfied. But it is most Easy at present, becaus GOD is'.[66] In part, Traherne writes from the point of view of his concept of felicity; gradually his senses (in which he includes the mind's processes) find satisfaction. The experience of felicity is one of '. . . repose and perfect rest'.[67] Louis Martz (1964) writes that the poet discovers his inward Paradise. But we are not informed as to the precise nature of the experience.

> The exact nature of this experience of 'satisfaction' remains unexpressed
> and, apparently, inexpressible: all we know is that Traherne has received
> a brilliant glimpse of the essential image toward which all these meditations
> have been leading, ...[68]

There is a partial collapse, within his writings, of the traditional duality of good and evil. He has this in common with Eckhart, and, to a limited degree, with Julian.[69] Traherne knows that good and evil form a polarity in day-to-day life. But God transcends polarity, being infinite and therefore beyond ambiguity. In the poem *Ease*, Traherne uses the word 'intermutual'. The final four of the eight verses of *Ease* are as follows.

> That all we see is ours, and evry One
> Possessor of the Whole; that evry Man
> Is like a God Incarnat on the Throne,
> Even like the first for whom the World began;
>
> Whom all are taught to honor serv and love,
> Because he is Belovd of God unknown;
> And therefore is on Earth it self above
> All others, that his Wisdom might be shewn:
>
> That all may Happy be, Each one most Blest,
> Both in Himself and others; all most High,
> While all by each, and each by all possest,
> Are intermutual Joys, beneath the Skie.
>
> This shows a Wise Contrivance, and discovers
> Som Great Creator Sitting on the Throne,
> That so disposeth things for all his Lovers,
> That evry one might reign like GOD alone.[70]

In view of the monarchical words which Traherne uses ('throne' and 'reign'), readers can be misled into overlooking the poem's radical side. For here are lines of relation: Of self and other, of God and self, and of God and other. Traherne presents what he considers to be the highest human good: The mutual giving and receiving of communion and, therefore, felicity. The sub-text is as follows: I *become myself* through awareness of *the other*. It is this experiential dimension of theology which underlies my attempt, below, to honour the wisdom tradition.

To Sophia

We speak of Sophia;
she is found neither in the unreal aspect of the world
nor in the rulers of the unreal aspect.
We speak of the mystery of Sophia,
foreordained from the beginning for our bliss.

– 1 Cor. 2: 6 & 7 (author's paraphrase)

Wherever I go,
you are there too:
nearer than air, closer
than teeth or hair,
you are not separate from me
yet I am not you. Deeper
than thought or feeling:
your life in mine,
my life in yours. You teach me
how to be aware
of who I am. Hidden in yours,
my life will be as human as it can.
I'll praise each open face,
the naturalness
of grace; I'll praise that everyday
occurrence, the mystery
of your presence.

Perhaps this poem is really about self-awareness, as indeed Traherne's poem *Ease* could be. The subject-object relation is breaking down; 'the Thou' is not necessarily 'other'. Such poems as these carry the risk of an irritating egocentricity, not to mention didacticism. Or so it might seem from these lines in part two of Traherne's *Insatiableness*.

This busy, vast, enquiring Soul
Brooks no Controul,
No Limits will endure,
Nor any Rest: It will all see,
Not Time alone, but ev'n Eternity.
What is it? Endless sure.[71]

The poet also claims much for his own soul in *Thoughts IV*, quoted earlier. We are given to believe that by means of mere thought, his soul can inhabit all the ages. Apparent hubris is balanced by vast, capitalized abstractions: 'Eternal', 'Joys', 'Wisdom', 'Love', 'Glory', 'Goodness'. As unpoetic as these words might be, they are Traherne's 'double vision' at work. Vast nouns signal his awareness that apparently ordinary events or things can be momentous. And so the impact of an excessively elevated diction can be ameliorated by a love for the quotidian.

Current sensibility has decreed that poems should be crafted in 'concrete' words. By contrast, Traherne prefers fusions of abstraction and plain speaking. *Thoughts IV* emphasizes that we are able to love things when we have seen them properly. The poem ends with something of a vision of God; sight and love combine. Line 83 states that 'His Omnipresence is all Sight and Love'.[72] Traherne had pre-figured this conclusion at the start of *Thoughts IV*, by quoting a (slightly faulty) version of Ps. 16:11. In the KJV which Traherne used, the verse runs as follows: 'Thou wilt shew me the path of life: in thy presence is fulness of joy; at thy right hand there are pleasures for evermore'. The poet sees communion between bodies, souls and spirits (which include unseen presences, here and 'elsewhere') devolving into communion with the divine. A living temple is created within the poet: '. . . a Living one within the Mind'.[73] His apparent Neolatonism re-enters the picture: The souls of those who have been purified are '. . . transformed to a Thought'.[74] This line takes its place in the concluding lines of *Thoughts IV*:

> O give me Grace to see thy face, and be
> A constant Mirror of Eternitie.
> Let my pure Soul, transformed to a Thought,
> Attend upon thy Throne, and as it ought
> Spend all its Time in feeding on thy Lov,
> And never from thy Sacred presence mov.
> So shall my Conversation ever be
> In Heaven, and I O Lord my GOD with Thee![75]

The poet's soul, which had inhabited the cosmos by means of thoughts, becomes 'a Thought'. He is thereby in God's presence, in 'Conversation' with God, but still aware that no 'absolute answers' will be forthcoming. As I try to infer in the following poem, this scarcely matters.

Sophian Song

> Beyond word
> and concept
> there's no answer
>
> but a void.
> In the void
> a fuller
>
> answer
> means no answer
> but a spectre:

let's call her
Sophia, or *Wise Other*,
to be proper

or traditional,
it doesn't matter.
Does she sleep

with me
in basement
bed-sits,

sleep with generator-
throb, vertical drop
of other folks'

effluvia,
pipe-hammer?
As dawn comes up

over tenements
and smoke hovers
low in heavy wisps,

do I begin to see:
Sophia, you're not other,
you're us, you're me, you're Mother?

The divine seems inclined to conversation; the subject/object relation is dialogical rather than dualistic. The sign of Logos is to the fore in Traherne; perhaps the sign of Wisdom is to the fore in my own work. Under either sign, the divine is felt to remain open to every creaturely response of openness. Traherne treats openness, in *Thoughts IV*, as both dialogical and devotional; I hope that I do the same. Devotion, surrender, yieldedness: the freely chosen joys/pains of asceticism are with a view to more openness and clearer 'sight'. There is mutual reciprocity. I will return to this in Chapter 3, when discussing Julian. In Chapter 5, reciprocity will be to the fore when discussing the pluralism of Raimon Panikkar.[76]

An 'eternal correspondence'

The open-hearted Traherne was perhaps a freer, less doctrinaire individual than some of the Calvinists with whom he was obliged to interact. Stanley Stewart (1970) affirms that a glance at Traherne's poems persuades the reader of the man's sweet disposition. More to the point, Stewart recognizes that the poet's thought moves outward in an open way, creating the impression that his body/mind/soul is coexistent with all other beings, on earth and in heaven. Stewart writes of Traherne's theme as one of reintegration preceded by a necessary disintegration '... as the boundaries of self and other, of subject and object, become more and more attenuated'.[77] Stewart's book served for decades as a rare summation of Traherne's legacy. It concludes by seeming to adopt the poet's perspective.

> Man's ultimate alienation from the world is felt most tragically in the loss
> of the sense of his identity with others. From such a death in life
> man can and must be resurrected: the poetic sequences culminate in
> visionary glimpses of the kingdom in which man's reconciliation
> to the world is complete. The soul is transfigured by a process
> of divine narcissism into a being able to love himself – his humanity –
> in others; the speaker is able to see in the glow of other men's faces
> the reflection of his own and God's love.[78]

Traherne's *ouvre* is redolent with the cosmic dance of connectedness. But also, at a personal level, he evinces a *felt sense* of identification with others. Perhaps, today, it is not an absence of 'objective' identification with others that is an issue, so much as the lack of a felt sense of trans-identification. Perhaps an absence of feeling has fed a fantasy of what could be called 'separativity'. This is a theme in my following poem.

On a Day of Still Heat

In the still heat
    a breadfruit ripens:
a multitude of tiny sunspots
    mounted on hexagonal platelets,
green leather skin
    and flesh of kneadable custard.

In the breadfruit
    is hidden the sun,
in the sun
    the breadfruit.
Before the heat reaches Earth,
    the flames have already died;
before being picked,
    the breadfruit is already rotten.

And all the unpurchaseable luxuries
    - beetles, thunder, pebbles, twigs -
whose lives say, simply,
    I *accept*,
are hidden in each other
    and hide all things.

In a book with the pointed title *Thomas Traherne: Mystic and Poet*, Keith Salter is absorbed by what he calls Traherne's 'illumination'. Salter believes that Traherne had reached '. . . the realization within him of a secret self, a self which is at the same time infinite and universal'.[79] The poems which might best exemplify this realization are *My Spirit* and *The Preparative*. Salter refers to Traherne's 'sense of his unlimited power to become the very object of his contemplation'.[80] He proceeds as follows.

> As the distinction between body and spirit disappears,
> so likewise is Traherne unable to distinguish between what is objective
> and what is subjective. . . . He creates and is created by the world
> around him, the world which seems to flow through him.
> The terms internal and external which are useful on ordinary levels
> of consciousness cease to be valid for him.
> The simplicity of this state of being, his 'naked, simple, pure intelligence',
> stands clearly for an absence of all dualism, a positive sense of unity
> in which the distinctions of spirit and sense, mind and body,
> subject and object become subordinate to an overriding conviction
> of an essentially mutual relationship existing between apparently
> individual and separate entities.[81]

Here we have a rare allusion, in the literature on Traherne, to his non-dualism. At times there is a theopoetic expression of non-duality between God and humanity. More often, the poet posits non-duality between body/soul and between the individual self and other entities. His readers receive an impression that spiritual growth occurs, not through willpower, but through non-dual imagination and awareness. Eckhart is similar in this respect, whereas Julian is more overtly devotional in her understanding of growth, while including imaginative awareness. But is not our inner growth a question of awareness, *always*?

The texture of awareness is difficult to describe. It would be foolish to blandly regard it as the perception of everything without boundaries. An informed grasp of 'emptiness' (Skt. *śūnyatā*[82]) is important here. An acceptance can develop that there is no such thing as an essential or enduring 'self'. In 'pure awareness' it is held that the sense of *inner* and *outer* no longer applies. Traherne's view of infinite love takes him to a similar openness. In the first sections of *Centuries 3*, he perhaps comes closest to an autobiographical account. False values have been instilled in the child; an awareness of another world, another creation, has to be *re-learnt*. But as far as *this* world is concerned, his poems invite us to *absorb* it. Since infinite love has orchestrated the world, what else would be appropriate? He even declares that 'you', 2nd person singular, are 'the Sole Heir of the whole World'.[83] This 'engaged mysticism' is Trahernian; it contrasts with, for example, the mysticism of John of the Cross and others both Catholic and Protestant who favour the soul's *retreat* from the world.[84]

Traherne's idea of spiritual nourishment begins with the enjoyment of life's temporal, material gifts. His register or hallmark of spiritual inclination and maturity is the extent of such enjoyment. Transcendence which is out-of-this-world does not attract him, notwithstanding his exultant paeans to a childhood which seems, at times, to float free of everything dismal. But Traherne is not a naïve sentimentalist who is fixated on nature, although he regards all of nature as deeply significant in the quest to find joy within immanent terms.[85] In his apparent acceptance of the human body as a unity (of spirit with matter), he adheres to a union of grace and nature which was more widespread in the era of Julian and Eckhart. He is able to represent himself as having felt an inward, bodily experience of the Infinite One. Nothing pertaining to himself, *per se*, is infinite, yet he feels inwardly embraced by infinitude. Indeed, Traherne regards all things as included in the Infinity which is God. A principle of oneness applies, no matter what the scale.

Breathing Boulder

I once knew a woman
who collected fragments
from French cathedral walls.

She claimed they cleaned the air,
which she could hear,
glistening,
on windless nights.

Sensing a subtle joy,
I called her *Balmy*,
although her carbuncular skin
was anything but placid.

Each morning, she liberated moths
trapped behind glass,
picked up earthworms
before they steamed to pretzels
on the path, shook ants form cut gladioli.

Balmy took me bushwalking
to see a certain boulder:
lichen-spotted, bull-shouldered.

I looked until I saw,
or thought I saw,
an infinitesimal
rise and fall:

igneous passion in motion,
stabilised for an aeon
and now stilled,
        or perhaps not.

I felt part of a backdrop
of presence,
as if all things participated
in a gossamered influence,
a cloud of utterance.

In the piece of writing above, I followed a Trahernian mystical mode, so called. But the words are grounded in very ordinary life, in what Traherne calls '. . . your Walk and Table'.[86] If the participatory 'cloud of utterance' has everyday relevance for us, it will be an *embodied* relevance. Along this vein, the Christian declaration (*kerygma*) is both an announcement and a celebration of present-time liberty. The *kerygma* does not concern itself with proposing a more convenient life in a body-free sector of the cosmos. Traherne claims and exudes an experience of liberty. He develops the consequences of the Eckhartian birth of the divine in the soul. We might imagine Traherne imagining Eckhart. In front of the poet is a fourteenth-century manuscript which seems to contain a radical perspective. If it is radical, it is also grounded in a traditional hermeneutic of the Gospel. Eckhart conveys to Traherne that what matters most is the birth of God in the soul. In developing the consequences of God's birth, Traherne's senses are heightened. He wants our senses to be heightened also.

By the very Right of your Sences, you Enjoy the World.
Is not the Beauty of the Hemisphere present to your Ey?
Doth not the Glory of the Sun pay Tribut to your Sight?
Is not the Vision of the WORLD an Amiable Thing? . . .[87]

You never Enjoy the World aright, till the Sea it self floweth
in your Veins; till you are Clothed with the Heavens,
and Crowned with the Stars: and Perceiv your self to be the Sole
Heir of the whole World: and more than so, becaus Men are in it
who are evry one Sole Heirs, as well as you. Till you can Sing
and Rejoyce and Delight in GOD, as Misers do in Gold,
and Kings in Scepters, you never Enjoy the World.[88]

Till your Spirit
filleth the whole World, and the Stars are your Jewels,
till you are as Familiar with the Ways of God in all Ages
as with your Walk and Table.[89]

Traherne's use of 'spirit' is different from that of Eckhart or Julian. He seems to elide divine Spirit with human spirit. Living in the religiously diverse seventeenth century, Traherne was able to write without the constraining pressure of a monolithic, inquisitorial church behind his shoulder. He does indeed 'cut loose', so to speak, in the expressions of his 'authentic self'. It is as a body that Traherne has 'come to share in the very being of God'. It is not as a disembodied spirit but within his body that he shares '. . . the mind of Christ' (1 Cor. 2:16 REB). In the words of Gregory of Nyssa, he begins to see 'with the eyes of the Dove'. Actual, literal doves are not concerned with finitude and mortality, so far as we can gather. A feathered dove does dove-things, in a real-time dove-body. If it is a female dove, she will probably reason her way to creating a small platform of softish twigs. Her concern is not with mortality but with natality. We imagine dove-desire; it connects with another real-time dove; their creativity is this-worldly. How does this relate to Traherne? The theme is the same: It is *newness now* that matters! Here is the opening verse of *Wonder*:

How like an Angel came I down!
How Bright are all Things here!
When first among his Works I did appear
O how their GLORY me did Crown?
The World resembled his *Eternitie*,
In which my Soul did Walk;
And evry Thing that I did see,
Did with me talk.[90]

Traherne dispenses with time and figures his childhood and his present and future life as resembling '*Eternitie*'. The reason for this does not become clear until the close of verse three: 'I nothing in the World did knowe, / But 'twas Divine'. This reads like an epiphany of Realization; not surprising, therefore, that '. . . evry Thing that I did see, / Did with me talk'. Traherne is not crediting a personal achievement of enlightenment; instead (again in verse three) he praises the infinite One: 'I felt a Vigour in my Sence / That was all SPIRIT'. He uses 'Sence' generically; it stands for each one of his five senses. He reminds us elsewhere that it is 'som thing infinit Behind evry thing' which talks with him.[91]

But Traherne knows that Infinity cannot be an object of understanding or experiencing. He is writing paradoxically and theopoetically. He is saying, in effect: 'I experience the collapse of the subject-object relation, in the Now'. When he writes of 'the Now', his diction sounds modern. He wants to expand our consciousness, so that we might have sufficient openness, in Spirit's presence, to enter the experiential knowledge of our graced participation in divine life. The isolated, egoic 'I' will be disclosed as not the real 'I'. The genuine 'I' is on intimate terms with 'the Almightie'. Later in this book, there will be increasing mention of the *Vedāntin* non-dual, supreme 'Self'. Within the sub-continental tradition(s), we are participants in this 'Self' but lack Realization of the fact. We are 'selves' within 'the Self', yet without loss to the Oneness of the 'Self'.

In keeping with his own vision of Oneness, Traherne recapitulates an infancy that was inseparable from '*Eternitie*'. Unequivocally, he wants us to grasp that God's pristine creation was 'present to him'. It is a non-dual recounting of a beatific state. The poem *Wonder* continues:

The Skies in their Magnificence,
The Lively, Lovely Air;
Oh how Divine, how soft, how Sweet, how fair!
The Stars did entertain my Sence,

And all the Works of GOD so Bright and pure,
So Rich and Great did seem,
As if they must endure,
In my Esteem.

A Native Health and Innocence
Within my Bones did grow,
And while my GOD did all his Glories shew,
I felt a Vigour in my Sence
That was all SPIRIT. I within did flow
With Seas of Life, like Wine;
I nothing in the World did knowe,
But 'twas Divine.[92]

No distinction is discerned between his spirit and the 'Seas of Life'. Indeed, there is no distinction drawn with the '. . . all Things here' of verse one. Traherne raises his Edenic non-dual vision to an explicit level. About four centuries earlier, Eckhart had expressed his theological certainty of our potential *union* with God. And Julian had aligned the soul with *participation* in both the sufferings of Christ and the resurrected glory of Christ. For Traherne, 'all Things' (including 'The Skies' and 'The Lively, Lovely Air' and 'The Stars' of verse two of *Wonder*) combine to nourish a non-dual perspective. He has a sense of greatly reduced separation. In the poem *The Salutation*, the unitary tendency is again prominent. 'The Earth, the Seas, the Light, the Day, the Skies, / The Sun and Stars are mine; if those I prize'.[93] He then confidently announces: 'Into this Eden so Divine and fair, / So Wide and bright, I com (God's) Son and Heir'.[94]

To be a daughter or son of God is to hold an 'Eternal Correspondence' with the divine.[95] Since Traherne regards the soul as infinite, his word 'Correspondence' has ontological as well as epistemological implications. He grants: 'Few will believ the Soul to be infinit: yet Infinit is the first Thing which is naturally Known. Bounds and Limits are Discerned only in a Secondary maner'.[96] He is confident that a child of the Father hears the Father talking with him. 'Eternity was Manifest in the Light of the Day, and som thing infinit Behind evry thing appeared: which talked with my Expectation and moved my Desire'.[97] The effect is conveyed that Traherne believes that the divine God speaks to him, within the inherent desires and expectations of his own spirit.

A radical economic theory is presented in verse six of *Wonder*. Traherne proposes a non-acquisitive, non-possessive economy.

Rich Diamond and Pearl and Gold
In evry Place was seen;
Rare Splendors, Yellow, Blew, Red, White and Green,
Mine Eyes did everywhere behold,
Great Wonders clothd with Glory did appear,
Amazement was my Bliss.
That and my Wealth was evry where:
No Joy to this![98]

He has already proposed an ecological practice based on inherent worth. This comes in the concluding lines of verse three: 'I nothing in the World did knowe, / But 'twas Divine'.[99] He has also, in the opening line of the same verse, staked a claim of 'A Native Health and Innocence . . .'.[100] This is naïve, on any superficial assessment. But, it is Traherne's way of adumbrating his view that all things enjoy a participatory share in the divine. The elements and colours, in the verse above, help to comprise the 'Splendors'. These, in turn, are part of 'my Bliss'. But (and here again is Traherne's non-dualism) everything is subsumed in 'Joy' which is both transcendent and immanent. The poet is passionately dissolving distinctions. In effect, he wishes to say to the reader: 'This is your reality. This is where you will find your true nature'.

In the seventh and penultimate verse of *Wonder*, Traherne's expressions of the undivided nature of the cosmos are mitigated by an awareness of this-worldly divisions. Here is one of Traherne's rare elaborations on sin:

> Cursd and Devisd Properties,
> With Envy, Avarice
> And Fraud, those Feinds that Spoyl even Paradice,
> Fled from the Splendor of mine Eys.
> And so did Hedges, Ditches, Limits, Bounds,
> I dreamd not ought of those,
> But wanderd over all mens Grounds,
> And found Repose.

The final verse returns to the unified vision.

> Properties themselvs were mine,
> And Hedges Ornaments;
> Walls, Boxes, Coffers, and their rich Contents
> Did not Divide my Joys, but shine.
> Clothes, Ribbans, Jewels, Laces, I esteemd
> My Joys by others worn;
> For me they all to wear them seemd
> When I was born.[101]

Superficially, here is an idiosyncratic narcissist, placing himself uppermost within every trope. But the 'For me', of the penultimate line, means 'to' me. Traherne indicates that his individuality has not been dissolved, and yet, all the 'Joys' are shared. On his view, all people are within the divine and can choose to share 'an eternal Correspondence' in the partnership of universal participation.

All things in one

The first comprehensive study of Traherne's theology was not published until 2009. Its author is Denise Inge, a theologian who writes within the Anglican tradition.[102]

Traherne wrote within a seventeenth-century version of the same tradition, although he is unlikely to have used the term 'Anglican'. The book by Inge is an exemplary assessment of Traherne's extensive prose corpus, including the rediscovered texts. Her choice to concentrate on the prose theology is understandable, given that Traherne wrote much more prose than poetry; further, that the prose *in toto* has drawn less scholarly attention.

Inge finds that 'Desire percolates throughout his writings'.[103] She calls Traherne's theology a '. . . theology of desire'.[104] God desires a reciprocal relationship of love. If we were true to our own deepest desire, we would 'want like a God' (Traherne's words) and find our hearts satisfied in God-like ways.

In the literature on Traherne, references to his non-dualism are surprisingly rare. As far as I know, Alison Kershaw (2005) and Arthur Clements (1969) are the only authors of full-length works on Traherne to mention 'non-dualism'. I look forward to being otherwise advised. Inge does not refer to non-dualism as such, yet is very aware of coexisting opposites in Traherne. She mentions his paradoxes frequently, without alluding to the strong variety of paradox (antinomy) whereby Traherne seems to put forward contradictory principles (such that the rules of logical paradox are inapplicable). I would suggest that he regards *both* principles as true, in different senses, when viewed theopoetically from the harmonizing perspective of the ultimate, unitive mystery.

Although not willing to refer to 'non-dualism', Inge thoroughly engages with Traherne's perspective on 'union with God'. She locates a distinction, in Traherne's thought, between 'union' and 'communion'. She writes:

> His deep exploration of desire and its place in the heart of God
> and thereby in the heart of Christianity is perhaps the most significant
> theological contribution he has made. . . . Felicity is not about regaining
> childhood innocence, or about deferring happiness to an afterlife,
> or about negating or subjugating the plethora of human desires.
> Because desire exists in God, felicity is about living in lack and longing,
> being simultaneously needy and filled. Final fullness *is* this interplay
> of want and satisfaction, heaven here and hereafter,
> having and wanting from and into eternity.[105]

This is elevated writing; implicitly, it praises imaginative representation. But Inge is non-specific regarding his testimony (as I see it) of actual, experiential non-dualism. Inge writes: '. . . we may understand Traherne's felicity not as an achieved state but as a participation in the dynamic of desire and satisfaction that for him marks the relationship of God and the soul'.[106] This is well-nuanced: No spiritual quality can be reduced to 'achievement'. On the other hand, a range of religious traditions testify to experiential knowledge (or Realization) of non-dual truth. For this to occur, one must 'achieve' an openness to divine grace, such that the body-mind organism occupies 'the window' through which Spirit can bestow its ineffable light. Inge is sensitive to this. Hence she can write of '. . . the dynamic of desire and satisfaction'.

As to her emphasis on desire, Buddhists will be reminded of the importance, in their traditions, of the mindfulness and compassion which mitigates desire's negative consequences. Inge alludes to Trahernian scholars who have preceded her. She states the following:

> Critics ... are right to note the unitive urge in Traherne's writings. ...
> The danger, however, of such a loose understanding of oneness
> in Traherne is that it can easily slip into a kind of fusing of all things
> into one indistinguishable sameness; God and the great oneness
> become synonymous. God is not a person at all but a kind of overarching
> unity, a concept.[107]

Inge is doubtful whether Traherne inscribes the transcendence of normal subject/object relations.[108] Cautiously, she views him as straddling the following tension '... on the one hand, subject and object relations and, on the other hand, a unity that is the origin and end of all'.[109] Dualism would appear to remain, with a view to an eschatological unity. Inge continues:

> I suggest that not only do subject and object need each other but that,
> in Traherne, subject/object division and ultimate unity need each other too.
> By the one we are; by the other we come to know who we are.[110]

A little later, Inge concedes that Traherne's work possesses a '... simple daring. ... The subject and object participate in a greater unity of perception and being'.[111]

Wearing his poet's hat, Traherne can avoid literalism. Inge's approach might be a touch inhibited by a degree of literality. For example, her personal, orthodox view of the Trinity is perhaps projected. Did Traherne adhere to the orthodox, paradoxical teaching that God is a person (who is but one person) yet simultaneously three persons? This would accord with the ecumenical Creeds, which are best treated (in my view) as deep theology which is both deeply symbolic and poetic. Did not Traherne see the theopoetic and *perichoretic* dimensions which lie 'concealed' within the orthodox position on the Trinity?

As quoted in the present chapter, Traherne's most exuberant poems tend to collapse the assumed objective world into boundlessness or ultimate formlessness. It is here that I propose kinship with Ramana Maharshi's version of *Advaita*. Traherne's poetry takes the recognizable doctrinal formularies of 'Western' tradition and moves theopoetically beyond them; or deeper than them. This is not to imply that he takes leave of his tradition, still less of Christianity. But within his own broad tradition, one can imagine Traherne being drawn to the thoughts on divinization or theosis with which he was familiar in the writings of the 'Eastern' Church fathers. Such was his view of transformative grace that he can effectively declare a person to be a micro-cosmos. Indeed, a micro-theos.[112]

In an unpublished thesis, Kershaw specifically uses the term non-dualism, albeit in passing references. This is justifiable, given that her thesis is a detailed analysis of

Traherne's prose work *The Kingdom of God*.[113] Kershaw mentions Traherne's 'subversion of dualism'.[114] She explores the implicit connection, in Traherne, '. . . between Christ and all things'.[115] The Logos is '. . . at the core of every being'.[116] Since the poet understands Christ to be the Logos, each human being can be configured as a co-possessor of the world. Traherne, as I have mentioned, begins *Centuries* by individualizing this trope. It is *you*, singular, who inherits the world. For example:

> Is it not a Great Thing, that you should be Heir of the World?
> Is it not a very Enriching Veritie? In which the Fellowship of the Mystery,
> which from the beginning of the World hath been hid in GOD,
> lies concealed! The Thing hath been from the Creation of the World,
> but hath not so been Explained, as that the interior Beauty should be understood.
> It is my Design therfore in such a Plain maner to unfold it,
> that my Friendship may appear, in making you Possessor of the Whole World.[117]

Traherne's vision is unitary; in a sense the world is construed as Christ's body. Thereby, a customary duality between 'earth' and 'heaven' is collapsed. In Kershaw's words, '. . . heaven is present on earth and earth is celebrated in heaven'.[118] With a surprising and fruitful touch, Kershaw brings Traherne into proximity with Jesuit scientist Pierre Teilhard de Chardin (d.1955). She writes that Traherne and Teilhard share a view that the Kingdom of God is 'present'.[119] More than that, they emphasize a union of the material and the divine by sharing what amounts to a 'realized eschatology'. The Kingdom is less a futuristic anticipation than something already realized through Christ's incarnation.

In a viewpoint which concurs with that of the first generation of Trahernian scholars, Alan Gould[120] favours retaining felicity as a key to Traherne's theopoetics. Felicity, writes Gould, is derived from true perception rather than personal acquisition. It is true perception which enables covetousness to be disarmed; the active engagement of the senses can permit a genuine ownership which manifests as self-possession. Gould is drawn to Traherne's exalted view of humanity, a quality unusual in Christians of Gould's acquaintance. He writes of Traherne as an 'exhilarated witness' of intimacy 'between the One and the All'. Gould believes that Traherne 'takes for his underlying situation' the idea of a threshold. That is to say, Traherne signals his awareness that temporal constraints have only served to heighten his apprehension of '. . . an ampler sense of the real'. According to Gould, this poet-theologian enjoys presenting his poetic arguments from the threshold of the human and the divine; from what I might call the divinely human.

Gould notes that Traherne can be 'intently self-regarding'. He adds: '. . . but this is because the poet's buoyant egotism is vital to his project, which is to disclose how the essential wonder of Creation is the way the presence of the All comes to be concentrated in the attentive powers of the One. Here is one of the profound attractions of any faith, and at one level it little matters whether that One is Deity, or TT himself'. Gould's appraisal carries the refreshing perspective of a writer with no prior commitment to Traherne's religious assumptions. The following extract (verse five) from *The Improvment* is corroborative:

> His Wisdom, Goodness, Power, as they unite
> All things in one, that they may be the *Treasures*
> Of one *Enjoy'r*, shine in the utmost Height
> They can attain; and are most Glorious *Pleasures*,
>   When all the Univers conjoynd in one,
>   Exalts a Creature, as if that alone.[121]

Is it a matter of letting the One who 'unite(s) All things in one' (lines 1 & 2, above) speak through our embodiment? Is it through surrender that we best create the embodied poem of ourselves?

A *perichoretic* cosmos

Traherne's confidence in his vision can be disconcerting, especially when he conveys his feeling of being imbued with 'Truth' and 'Love' from birth.[122] These are traditional nouns, often employed to denote God. Although his 'Infant Soul', admittedly, did not comprehend the greatest truths, it nonetheless possessed them. The 'most Enriching Truths' were within his soul.[123] There is, therefore, the expression of a latent union with God. The Plain Style of the period combines well with an established meditative tradition. Traherne's often unadorned language might be said to mimic the way in which he envisages the Creator declaring the plain Word of creation. The opening lines of *Centuries* 3:2 were quoted earlier. Here is a further extract:

> I Knew Nothing of Sickness or Death, or Exaction,
> in the Absence of these I was Entertained
> like an Angel with the Works of GOD in their Splendor and Glory;
> I saw all in the Peace of Eden; Heaven and Earth did sing my
> Creator's Praise, and could not make more Melody to Adam,
> then to me. All Time was Eternity, and a Perpetual Sabbath.
> Is it not Strange, that an Infant should be Heir of the World,
> and see those Mysteries which the Books of the Learned never unfold?[124]

The unpromising repetition of abstract words does not swamp the passion. His metaphysics might be out of favour today. We are nervous about assumptions and schemes that purport to look for truth in abstract propositions, without reference to the conversational contexts now felt to be indispensable. But Traherne's use of absolute statements and abstract concepts is not a pious reiteration of received positions, whether biblical or institutional. It is one of the strategies of his religious imagination. He wants to point to the significance of human beings with all five senses 'operating'.

By means of our senses, he wants us to apprehend the mystery of creation and of redemption. My senses (as Traherne everywhere implies) will unite with grace to allow me to enter the felicity of Paradise while here on Earth. His position is this: Nature is inherently worthy and worth attending to, for its own sake. Nature is also the forecourt on Earth of the full manifestation, in the age to come, of the Kingdom of God. But the human spirit can exult in Earth-centred joy (albeit this joy points to Spirit and to the Trinitarian dance).

An awareness of essential unity can be mitigated by a resurgence of factors which generate a sense of individualized possessiveness. But not for long; Traherne quickly reverts to 'Joy'. Together with 'Delight' and 'Love', the word 'Joy' spirals towards 'Felicity' throughout much of his work. Perhaps he was weary of encountering Christians who evinced the sense that God, somehow, did not approve of them. In the fourth *Century* he addresses such a disjunction, by indirect means, when he refers to self-hurt or self-bereavement.

> From His Lov all the Things in Heaven and Earth flow unto you;
> but if you lov neither Him nor them, you bereav your self of all,
> and make them infinitly evil and Hurtfull to you and your self abominable.
> So that upon your Lov naturally depends your own Excellency
> and the Enjoyment of His. It is by your Lov that you enjoy all His Delights,
> and are Delightfull to Him.[125]

His observation of negativity is a cause for *angst*. As with Eckhart and Julian, he has a pastoral intention. He wants all people to know they are 'Delightfull' to divine eyes.

> To know God is to know Goodness; It is to see the Beauty
> of infinit Lov .... Whatever knowledge else you have of God,
> it is but Superstition.... He is not an Object of Terror, but Delight.
> To know Him therefore as He is, is to frame the most Beautifull
> Idea in all Worlds. He Delighteth in our Happiness more than we:
> and is of all other the most Lovly Object.[126]

Later, in the third *Century*, Traherne uses the term 'Enlarged Soul'. A person whose soul is enlarged is compared to a fountain, of which God is the source. The fountain bursts out with love. This love is returned to God; it is also conveyed to all creatures, attenuating boundaries and establishing unity. Discussing the poem *Shadows in the Water*, Stewart writes as follows: 'A proper understanding of the world and the imitation of the divine self-love are one and the same thing. The truth emanating from the world is that love annihilates the boundaries between the self and the other ....'[127]

Traherne's 'Enlarged Soul', with its quality of boundlessness, harmonizes both wisdom and compassion within itself. Originating in God, the soul has a share in the divine, embracing all of the world's beings in wise love and compassion. It appears that the soul will eventually be immersed in, or perhaps absorbed by, God's infinite life. The first verse of Traherne's six verse poem *Goodnesse* includes the following lines:

The Face of GOD is Goodness unto all,
And while he Thousands to his Throne doth call,
    While Millions bathe in Pleasures,
    And do behold his Treasures,
        The Joys of all
        On mine do fall
And even my Infinitie doth seem
A Drop without them of a mean Esteem.[128]

To further develop Traherne's position, it is the *perichoretic* nature of relations between the traditional 'persons' of the Trinity which engenders a joy which is based on Earth. The invisible dancing within the divine is reflected in our interconnected human relations of reciprocity and gladness. In this way, Traherne sees all humanity as participating in the reinstatement of the divine image. For example, the interpenetration of the divine 'persons' might be seen in the accountability of one human being for the next human being and of one community for the next community. In other words, our behaviour as persons is *perichoretic*. In Christian parlance, our actions are those of *agapeic* love, expressed from body to body; to and from your body and mine. It takes place between, within and among all persons and all other creatures within their contexts. On this existential or process-oriented interpretation, the traditional teachings regarding Trinity (and regarding incarnation) have ongoing value. Especially so, if and when these teachings are rescued from the weight of an excessively gendered history and emerge as, literally, holy/wholly communion.

Turning now to the style in which Traherne expresses passionate 'Lov' for all things, the reader cannot avoid reiterations of capital letters. Unexpectedly, these can transmit his passion. The writing below is taken from a didactic meditation which is cast in a superficially poetic form. Its title is 'Thanksgivings for the Blessedness of his LAWS'.

      The SUN is a glorious Light,
Whose Beams are most Welcom, Necessary, Useful,
    To me and all the Sons of Men;
But thy Laws surpass the light of the Sun,
    As much as that of a Gloe-worm;
        Being the Light of Glory,
        Teaching us to live
           On Earth in Heaven.[129]

When Traherne refers, above, to 'The SUN', he means Christ. As the expressive Word of the Father, Christ is viewed by the poet as surpassing the likewise necessary light of the cosmological 'Sun', mentioned further down. By means of the 'Light' of Christ, humankind is taught how to live 'On Earth in Heaven'. Here is an Earth-honouring reversal of the traditional duality of a torrid life on Earth followed by Heavenly bliss. The expansive expressions within Traherne's diction have already drawn us towards a unified use of language, or rather, a universalized approach to language. For example, he elides or conflates his terms (SUN, Sons and Sun; Light, light and Light) to bring out his non-dual intention.

A little later in 'Thanksgivings for the Blessedness of his LAWS', Traherne intuits that the Word of God 'operates' in conjunction with his own words. Together, they teach him.

> They teach me to live
> In the Similitude of God,
>> And are the inward Health
>>> And Beauty of my Soul,
>> Marrow, Wine, and Oyl,
>>> WITHIN!
> They teach me to live in the Similitude of thy Glory.[130]

The reference to 'marrow' is taken from Ps. 63; the references to 'wine and oil' are drawn from Ps. 104. But unlike these Psalms, Traherne specifically locates these three substances within himself. Further on, he implies that the marrow, wine and oil are part of 'THINE INWARD GOODNESS'. The poet's capitalization prevents us from evading his emphasis.

There are nine pieces of writing which Traherne called 'Thanksgivings'. Bellette[131] considers that they were written by way of imitation of God's creativeness. There is no consistent framework and no predictable sequence. Bellette adds that the poet '. . . conveys almost like a musical score the unity within division which is God's presentation of himself'.[132] I have alluded above to the fact that Traherne implicitly aligns his work with the so-called Plain Style movement. Bellette describes Plain Style as a rejection '. . . of all that is contrived and fanciful in style'.[133] He continues: 'The shift from the authority of words to the authority of experience implies not just a rejection of the formulations of the past but also a willingness to rethink the very nature of the world'.[134] Traherne seems to assume that truth is conveyed to us 'plain'. The truth is 'plain' in the sense of being self-evident to those who wish to receive it. He also assumes that when the appropriate language is found, the truth can be democratically accessible to all people.

I have mentioned the book *Religio Medici*, by Browne. It propounds 'the two books': that of scripture and that of nature. Yet despite his assumed knowledge of Browne's book (together with Browne's well-admired life of 'lived spirituality'), Traherne tends to favour a single act of divine revelation. A unitary Word/word creates and discloses, or discloses as it creates. The divine and the human are co-opted, so to speak, to make manifest the one 'Lov'. This 'Lov' is active in the ongoing creation of Creation. Towards the end of 'Thanksgivings for the Blessedness of his LAWS', Traherne refers specifically to the 'one Work' which includes 'all things'. These 'all things' issue from the Word; they are brought to light (or to sight or to mind) by the human words which work in conjunction with the Word. The poet has asserted that an infant carries the knowledge of both the divine and the earthly, as if by inherent gift or intrinsic grace. But exposure to the world of adults, with their sense of separation and orientation towards individual possessiveness, can blight this Edenic state. In one of his few references to humanity's negative propensities, Traherne concludes 'Thanksgivings for the Blessedness of his LAWS' by telling us that 'If my delight had not been in thy Law, I had perished in my Trouble'.[135] We are not told the nature of the trouble. It is clear that we are not meant to dally, overmuch, with private suffering. Rather, we are to *know* that Spirit is with us, to transport us around the cosmos.

An empathetic reader will see that Traherne's 'abstract art' is a quest for clarity. Unlike Donne, for example, with his complex allusiveness, Traherne focuses on divine inseparability from you and from me. Stewart[136] is correct, in my view, when he states: 'Traherne's is an artistry of abstraction: abstract nouns in great numbers, apocopated conjunctions, intransitive verbs. In language Traherne attempts something like the aim of the 'action' painters of the 1950's. He bases his entire strategy on the idea that one cannot think of the whole as apart from its smallest segment'. Nonetheless, it is true that Traherne does not, in every poem, match his vision with a poetic embodiment. A critic might sometimes conclude that his repetitions, his use of capitalization and punctuation (or lack of it) draw attention to the drama of his words in an eccentric manner. Such lines as 'I felt a Vigour in my Sence / That was all SPIRIT' (from verse three of *Wonder*, quoted earlier) might be vulnerable to such a charge. But these lines succeed (for me) when taken as part of the complete poem's passionate impression. Even by means of images that have minimum sensuous appeal, Traherne convinces me that he truly believes that he affectively experiences Spirit. Bellette writes as follows: 'That curious mixture in Traherne of abstraction and celebration represents a process in which self discovers itself, then moves outward to identify with all that is other, then returns to reclaim the initial experience of infant joy'.[137] Bellette's words might serve as a picture of the *perichoretic* dance of participation.

Traherne writes about the integral goodness of all things. If his readers should believe otherwise, and hold a dimmer view of humanity, Traherne would advocate a wise unknowing. He would bring the duality of divinity and humanity closer together. In so doing, he would redefine the boundaries between 'self' and 'other'. I have quoted lines that are low in metaphor, high in abstraction and replete with the kind of imprecise imagery that has since become unpopular. But Traherne embeds himself in his theology. It is from that base that he projects a daring and enthusiastic blend of spirit/matter onto the reader's imagination. In his poems, he scarcely acknowledges Spirit as *ultimately* separate from matter, although of course his doctrine of creation does do so. His passion for humanity as a single sacred community (and inseparable from the rest of the created order) is palpable.

As with Eckhart and Julian, Traherne understands humanity to be distinct from the Ground of Love, yet not separate from it. But he wishes to take the reader beyond any description of unity. He wishes to convey all of us, in reciprocity with the divine, to what he calls 'Joy eternal'. Despite the proliferation of concepts, Traherne is keen to represent himself as experience-centred. His words still retain energy, vivacity. His spirited language still asks questions.

Meister Eckhart

One Spacious Day

Here walks the heretic, al-Hallaj,
who sees God in everyone
and everyone in God.
He can't keep quiet.

Before his crucifixion,
these final words:
One spacious day, quite soon,
when inner things unite,
the spirit will predominate.
We'll feed less on food,
more on light.

Here walks al-Hallaj,
who claims the freedom to be himself.
They lead him out of the city,
toward the sound of harsh carpentry.

Meister Eckhart was aware of the fate of those who spoke in clear, non-dual terms. He was aware of the life and witness of al-Hallaj, the subject of my poem, above. This Sufi mystic (Husayn ibn Mansur al-Hallaj) was crucified near Baghdad in 922 CE. He was arrested in Basra after repeatedly announcing the words *ana'l-haqq* (literally: 'I am the truth'). Such an abolition of distinctions connects with Eckhart's position.

There are passages in Eckhart where his non-dual tendency becomes explicit. For example, 'There is nothing but one, and where one is, there is all, and where all is, there is one'.[1] It would seem that Eckhart dislikes the rigidity of either/or, preferring that we develop an insight, and then a wisdom, which goes deeper than conventional understandings. Perhaps a sub-text is as follows: If we cling to one side of a duality (if, for example, we favour 'mind over matter'), we are less likely to emerge into wholeness. The following sermon extract is startling, if convoluted, in its expression of non-duality.

In the love that one gives there is no duality, but one and unity,
and in love 'I am God' more than I am in myself.
The prophet says: 'I have said you are gods and children
of the Most High' (Psalm 82:6). That sounds strange that
'a person can become God in love', but so it is true
in the eternal truth.[2]

Eckhart's non-dual Christian discourse is distinct from the dualism of the 'East', where non-duality is a central term with standard definitions. Neither Traherne, Eckhart nor Julian unambiguously discuss the moderate non-dualism which they share. Its origin, for them, lies in the non-dual statements attributed in the Gospels to Jesus. Its effect is to partially collapse the classic Western dualisms of creator/creature, subject/object and spirit/matter.

The ambiguity in Eckhart stems from his view that God's absolute unity and simplicity means that God escapes all conceptualization. God is 'undifferentiated unity' whereas human thought and speech cannot avoid the postulation of a subject and a predicate. Duality and multiplicity are always present; this statement itself involves a duality between the subject and that which is postulated concerning the subject. But Eckhart also holds that we are 'one with God', both now and in terms of future destiny. He seems to mean a real form of identity with the divine. The innate desire of each soul is to return to the One from which it originally came. It therefore appears that, in the first place, God is One and not 'three' ontologically. In the second place, God manifests in a triune manner, such that the union of humanity with God is possible. If I desire to Realize that union (in immediate, experiential knowledge), an old 'I' must be left behind. The injunction within Eckhart's sermons can be summarized as follows: '*Gang uz dir selbst uz!*' ('Go out of yourself!'). But Eckhart undercuts desire and spiritual ambition. He surrounds his 'Go out of yourself!' with '*sunder war umbe*' ('without a why'), to which I will shortly return.

Letting-be

A guiding theme of Eckhart is *Gelâzenheit*, sometimes translated as 'letting-be' or as 'detachment'. Reiner Schürmann[3] considers the most appropriate translation of *Gelâzenheit* to be 'releasement'. Releasement functions in Eckhart as part of the preparation for the birth of God in the soul, which is Eckhart's main theme. Eckhart's passion is that we should 'make actual' the implicit 'seed of God' within us; that is to say, we should allow the divine birth in our souls. This might or might not yield unusual experiences; Eckhart is less concerned with the nature of an actual experience of union than he is with the underlying principle of unity. He mentions Paul's ecstatic experience,[4] but does not deal with anything resembling a phenomenology of ecstasy. He is prepared to take theological risks: he has an elevated understanding of humanity; he has a non-dual tendency.

To prepare the way for non-dual spiritual experience, Eckhart explores the meaning of *Gelâzenheit*. This exploration forms a key part of the biblical exegesis and exposition which is central to his philosophy. Beyond abstraction and beyond image, he desires to present the ultimate mystery: The divine Subject, the Infinite. Then his claim is that the soul is destined for mystical union with the divine, not only in the hereafter, but within this life. This concern would remain abstract, if not abstruse, without the emphasis on the divine Subject being peculiarly accessible within a life of releasement.[5]

> When I preach, I am accustomed to speak about detachment,
> and that a man should be free of himself and of all things;
> second, that a man should be formed again into that simple good
> which is God; third, that he should reflect on the great nobility
> with which God has endowed his soul, so that in this way
> he may come to wonder at God; fourth, about the purity of the divine
> nature, for the brightness of the divine nature is beyond words.
> God is a word, a word unspoken.[6]

God and the experience of God are 'past telling of tongue' (G. M. Hopkins). But this does not inhibit Eckhart from 'telling' at considerable length. His insistence on *Gelâzenheit* is clearly stated in the extract above; the outlook is drastic. The short treatise *On Detachment* implies that detachment or releasement is a deeper quality than even love itself. The noun *Gelâzenheit* is from the verb *lassen*, which means 'to leave aside'. Eckhart's use of the noun is thought to be original. In popular imagination, this is the nub of the Eckhartian parallel with Asian thought. Detachment (or, better in the Asian context: 'non-attachment') is a mutually held key concept. Hee-Sung Keel describes Eckhart's view of *Gelâzenheit* in terms of a radical breakthrough.[7] He explains:

> The self-denial he has in mind does not simply mean the denial
> of a particular desire or action but the denial of desire itself,
> or the will itself, including the will to do God's will.
> It means freedom from will as such, the self-will.
> Detachment, then, means for Eckhart abandoning self-will
> and possessiveness in thought and action.[8]

In a famously unusual interpretation of the words that Jesus reportedly says to Martha ('There is need of only one thing' Lk. 10:42, NRSV), Eckhart states that '. . . whoever wants to be free of care and to be pure must have one thing, and that is detachment'.[9] To Eckhart, God himself is detached. From the tradition of divine timelessness, he deduces that God is unmoved by transitory events.

> This immovable detachment brings a man into the greatest equality
> with God, because God has it from his immovable detachment
> that he is God, and it from his detachment that he has his purity
> and his simplicity and his unchangeability.[10]

Eckhartian *Gelâzenheit* is mainly detachment from images and objects, not a retreat from creating and fostering communion and community.[11] The person who chooses to participate with the divine God will not be found trying to escape from the world's conflicts and sufferings, but will, by identifying mystically with the Son (who suffers at the hands of the world), be reunited mystically with the Father (with whom always the Son identifies). An ongoing 'inner work' is required. This will involve action and contemplation, as inseparable. The person who is an 'active contemplative' will have, as his or her inner foundation, *Gelâzenheit*. Keel states that this 'inner work':

> ... has nothing to do with indulging in any peculiar religious
> experience, ecstatic or enstatic. Its sole purpose is to enhance
> detachment from all things, including religious exercises
> and experiences themselves, only to be engaged in active life
> rooted in the ground of one's being.[12]

Eckhartian non-dualism relates to both *Gelâzenheit* and to a concept of 'nothingness'. The soul is required to become 'nothing' (MHG: *niht*, or in the L sermons *nihil*) if union with God is to be realized. This is because: '... the divine being is equal to nothing, and in it there is neither image nor form'.[13] Elsewhere, Eckhart states that '... to be empty of all created things is to be full of God, and to be full of created things is to be empty of God'.[14] Such detachment frees the soul to be able to 'break through' to its Ground, and thereafter to 'break through' to the Ground of the Godhead.

Eckhart puts forward something of a distinction between God and the Godhead. Those who interpret Eckhart as making a clear distinction would tend to describe it as follows. God is the principle of 'Being' and the personal deity of scripture, whereas the Godhead is the impersonal Absolute which 'dwells' in the unqualified dimension of 'Beyond-Being'. But it needs reiterating that the Godhead (or in other words, the unqualified Absolute) is expressed in the traditional tripartite way. Father, Son and Spirit are figured as *kenotic* expressions of the Infinite which is also One. If Eckhart equates the Godhead with 'absolute nothingness', he is not alluding to a vacuum. He is finding language with which to approach reality; he wants to talk about the field, or the matrix, from which everything emerges or flows.

German Sermon 52 includes the well-known injunction to pray to God that we might be free of 'God'.[15] Assuming that his audience grasps the context of *Gelâzenheit*, Eckhart reiterates the apparently disturbing notion.

> When man clings to place, he clings to distinction.
> Therefore I pray to God that he may make me free of 'God',
> for my real being is above God if we take 'God' to be the
> beginning of created things. For in the same being of God
> where God is above being and above distinction,
> there I myself was, there I willed myself and committed myself
> to create this man. Therefore I am the cause of myself
> in the order of my being, which is eternal, and not in the order

of my becoming, which is temporal. And therefore I am unborn,
and in the manner in which I am unborn I can never die.
In my unborn manner I have been eternally,
and am now, and shall eternally remain.[16]

The stated desire to be free of 'God' appears to be a way of underlining Eckhart's view of an apparent distinction between God and the Godhead. This move on Eckhart's part seems to avoid equating God with Presence. God is that which enables Presence, which in turn enables Love; God is *agape*, but redemption is also configured as *agape*. As with Traherne and Julian, the language of Eckhart at this point is personal and relational. (By way of counterpoint, the language of Ramana Maharshi's version of *Advaita Vedānta* is both personal and impersonal. See Chapter 4.)

A stripping of self-images

The letting go of images and objects does not represent a withdrawal in order to cultivate a particular experience. It is a sign, rather, of an equanimity that remains open and receptive, irrespective of one's experience. Regardless of the external situation, there can be a 'breaking through' (*durchbrechen*) to a serene acceptance of whatever, at any given moment, is the case. The setting for such openness, in Eckhart's view, is the givenness of our incorporation into the kingdom of God.

John Caputo, in the proximate context of observing that the church is always deconstructible, but that the kingdom of God is not, interprets *Gelâzenheit* as follows.

> This letting-be (*Gelâzenheit*) . . . is essentially a letting go of human self-sufficiency . . . which would deny the very meaning of the time of the kingdom as the time of God's rule, not ours. In the kingdom, time can be experienced authentically only by taking time as God's gift and trusting ourselves to time's granting, which is God's giving. . . . By letting go of our own self-possession, by opening ourselves to God's rule, we release the day from its chains. . . . The temporality of the kingdom . . . is free, open, unbound, unchained, a day or time that is savoured one day at a time, experienced, lived for itself, in its own upsurge, instant by instant, day by day.[17]

Caputo understands Eckhart's God to be involved in human affairs, although this God is unknowable in essential ways and cannot be described. Eckhart is viewed by Caputo as pastorally concerned for community cohesion and for the shared practices of Christian life. Reading him, I have the impression of a warm-hearted ascetic who is not overly anxious about personal belief as such. One might imagine him opposing today's spiritual narcissism, whereby we are encouraged to feel elevated thoughts within the parameters of a self-preoccupation unchallenged by social and environmental responsibility.[18]

Eckhart advocates that all activities be attended by *Gelâzenheit*. I am exhorted, not to look for divine remunerations, but to face up to the illusory quality of my separate self (small-s). The letting-be of releasement will be painful to the extent that I have attached myself to unreality; in particular, to the unreality represented by my isolated and isolating ego. Using older forms of words, Eckhart, Julian and Traherne are agreed in their broad attempt to partially collapse the dualisms of creator/created, subject/object and spirit/matter. It cannot be assumed that they share precisely the same type of non-dualism; neither of them is concerned with definitions here. In the poem below, I try to express a moderate non-dualism which is indebted, in part, to an excerpt from the anonymous fourth-century spiritual writer Pseudo-Macarius.[19]

One Light, Many Lamps

Caught short
by nightfall
in a forest;
chancing upon fungi,
luminescent.
Intense bluish-
white shards
would in the morning
be as cold as
crockery.
Peaked strata,
suspended
like tiered
cave-homes
in Cappadocia,
where in silence
a countenance
was seen
and known,
and known to be
seeing back.
Just so,
the wilderness
sees those
who see it
on a late summer
night with stars,
a night to be brought
to sense
by sight
of the earthly.
This fungus:
a hardening

of light.
Beyond its bluish
glow, tiny beings
call their
complement.
Each of them,
a lamp;
each lamp
the embodiment
of one light.

Separation from 'the One light' is what Eckhart and Traherne seem to understand by 'the Fall'. Neither writer is concerned with elaborating a dualism of good/evil. They view human identity as a unity; it is beyond the zone of opposites. It is participatory, as expressed in 2 Pet. 1:4. The follower of Christ, according to that verse, has '... come to share in the very being of God' (REB). There is an identity to humankind which is more immediate, or more subtle, than the process of thought and of thinking itself.

Beyond metaphysics, creeds and institutions, Eckhart (likewise Julian and Traherne) implies understanding and compassion will be harmonized in direct personal experience. We are drawn by Love to a kind of crisis point. Once there, we might glimpse the difficult truth that our separate ego has an illusory quality. For Eckhart, it is attachment which prevents the experience of Love and of Reality, through which the illusory aspect of separate existence is transcended. To countermand *Eigenschaft* (self-attachment), Eckhart puts forward the interior activity of 'cutting loose' *abegescheidenheit*, which literally conveys the idea of decease, as in dying. *Gelâzenheit* is likewise characterized by inner work; there are implications of a peaceful, trusting surrender that seemingly requires nothing from God and asks for nothing.

Although Eckhart told his congregations that a prayer of petition could have a legitimate side, he himself seems uncomfortable with the idea of petitioning the divine.[20] Rather, he teaches an emptying out of personal desire. This is a reflection of his central idea, namely, that God can fully enter the human subject, so that the subject can be said to disappear and merge with the divine object. In other words, 'the birth of God in the soul', to which I will need to return.

What is the *means* by which the human subject may disappear and merge with God? Part of the means has to do with the metaphors 'spark' (MHG: *Vünkelîn*) and 'small castle' (MHG: *Bürgelîn*), both of which convey in Eckhart the soul's highest/deepest part. Each soul possesses such a 'spark' (or 'castle') which is God-given and remains connected to God. As the soul's highest/deepest part, the *Vünkelîn* has the capacity to disentangle the soul from the absorption in created things which obscures the understanding and experience of God. Through grace and through many choices to loosen our attachments, we can (through the *Vünkelîn*) expand 'into the divine'. Here Eckhart is drawing together a classic Western dualism. Here, in Eckhart's theo-philosophy, is the equivalent of the *Vedāntin* teaching of *Tat tvam asi*.

Union with God, however, does not imply that we are transformed into God. But the question arises: Does our 'expansion into divinity' occur at the expense of individual personality? There is no ready agreement on this question; interpreters of Christian 'mystics' will continue to differ on the question of the demise of personality. Eckhart repeatedly says that we are 'nothing' in and of ourselves (MHG: *niht*, or *nihil* in the L sermons). He is not necessarily suspicious of bodiliness. His presuppositions are influenced by Greek philosophy; the negative status of humanity is countermanded by the positive realization of the Absolute. And in his overall theology, Eckhart asserts a vulnerability in God which arises from God's relational 'dependence' on humanity. We are unique expressions of the divine, created for divine union. On a non-dual basis he insists on our nothingness, but also on our participation with or in God.

Divine birth

The idea of a separate, autonomous personhood arises in us as a thought, as a feeling and as a sensation. Our cultural background conspires to confirm that we have accurately gauged 'the truth' of the matter, namely, that we are separate individuals. Eckhart's understanding of Oneness would query this. In modern non-dual language, the thought, the feeling and the sensation of possessing a separate personhood would be regarded as 'objects in awareness'. The person would be viewed as 'That' to whom these objects appear. This leads to a possible claim, by non-dualists, that we are Awareness itself, in some absolute sense.[21] Eckhart, Julian and Traherne do not employ such language, but Ramana Maharshi does do so, even though his tradition is likewise premodern. But if the Christian use of 'Oneness' is treated as 'Awareness', then Oneness in the three Christian teachers might be viewed as 'That' in which the thought, feeling and sensation of separateness appears. The Oneness/Awareness is not an object, but is the background 'on which' objects appear. Accordingly, in terms of the absolute truth-level, this Oneness/Awareness is our true nature. We appear within That, within the One. A traditional Christian ontology might wish to add that the One is the *I Am*, whose nature is the creative love of *agape*. A Christian inclined to non-dualism might wish to affirm: 'The divine *I Am* is my being (absolute level of truth) but I am not (conventional truth-level) the being of the *I Am*'.

In view of the above, and at the risk of facileness, the word 'non-separation' can serve to summarize the outlook of Traherne, Julian, Eckhart and Ramana. Nothing exists independently; that which might appear solid, or personal, is really transparent and impersonal (from the perspective of the absolute truth-level). It is the emphasis on unitive reality or unitive consciousness which brings Ramana into proximity with the three Christians. In the *Advaitic* teaching of Ramana, the phenomenal or empirical self is lured by the non-dual, supreme Self (capital 'S') beyond all false self-identification. The aspirant acquires the experiential knowledge that she *was always* a participant in the infinite substrate of the universe. Eckhartian language converges here, inasmuch as the Meister believes that the individualistic self, with its idea of separateness, *falls away*. This happens in the process of learning to participate in the divine. The 'separated self' or ego[22] is ultimately illusory (albeit *natural,* inasmuch as it produces the day-to-day functioning sense of 'I-ness').

Within the Upanishads, the Self (capital 'S') might serve as a synonym for 'God'. Ramana tended to use the word 'God' as interchangeable with 'Absolute Being' and 'Self'. But his understanding of 'God' is *Advaitic*: That is to say, it is not so much 'personal' as transpersonal and interpersonal. It might be characterized as 'limitless Awareness'. Traherne capitalizes the word 'Self' at times, but probably does so as part of his seventeenth-century style. Eckhart uses the phrases 'our true nature' or 'our higher self', both of which might suggest that analogies be drawn with the Self of the *Upanishads.* Although Eckhart and Julian teach that humankind needs to revert to participation in the divine, they also believe that God is infinitely greater than anything that can be thought about God. If someone presumes to think that they have reached a conception of a divine property, it is likely to be more false than true. Contrariwise, Julian's maternal imagery is so graphic and unqualified as to leave room for literality. Below, I allude to the impossibility of 'speaking the divine'.

Without images

the sight of the invisible

will be no blazing illumination

but inner sight I mean to say insight

which means seeing without images

the sight of the invisible

will be possible only to eyes large enough

or rather enlarged enough to see the sacred

everywhere

On this view, the *kenotic* self will have little use for images or projections. It will 'see the invisible without seeing it'. Such a self might perhaps be viewed as a Christian equivalent of the Buddhistic 'non-substantial self' (Skt: *anātman*; Pali: *anatta*). An epithet by Dōgen expresses a parallel teaching within a Zenist context: 'To learn the Buddha Way is to learn one's self; to learn one's self is to forget one's self'.

We can now consider Eckhart's idea of the divine fully entering the human subject. This is reciprocal. The subject simultaneously merges with the divine object. When Eckhart uses the word 'God' and the transcendental predicate 'the One' (*ein* in MHG, or *unum* in the L sermons), he seems to mean a static One (which, dwelling in mystery, is beyond enumeration) *and also* a dynamic process (likewise partaking of mystery). In the mode of 'Father', God eternally gives birth to his 'Son'. By extension, as 'one birth', God also eternally gives birth to the 'Son' in us. That is to say, the birth of God in the soul is not separate from the birth of the 'Son', who is not involved in time's constraints but 'was' and 'is' eternally born. In German Sermon 12, Eckhart specifically states: '. . . we are this same Son'.[23] He continues:

> When God sees that we are the only-begotten Son,
> he is very quick to pursue us and acts as though his divine being
> were going to burst and completely vanish,
> so that he might reveal to us the utter abyss of his divinity
> and the fullness of his being and nature.
> God hastens to make it all ours just as it is his.
> Here in this fullness God has delight and joy.
> Such a person stands in God's knowing and in God's love
> and becomes nothing other than what God is in himself.[24]

This sermon is a fine example of Eckhart's non-dual tone. The birth of the 'Son' in each human soul will manifest itself as transformed behaviour. We will no longer attempt to maximize every circumstance of our lives. Instead, we will realize ('in our Ground') who we really are. Dispossessed of the illusory, separate self-identity, we will find ourselves 'repossessed' by the One who gave us 'second birth'. This is the 'Oneing' which Julian takes up, about 50 years after Eckhart's death. There is a reconciliation of opposites. Conflictual impulses within the soul are no longer pitted against each other. The soul finds its primordial and natural unity in and with the divine.

Among the NT passages cited by Eckhart to corroborate his non-dual tendency is 'The Father and I are one' (Jn 10:30, NRSV) and '. . . the Father is in me and I am in the Father' (Jn 10:38, NRSV). Eckhart is nonetheless clear that, in the awareness of Jesus, God is an 'I' distinct from his own 'I'. The Gospel accounts assert that Jesus refers to that which in modern jargon we might label as 'the Other who is not wholly other'. It is from this Other that Jesus is said to have come (and will return to). But the relationship, especially in John's Gospel, is profoundly mysterious. Jesus is portrayed as maintaining constant awareness of God as his Father, and simultaneously as seeming to 'locate' the Father as inseparable from his own 'I'. Chronologically, the Gospel accounts are held to have been written after the Pauline Epistles, which allude to non-dual tendencies within the infant Christian communities. For example, Ro. 8:14–17 (REB): 'All who are moved by the Spirit of God are sons of God . . . the Spirit of God joins with our spirit in testifying that we are God's children; and if children, then heirs. We are God's heirs and Christ's fellow-heirs'. Other instances could be cited, such as 1 Cor. 6:17 and 13:12b (NRSV): 'But anyone united to the Lord becomes one spirit with him'; 'Now I know only in part; then I will know fully, even as I have been fully known'.

Although full knowledge is always 'up ahead', Eckhart finds concurrence with Julian and Traherne in his confidence that the state of beatitude is not only post-death. The three appear to agree that one of the obstacles to a joyful realization of beatitude is the notion that such a condition is reserved for the future. Their spirituality is oriented around understandings and affective experiences that take place *here*. Therefore, 'Realization' is involved, to somewhat co-opt the sub-continental meaning of an immediate and 'lived-out' embodying of truth. Such 'Realization' runs far deeper than our fleeting identification with the various roles which we assume in the world of outward consciousness. I have mentioned that Eckhart underlines human contingency; we are *niht* (or *nihil*) in and of ourselves. Reference will be made, in later chapters, to the underlying coherence of *kenosis* (self-emptying) and *śūnyatā* (emptiness). Within their respective traditions, these concepts are indispensable to 'Realization' or 'non-dual awakening'.

Eckhart's 'birth mysticism' is positive towards the human body. Neither he, nor Julian nor Traherne preach self-denial. Eckhart's congregations are not required to make a dualistic choice. They do not have to choose between cultivation of the soul at the expense of nurturing the body. There is no focus on eternity at the expense of responsibility for what happens in the present time. Eckhart is capable of being distinctly practical. He opposes, for example, a popular idea that contemplation is a passive activity, fit for a recluse. The 'true seeing and true knowing' of contemplation is intended to nourish, not a 'gazing at being', but a 'participation in being'. Eckhart's hearers are expected to be *verb-oriented*, giving birth to the 'Son' by actively becoming and begetting. This would have resonated with Traherne. It appears to me that both men eschew 'prayer', in the sense of requesting something from God. For if we are 'full', we have no need to pray in that sense.

'Without a why and wherefore'

According to Charlotte Radler the ethically oriented teachings of Eckhart can be described as apophatic.[25] Apophatic or negative theology has a variety of meanings, because negation, as a means of working towards a description of the divine, arose in diverse traditions in different eras.[26] But broadly speaking, and as far as Eckhart is concerned, the apophatic method deliberately includes the possibility of undermining itself. With his persistent attitude of *openness* as far as referential positions are concerned (and aware that he is writing 'that which cannot be written'), Eckhart effectively blurs the distinctions between subject and object. Apophatic theology tends to 'take back' whatever it has asserted, and then (perhaps) take back the taking back. But on the face of it, Eckhart simply desires that his hearers and readers should question their assumptions and preconceptions with regard to the conventional truth-level and the complete duality it posits, as between creature and Creator. Radler can claim an apophaticism for Eckhart because his writings are almost devoid of specific ethical instruction. She writes:

According to Eckhart's apophatic ethics, it is out of the inner ground
that the detached human being performs works without a why
(*sunder war umbe*), not for the sake of something but for the sake
of no purpose and nothing, that is, God. The only option for a detached

person, who rests content in the emptiness of the divine, is to live and work
a way-less and why-less life toward God as the final goal. In living this way
the detached human being does not totalize or fracture the integrity
of the neighbour, by instrumentalizing him or her, but truly recognizes
and acknowledges the communal identity of being.[27]

Political theologian Dorothee Soelle (d. 2003) explores the implications of Eckhart's
idea of living *sunder war umbe*: 'without a why'. Soelle maintains that 'the way-less
way' can help to contain the ego and reduce world-wide violence. She writes as
follows:

This 'without a why or a wherefore' that we should live in, that life
itself lives in, what does it mean? It is the absence of all purpose,
all calculation, every *quid pro quo*, every tit for tat, all domination
that makes life itself its servant. Wherever we are torn between being
and doing, feeling and acting, we no longer live *sunder war umbe*.[28]

The seemingly all-pervasive alternative is bleak:

Instead, we measure expenditure and success, calculate probability and benefit, or
else obey fears we do not understand. I say this with a view to the goal-centred
rationality that pervades our highly technologized world. Such a rationality
prohibits any form of existence for which there is no purpose: we eat certain foods
in order to lose weight, we take dancing lessons in order to keep fit, and we pray in
order to facilitate specific wish fulfillment by God.[29]

When language is conducted 'without a why and wherefore', it obviously carries less
intentionality, less purposiveness. It carries, instead, more of a tone of celebration:
Of acknowledgement for the sake of acknowledgement. Language, in other words,
can bear the character of praise. It can speak of the letting go of my preoccupation
or distraction. There can be a letting go of what Eckhart calls 'what is one's own'
(*Eigenschaft*). Soelle continues:

While praise may have its reasons – and mingles with thanksgiving in the
language if liturgy – in reality it always has the character of the *sunder war umbe*.
For example, in praising the moon as it rises, in praising someone who is loved
or, indeed, in praising the source of all good, the ego that is possessed by goals
and that craves dominance vanishes. It has stepped out of itself. It has scuttled
itself.[30]

Soelle makes use of Simone Weil's often-quoted and traditional statement to the effect
that true attention-giving, in its detachment or 'emptiness', is the substance of prayer.
She describes Weil's statement as a clear example of Eckhart's *sunder war umbe*. In my
view, Soelle rightly discusses Eckhart as an exemplar for this third millennium. She
writes of Eckhart in terms of a critical, Christ-infused, practical mysticism. Whatever
we make of Eckhart's 'Godhead beyond God', the assumed 'beyondness' does not

preclude either access or union. Wherever we are at this moment, we are *re-called* to union with ultimacy. I hope to infer as much, in my poem below.

The Potter and the Prison

Simply to be here is more than a pleasure,
writes a Japanese potter on a jug he has made
in the Shogun's prison. He is living out
his teacher's words: *If enlightenment*
is not where you're standing,
where will you look?

It is not hard to imagine Julian and Traherne agreeing with Eckhart that even an *engaged* mysticism must conceive of the divine as unknowable in an absolute sense.[31] God allows 'God' to be experienced in the kind of communion that is manifested in the love between people and in the kind of prayer that manifests an awareness of already-existing union. As the process of union with God begins to take place, Eckhart infers that joy emerges as a natural response. The unity can be 'known' by the human subject with the aid of reason and with the assistance of that to which reason points. The word 'known' would seem to equate with an awareness of a 'unity', both within ourselves and within the 'exterior' world. Inherent to this 'knowledge' is the awakening of an *I Am* consciousness. The paradox is that this *I Am* is not egocentric. It 'knows' itself, only insofar as it knows itself to be part of what *Advaita Vedānta* calls the universal non-dual Self. But of course my three writers express this in classically Christian triune terms. Eckhart appears superficially to advance a Buddhist tenet, when he declares that there is no such thing as a separate *me*. In our more enlightened moments (he states), we all *know* this to be true. The enlightenment to which he refers is instigated and brought to maturity by the Spirit of Christ within. To 'find' this inner Christ is to find oneself, since to find oneself is to find the True and the True is 'God'.

It would seem to me that theories regarding truth (what to rule in; what to rule out) might not concern Eckhart so much as the question of practice (what should we do?). The allied question (what should we be?) likewise concerns Julian and Traherne. Eckhart mentions 'truth' frequently; perhaps the impression is purposefully conveyed that truth should always be up for discussion.[32] On the other hand, Eckhart might be best understood when we choose to inhabit his perspective on truth, even if this entails suspension of disbelief. Neither he, Julian nor Traherne overtly deny a separate *me*, but the tonal register is one of non-separation. In his few negative passages, Traherne mentions the ugly side of getting, calculating and spending wealth. But his forays into negativity are to counterpoint non-separation. In the next chapter, I discuss Julian's hopefulness with regard to human transformation. Her belief in God's maternal care takes her beyond a close focus on the crucifixion to an all-inclusive positivity. Eckhart is also positive, but more abstract to the extent that he is more concerned with transcendence through divine birth in the soul.

Entering the life divine

When Eckhart alludes to transcendence, he is not necessarily thinking of the supramundane, or of a situation that might obtain after death, such as heavenly transcendence. Nor is he thinking, primarily, of the indwelling of God in this life. If Eckhart has a theme or 'a single great idea' from which all his other ideas develop, it is God's birth in the soul.[33]

> If anyone were to ask me: why do we pray, why do we fast,
> why do we all perform our devotions and good works,
> why are we baptized, why did God, the All-Highest,
> take on our flesh? – then I would reply: in order that God
> may be born in the soul and the soul be born in God.
> That is why the whole of Scripture was written and why God
> created the whole world and all the order of angels:
> so that God could be born in the soul and the soul in God.[34]

According to Philip Sherrard, a significant number of the Greek Fathers accepted that each person possessed 'an inherent capacity to be divinized'.[35] Eckhart's equivalent to the Patristic emphasis on divinization is the birth of God in the 'ground of the soul'. He often uses this phrase. The word *Grunt* or ground, or ground of being, does service as a synonym for the deepest 'heart' of each person. This 'ground' is beyond name and form. It is both *in* the world, *yet* transcendent. The doctrine regarding incarnation implies full participation in the human 'ground' by Christ as the 'Son'. Cyprian Smith elaborates:

> What must I do to get into my own ground? I have to strip away
> the 'images'. I have to let go of all that I normally consider as 'myself',
> all the external part of my nature which is conditioned by outward
> circumstances, all my individual habits of mind, patterns of behaviour,
> assumptions and expectations. But if I do that, I shall have let go
> of all that is *distinctively* me, all that separates and distinguishes me
> from other people. . . . At this level all distinctions between human
> beings fade away; at this level they are all one.[36]

Eckhart believes that we not only encounter the 'Son' when we enter the 'ground', but that in a sense we *become* the 'Son'. We revert to being the children of God that we were created to be in the first place. Smith continues:

> If we strip away from ourselves all that is accidental, relative and individual in
> ourselves, we shall attain that 'universal human nature' which has been united to
> Christ, and the Incarnation will thus become a present reality for us, here and now,
> in our lives.[37]

A physical incarnation, accepted as an actual historical moment, is less significant to Eckhart than an 'inward' incarnation. If the 'ground of the soul' simultaneously transcends the world and is within the world (and 'available' within the depths of each person), a present-moment transformation of life is possible. This would apply, irrespective of any historical claim. Such a conception was taken up by Feuerbach who, as he moved from Idealism to a form of speculative naturalism, offered a perverse version of Eckhartian thought.[38] Smith assumes a Christian readership when he states that:

> Eckhart ... does not encourage us to become 'Christ-centred' in the sense of being exclusively preoccupied with the historical figure .... He wants us rather to encounter Christ as a living, active force within ourselves, in the present moment.[39]

Therefore Smith can conclude: Rather than merely 'follow' Christ, or 'believe' in Christ, we *become* Christ.[40] It is not difficult to understand why powerful men of the Church sought to discredit Eckhart. Eventually, part of his work was condemned. Many others, in Germany and beyond, found themselves drawn to a deeper life, and to involvement with household churches and with other communities, as a result of Eckhart's preaching.

As stated earlier, Eckhart's God is One (*ein* or *unum*) but manifests as a triunity which, as with God-as-One, is beyond enumeration. There are not three 'instances' of God. Such mysteries are made possible through that which, in God, can be called 'mind' or 'intellect' or 'act of understanding'. This 'intellect' (MHG: *vernünfticheit*, or, in the L sermons *intellectus*) is consistently given priority over 'being'. That which is called 'the One' is the cause of 'being'. Eckhart is consistent with medieval usage in distinguishing between 'intellect' and 'reason'. The 'intellect' relates to the capacity to understand and to the act of understanding. The 'reason' refers to that which might devolve from acts of understanding. The Latin *esse* is translated by McGinn as 'being' or 'existence' or as 'act of existence'. Others have rendered the MHG *Isticheit* as 'Is-ness' and sometimes translated *esse* as 'Isness'. In itself, 'being' is derived from 'intellect'. That is to say, wherever Eckhart uses *vernünfticheit* or *intellectus* in his attempt to characterize God's inner life, he takes 'being' to be derived from it. The following two passages are from Frank Tobin's translation of German Sermon 9.

> God works above being in vastness, where he can roam.
> He works in nonbeing. Before being was, God worked.
> He worked being when there was no being.
> Unsophisticated teachers say that God is pure being.
> He is as high above being as the highest angel is above a gnat.
> I would be speaking as incorrectly in calling God a being
> as if I called the sun pale or black.[41]

> When we grasp God in being, we grasp him in his antechamber,
> for being is the antechamber in which he dwells.
> When is he then in his temple, in which he shines as holy?
> Intellect is the temple of God. Nowhere does God dwell more properly
> than in his temple, in intellect ... remaining in himself alone
> where nothing ever touches him; for he alone is there in his stillness.
> God in the knowledge of himself knows himself in himself.[42]

Here, Eckhart juxtaposes divine intellect and human intellect. By the word 'intellect' we know that he means, not the modern usage, but the act of understanding as having priority over 'being'. In relation to humanity, 'intellect' therefore means the workings of a spiritually alert mind, in tune with Spirit. There is a sense, in Eckhart, in which this 'intellect' is uncreated; in other words, divine. The metaphors 'spark' (*Vünkelîn*) or 'small castle' (*Bürgelîn*), which characterize the soul's latent power, appear connected with that which is 'uncreated'. It is as if these metaphors represent the soul's highest or deepest part: That which retains a connection with God. On the question of the priority of 'intellect' or 'act of understanding' over 'being', Keel elaborates:

> Like divine intellect, human intellect is free from the distinctions
> and particularities characterizing finite beings. In its clean and
> empty nature, intellect is not a being but rather nothingness (*nihil*),
> like divine nothingness. It is precisely this empty, nothingness-like
> nature of intellect that enables it to cognize things universally,
> not being confined to a particular category of beings.[43]

It is difficult to grasp what 'nothingness' and 'divine nothingness' might mean here. Since Keel also uses the word 'empty', does he mean Buddhist emptiness, *śūnyatā*? It is clear that apophatic theology should attempt to avoid assigning words to that which is ineffable; it is also clear that we all necessarily have recourse to words. There will always be definitional impotence.

One reason for Eckhart's popularity today might be that his metaphysics is based on *vernünfticheit* or *intellectus* rather than on 'being' as such. As implied earlier, Eckhartian rhetoric (if not precisely Eckhartian theology) puts forward a fusing, within the one Ground, of the human 'intellect' with the divine 'intellect'. Such a perspective on 'intellect' is, *prima facie*, inseparable from an apparent belief that the soul has something 'uncreated' about it. McGinn places this disputed point into a mollifying context:

> The 'uncreated something' is *intellect as intellect*, as virtual being, not as formal being
> in the world. It is something *in* the soul (or perhaps better, the soul is really *in* it) . . . .
> . . . The 'uncreated something' is not and cannot be a part of any-*thing*. It is as
> mysterious and as unnameable in us as it is in God.[44]

Mysterious indeed; nonetheless Eckhart views humanity as part of God's manifestation. In myself I am 'nothing' (*niht* or *nihil*). But to the degree to which I am *aware*, I can become by grace a participant in 'the One'. My phenomenal self will be eased to one side; I will realize my 'share', so to say, within 'the One' (*ein* or *unum*). Perhaps this is a prominent aspect of the influence of Neoplatonism on Eckhart. Humanity returns to 'the One'. Humanity can, through the grace of increased awareness of the true situation, return to its 'share' within the One. Further, it seems that Eckhart believes that humanity was never *truly* outside 'the One', in the first place.

The Eckhartian aporia, in which non-dual statements can be taken to suggest a shared ontology between God and humanity, has raised eyebrows since the early fourteenth century. A tentative 'solution' is that Eckhart is best assessed, today, as a theopoet. There appears to be scant support for such a view in Eckhartian scholarship. One exception is Oliver Davies who finds poetic characteristics in the sermons (both MHG and L) and thereby eases the perplexity surrounding the less temperate non-dual statements.[45] Assessments by Denys Turner likewise tend to support a theopoetic interpretation of Eckhart. For example, Turner suggests that the increasing use of the vernacular in Eckhart's day led to '. . . a distinctive theological rhetoric'.[46] Noting the possible influence of Marguerite Porete's *Mirouer des Ames Simples*, Turner hints that because both wrote with pastoral intent in their respective vernaculars, both were given to rhetorical hyperbole.[47]

Eckhart's suggestion that the intellect is uncreated is regarded by Turner as a legitimate implication from Neoplatonic doctrine. It was common, in medieval theology, to hold that all beings existed 'virtually' in God's mind, from eternity. What we *are*, in contingent life, is what we *were* in God's mind. Turner summarizes Eckhart's use of the tradition as follows:

> . . . what I most fully and truly *am*, in my contingent, created existence, is what I *was* in my source. My true being, intellect, is not merely divine but identical with the Godhead in which there can be no possibility of distinctions.[48]

Julian makes a parallel move. She writes, not of 'something uncreated' in humanity, but of the 'substance' of the soul being inseparable from the 'substance' of God.[49] In the next chapter, I will look briefly at this puzzle. Julian's apparent radicalism is mentioned by Turner, but he believes that it 'carries no risks for Julian'.[50] On the other hand, Eckhart openly espouses a form of non-dualism.

> . . . Julian can confidently play with formulas little short of Eckhart's in audacity while remaining firmly within the common Neoplatonic tradition, while Eckhart's version of them departs from the tradition.[51]

To the extent that 'truth' is accessible, Eckhart declares it to be accessible through paradox. Both *via positiva* and *via negativa* are necessary; even by Eckhart's time, the negative theology of apophasis was a highly traditional method for attributing (or rather, denying) qualities to the divine.[52] Eckhart uses the method, at least in part, to break down what he considers to be the idols of human imagination. These idols masquerade as versions of what God *is*. Most obviously, Eckhart works with his hearers' intuition that God is infinite by negating that God is finite. This need not imply that affirmation is abandoned. An authentically 'spiritual' life (on this view) requires both affirmation and negation, similarity and dissimilarity. God will be found within, and not only 'out there'. Our true nature, as lodged within the Ground, is inseparable from the divine. Accordingly, the concept of 'our true nature' might be said to function, throughout Eckhart, in a similar way to that of the non-dual Self (capital 'S') in the Upanishads. God remains transcendent, yet God is within. Eckhart and Julian hold these two positions simultaneously: Absolute transcendence, and yet, an immanence that is realizable in lived experience. (For, how could the former ever be distinguished from the latter?) For his part, Traherne is also very concerned with lived experience *now*. Heaven comes to Earth: we do not 'ascend' to a sphere which lies beyond, so much as 'descend'. The first verse of *Wonder* bears quoting once more.

> How like an Angel came I down!
> How Bright are all Things here!
> When first among his Works I did appear
> O how their GLORY me did Crown?
> The World resembled his *Eternitie*,
> In which my Soul did Walk;
> And evry Thing that I did see,
> Did with me talk.[53]

Neither Traherne, Julian nor Eckhart succumb to any 'religious' impulse to denigrate the body or the world. They complain only of an aspect of the human will that inclines humanity towards what is now called narcissism. Hence the need for *kenosis*. It is in acts of self-emptying that *metanoia* (openness to conversion) is expressed. *Metanoia* is understood as a life-long process of moving beyond the mind's tendency to be content with its current thought-patterns. On this view, we continually recover our true self/Self. As a result of *metanoia*, there is *koinonia* (fellowship: The manifestation of 'inter-being').[54]

To recapitulate the position developed by Eckhart (and perhaps implied by Julian and Traherne): the receptive self meets up with the divine, *all-ways*, but without comprehending it. And in order for the human subject to *re-merge* with the divine object, the notion 'God', as a notion, should be abandoned. The soul then remains as free from 'knowing' as it was before the person was born. Eckhart, Julian and Traherne hold the traditional view that God is beyond comprehension, but not beyond experience.[55] On one hand, God cannot be described, except in terms of mystery; on the other hand, all things reveal God. It is a question of seeing; those who pay the closest attention become the pure in heart. What they see is *carried alive*, so to say, into their hearts and into their actions, by means of their *passionate seeing*. Is this not another way of saying that faith is an act of imagination? In secular terms, is it a way of saying that 'the good life' consists in imaginative seeing?

Does the Eckhartian theo-philosophy of releasement, of 'uncovering', bear analogy with a particular sub-continental philosophy? In my view, yes. Did Traherne know Eckhart's work? Was Eckhart's near-contemporary, Julian of Norwich, familiar with it? The answer to these lesser questions remains unclear. The three mystics (if that imprecise word is appropriate) employ words which point to humanity's participation within the Infinite. This is conceived as a cosmic transcendence which contains the finite without itself being containable. At the same time, their God is irrepressibly immanent. As Living Spirit, their God generates communion between all of life. This is relevant in today's trans-religious attempts to put forward a non-exclusivist and non-oppositional narrative. Such a narrative might serve as an option for reasoned commitment.

The temerity with which Eckhart claims that the divine Subject is accessible within a human object has resonances with the Upanishadic tradition. This tradition prominently includes a speculative philosophy of identity between the divine and human. The emphasis on overcoming distinctions between the perceiving subject (e.g. the divine Subject) and the objects of the world (e.g. the devotee) is with view to *Brahmanic* union. *Brahman* is perhaps best understood as 'the Infinite' (which in some way includes the finite) and not as 'the Absolute' (which implies distinction from that which is relative). *Brahmā* (with the macron over the final 'a') is best understood as the appearance of *Brahman* in the cosmos, in order to produce beings. If the world of beings that *Brahmā* produces is regarded as absolute, then that is illusion. That is to say, the world is only illusory when regarded erroneously as absolute. Between *Brahmā* and the beings which *Brahmā* generates there is an accepted dualism. On the other hand, *Brahmanic* union is taken by thorough-going *Advaitins* to mean the complete absence of differentiation.

It is important to observe that the *Ātman* ('the Self' or 'Consciousness') of the Upanishads refers to the innermost principle or ultimate ground of humanity. Accordingly, 'the Self' might be equated with *Brahman*. But not always. A degree of flexibility in language allows 'the Self' to be construed as both non-dual and dual. An angle of vision which is non-dualist is not the same as a monist account of reality. In India there is widespread devotion to manifestations of the Self (capital 'S'). Devotion implies a dualistic element, even though the Self (as our innermost principle) is commonly held to be non-dual. It should also be said that within devotional Hinduism, when a devotee identifies with the Self, this is not necessarily a declaration of being *identical to* the Self. Rather, to 'identity with the Self' implies the uncovering of one's primordial, infinite Self. Such a relation has its parallel in Eckhart's 'true nature' and in Christianity as a whole. The devotee of Christ is encouraged to identify with Christ. This connotes, not a belief in *being identical*, but a vision of finding oneself, one's true self, through relationship. The divine is not only considered to be 'out there', accessible to faith, but is regarded as 'in here'. I understand this to be the viewpoint of Eckhart, Julian and Traherne.

An impulse to find resonances between Eckhart and the Upanishadic tradition can be intemperate. Verbal elision is fraught. The Upanishadic 'Self' and the Eckhartian 'our true nature' share a transcendent viewpoint. But there are varieties of transcendence, some of them linked with patriarchal assumptions and projections.[56] The transcendent viewpoint in which I am interested can be thought of as 'grounded', while at the same time being paradoxically boundless, inasmuch as it embraces both the relative and the absolute. In Christian understandings, it is the relationality of the divine *perichoresis* that 'grounds' the divine transcendence, which has no boundaries. As discussed in the previous chapter, the breaking down of boundaries is very important to Traherne. He does not elaborate a theopoem of transcendence as such. But one of the paradoxes in Eckhart is that while he heads in the direction of breaking boundaries, his 'conclusions' do not 'touch' a pure transcendence. And yet, when he treats of 'intellect', understood as a spiritually alive mind, this 'intellect' seems to participate in a pure transcendence.

But the main paradox for Eckhart (and for both Julian and Traherne) would seem to be this: Divine transcendence is 'realizable'. It manifests as immanence: A seemingly inevitable (and to that extent, unremarkable) immanence within creaturely life. The practice of devotion, or surrender, is the *perichoretic* avenue through which divine transcendence becomes grounded.[57] This is also the case within the Upanishadic milieu. Through divine grace, a human being can Realize some kind of identity with the Infinite.[58] As to my three Europeans, a progression is put forward, beginning with the dualism of devotion and moving in the direction of 'devotion without difference' (Skt. *abheda bhakti*). The 'culmination' is union. The unitive mystery is *perichoretic* in origin and outworking. It is not remote from other contingent creatures. It is not separatist; nor does it lack communal concern.

The many representations of deities in India can evoke distaste. This is especially the case with people who regard themselves as monotheists. But monotheists (in my experience) often fail to imagine that the One God might be represented under myriad forms, without recourse to idolatry. A sense of monotheistic superiority, common to 'Western' sensibility, is dispelled when the many representations are accepted as pointers to the one truth, namely, that the Infinite is beyond all possible representation. A full transcendence of the Infinite is acknowledged; a full immanence is also acknowledged. Traditionally, it is heretical within the Abrahamic religions to blur the boundary between Creator and creature. But within mystically inclined movements, an over-arching theme can be imagined, of 'Consciousness' (capital 'C') or at least of 'consciousness ever-evolving'. This would imply that we are part of the subjectivity of the universe. As subjects, we experience our own subjectivity in a manner that cannot be explained by anything else. No adequate metaphor can be used to describe our own subjectivity, since it is primary and 'untranslatable'. Perhaps it could be said that we are 'more than conscious' or part of Consciousness itself. In traditional Indian usage, the *Ātman* is Consciousness (capital 'C') or the Self (capital 'S'). The word is a pointer to infinite Mind, the ultimate substrate or principle of the universe. It is just possible to interpret Eckhart as alluding to both a conventional self and a transcendental self, where the latter approximates the *Ātman*.

But is there a meaningful sense in which a claim could be made that we *are* consciousness, at least with a small 'c'? The subject remains opaque. Perhaps there are internal distinctions within consciousness (small 'c') that are yet to be adequately described. Meanwhile, 'consciousness' might continue, *pro tempore*, to approximate heightened awareness which is tilted towards immediacy. This is intimated in the following lines from Traherne's *Fifth Day*.[59]

Armies of Birds out of the Waters rise.
And soaring mount towards the smiling Skies.
Here skipping Fishes cut the lambent Air,
There living Castles mighty things declare;
And swiftly rolling through the spacious Main,
This Day proclaim, with all their finny Train.

In the poem above, Traherne is not interested in particular names or classifications. He wants us to go beyond the conventional truth-level. He desires that we might sense the Presence which underlies all that is temporary. The concept and practice of non-dual devotion (*abheda bhakti*) might serve as a point of balance between absolute and relative truth. It might also assist those whose preoccupation with absolute truth is to the detriment of emotional integration in their personal lives. I mean to hint at such a balance in the following poem.

Today could be Saturday

I clap because I must clap.
I sway because I must sway.
I laugh because I must laugh.
I dance because I must dance.

And sometimes, just sometimes,
I enter the vibrant present tense,
as clear-eyed as a salmon,
as spacious as a cloudless sky.

One without boundaries

The Eckhartian relationship between the divine and the human is distinguishable, yet indivisible. I have mentioned this paradox by using both 'the language of identity' and 'the language of participation'. Eckhart's assertion that God is One, with no distinction possible, relates to his use of *Grunt* with regard to God. In this 'ground', God is undifferentiated, and yet the 'ground' gives rise to the potentiality of the Trinity. It also allows for the mysterious oneness of the soul within the Trinitarian differentiation. The clearest exposition of the 'workings' of the Trinity comes in German Sermon 39. Eckhart does not provide a picture of a hierarchic Father in heaven who might inadvertently generate a male-oriented idolatry here on earth. The following is an extract from Frank Tobin's translation of Sermon 39.

> All that is in God moves him to give birth. His ground, his essence,
> and his being all move the Father to give birth. . . . Whenever the Son
> appears in the soul, the love of the Holy Spirit also appears.
> Therefore, I say: The Father's being consists in giving birth to the Son;
> the Son's being consists in my being born in him and like him;
> the Holy Spirit's being lies in my catching fire in him and becoming
> totally melted and becoming simply love. Whoever is thus inside of love
> and is totally love thinks that God loves no one but him alone,
> nor can he love anyone nor be loved by anyone than by him (God) alone.[60]

But humanity can only have access to the *Grunt* when 'knowing' gives way to a complete 'unknowing'. Only then can God's 'ground' and the soul's 'ground' be treated as 'one ground'. McGinn writes that Eckhart uses *Grunt* variously, but with one end in view, namely, to characterize the 'simple One' as including both God and humanity.[61] If Eckhart goes so far as to say that God and humanity share an 'indistinct identity', this is writing which attempts to write from God's point of view. McGinn believes the *Grunt* metaphor (and synonym) to be a key to Eckhart's thought, because of that to which *Grunt* gives rise. Outside the 'ground', the divine and the human could not relate to each other or be mystically united. It allows for a dynamic harmony and mutual participation. The liturgical tradition expresses this in the Doxology of the Eucharistic Prayer: 'Through him, with him, in him, in the unity of the Holy Spirit. . . .'

In the following piece of writing, I have tried to blend the conventional desire for a soulmate with a desire to find the ultimate reflection of one's face.

Come, Come. Go, Go.

This glance
charged with
direct desire,
intensity:
this impulse
   – embracing,
        embraceable –
is also tender
possibly,
without calculation.

Eyes of oneness ask:
are you my face of faces?
From a body of oneness
   – depths,
       shallows –
they ask: *are you my true lover*
at last, and
at the last?

Eckhart asserts that the soul can recover 'indistinction'. God ceases to be an object to be known and loved and served *ex parte*. Instead, the soul will affectively 'actualize' its oneness with God by entering its own nothingness (*niht*/*nihil*).

> You should love him as he is a non-God, a non-spirit, a non-person, a non-image, but as he is a pure, unmixed, bright 'One', separated from all duality; and in that One we should eternally sink down, out of 'something' into 'nothing'.[62]

Traherne and Julian also tend to support the unconventional teaching that we will emerge from this relative life as 'one with God' in some sense. We are invited to the experienceable (*erfahrbar*) truth that the divine is not (only) a 'being' or 'person' outside us. It is important to note that when the Eckhartian soul is 'voided' of all things pertaining to creatureliness, it *reverts* to a form of identification with God. McGinn states that the language of identification, or of indistinction, represents the dialectical and inadequate play of language.[63] McGinn precedes some of his translations with this *caveat*: 'Of course, from the perspective of the soul's created being there is no mutuality at all – pure existence has nothing in common with nothing'.[64] Well-known Eckhartian phrases, such as those below, must therefore be regarded by McGinn as hyperbolic. I would tend to see them as theopoetic statements of trans-identification which are intended to underscore a theme of non-separation.

The eye with which I see God
is the same eye with which God sees me:
my eye and God's eye are one eye,[65] one seeing,
one knowing, and one love.[66]

You must know that this is in reality one and the same thing:
to know God and to be known by God,
to see God and to be seen by God.[67]

Aware of the limits of language, Eckhart's readers (McGinn infers) need to grasp that, in some way, they are in a continuous state of union with God. But then, they also need to see that this union '. . . is not an *experience* in any ordinary sense of the term – it is coming to realize and live out of the ground of experience, or better, of consciousness'.[68]

Among writers in English, the twentieth-century renaissance in Eckhartian studies was led by Carl Kelley who translates short sections, around which he builds the claim that Eckhart consciously writes from 'God's standpoint'. Kelley appears eager to state, and to restate, that Eckhart sees a real distinction between God and the self, from the human point of view. And yet when Eckhart adopts God's standpoint, Kelley has to concede that Eckhart can write: 'In truest reality there is no duality'.[69] Again, writing from God's perspective, Eckhart can make the extraordinary statement that 'the finite is the infinite'.[70] According to Kelley, this does not compromise the otherness of God. The Eckhartian understanding of God can be spelt out as 'Pure Spirit, unconditioned Isness, infinite Selfhood, the unlimited Knower . . . or the divine Self, which is identically the unrestricted Principle'.[71]

Kelley draws out Eckhart's distinction between 'is-ness' (MHG: *Isticheit*, or, in the L sermons *esse*) and 'essence'. It is more common, in any translation from Latin, to render *esse* as 'being'. I have mentioned 'intellect' in Eckhart, and his placement of 'intellect' above 'being'. Whether or not *esse* is rendered as 'is-ness' or 'being', it precedes 'essence' and is higher than it. On the other hand, since 'essence' is the seed of all manifestation and is grounded in 'is-ness', it can be said to be identical with it. But it is only within 'the One' (or the indivisible and all-inclusive Principle) that 'essence' is identical with 'is-ness'.

German Sermon 6 became controversial because it includes the following: 'What is life? God's being is my life. If my life is God's being, then God's existence must be my existence and God's is-ness is my is-ness, neither less nor more'.[72] According to Kelley, the *manifestations* of 'is-ness' should be characterized as 'differentiated' essence. He writes: 'But the undifferentiated essence itself contains the differentiated, as the infinite contains the finite'.[73] And so, to blithely claim (supposedly with Eckhart) that 'my innermost Self is God' is tantamount to ignoring Eckhart's discriminative precision. 'For him (Eckhart) the essence of ignorance is to superimpose finiteness upon God and divinity upon the finite'.[74] Kelley maintains that the relation of the manifestations to God is a *real relation* (my italics) yet from God's standpoint '... there are not two separate realities ... '.[75] Eckhart's position remains difficult. Kelley translates one of Eckhart's most radical statements as follows:

> I, without my temporal self, always am. I am eternally in God. And inasmuch as that which is in God is not other than God, then in principle my truest *I* (or innermost Self) is God.[76]

Kelley describes such declarations as 'elliptic statements'. They 'do not represent an ontological opinion'.[77] It is certainly the case that Eckhart qualifies his seemingly radical non-dualism. He does this by references to the grace whereby humanity is first transformed into the likeness of Christ, in order to become participants in the life of the Godhead. Here again is a translation by Kelley.

> In God there is nothing but God; in ourselves, however,
> we consider all things in an ascending scale, from good to better
> and from better to best. But in God is neither more nor less.
> He is just the simple, pure, essential Truth.[78]

Ambiguity is evident when language is so stretched that Eckhart can seemingly declare humanity to be of the same essence (*essentia*) as God. But again, Eckhart makes a distinction between essence and 'is-ness' (*Isticheit* or *esse*). The 'isness' precedes and is higher than the 'essence'. Only from the divine standpoint can essence and 'is-ness' be identical. And so, *from this standpoint*, Eckhart appears to conclude that each person can, putatively, be of the same essence as God.

In a foreword to the 2009 edition of Kelley, William Stranger offers a warning. He writes:

> ... it is extremely important to understand that we cannot simply choose to be identified with God – a will-less event that by definition no ego can willfully accomplish. Although Eckhart calls us to 'think principially', his non-dual teachings do not relieve us of the necessity of the profound moral, religious, and, eventually, spiritual preparatory disciplines required of all true aspirants, however apparently dualistic such a submission might appear to be.[79]

In my view, it appears that McGinn is comfortable with Eckhart's non-dualism but Kelley is nervous about this trend in Eckhart's thought. Further, that Kelley is reluctant to concede affinities with any form of sub-continental philosophy.

Be that as it may, Eckhart cites NT passages which might allude to a relative absence in the primitive church of dualistic thought. He mentions passages in Matthew, Luke and John in which Jesus seems to imply that children are at one with the divine. As a child might naturally extend its arms to find the embrace of her mother or father, so Eckhart advocates *epektasis* on the part of adults. Literally, the word means 'a stretching forward', in this case towards the divine embrace. He quotes from Paul's letter to the Philippians: 'Beloved, I do not consider that I have made it my own; but this one thing I do: forgetting what lies behind and straining forward to what lies ahead . . .'.[80]

Kearney[81] considers that 'the dis-possessed soul, emptied of ego and naked as a child . . . becomes a lodging for the in-dwelling of God'. Kearney is here reflecting on the journal of Etty Hillesum, who died in the Holocaust. In so doing, he states his Eckhartian aspiration to 'allow the infinite to beget itself in my persona'. Alluding to Eckhart's use of the 'outward' and 'inward' person, he writes:

> The inner person is the divine 'word of Eternity' giving birth to itself in us. Using the illustration of the swinging door, (Eckhart) explains: 'A door swings to and fro through an angle. I compare the breadth of the door to the outward man and the hinge to the inner person. When the door swings to and fro, the breadth of the door moves back and forth, but the hinge is still unmoved and unchanged'. . . . The most curious thing about this passage (Eckhart's discussion of disinterest) is, arguably, that while God seems identical with Himself as 'he-who-is', this does not, as we might expect, rule out the possibility of human beings identifying with God by attaining to this same inner point of silent, still disinterest. On the contrary, it secures it.[82]

The reference to 'he-who-is' (above) relates to Yahweh's disclosure to Moses on Mount Horeb in Ex. 3:14. The Hebrew of the verse is widely accepted as inconclusive. The declaration by Yahweh can be translated as 'I Am That I Am' (KJV) or 'I Will Be Who I Will Be'. The NRSV has: 'God said to Moses, *I Am Who I Am*'.[83] The *I Am* became pivotal for both Judaic and Christian theologizing.[84] Judaism became committed to a relationship between Yahweh and humanity, and committed to a union of humanity with the wider created world. For its part, Christianity's story of incarnation led it to a more horizontally conceived union of the infinite with the finite. Earlier, reflection on the *I Am* had led to an expansion of the field of the ethical. In addition to asking: 'What should I do?', semitic groups (and, before them, Indian *rishis*) began to ask: 'What should I *be*?'[85] I have mentioned Rublev's vision of a world subsumed in *perichoretic* love, expressed in his icon *The Holy Trinity*. We might imagine Rublev's interest in those who saw his work: What will become of them? Or rather, what will they become? In addition to asking 'What is it right to do?' Rublev asks the ontological question, 'What is it good to be?'[86]

Kearney prefers the following variant translation of Ex. 3:14: 'I am who I may be'.[87] He states that '. . . most orthodox theologies read the Exodus passage as the mark of absolute *separateness* between a transcendent God and transient humans eager to grasp his name'.[88] By contrast, Eckhart 'appears to claim a radical *identity* between the two. The human person who abandons its own outer will and enters fully into the desert of its own emptiness becomes one with the Godhead of God'.[89] Such an interpretation seems to draw near to Śaṅkara's doctrinal *Advaita Vedānta*,[90] and to the viewpoint of Ramana Maharshi, who is widely regarded as a leading twentieth-century exponent of experiential *Advaita*. Aspects of Ramana's teaching will be discussed in Chapters 4 and 5.[91] One significant difference is clear: When Eckhart makes a radical claim about oneness with God, he will nuance it by regular mention of the grace of adoption. That is to say, Christ is the Son by nature, but you and I are Daughters and Sons by the grace of redemption. In *Vedānta*, the grace of the divine is also crucial. But there is no single redemptive act which brings about adoption within historical time. You and I will Realize our true nature as we appropriate, through grace, the experiential knowledge that Reality is non-dual. To express this in a more theistic way, we recover the salvific knowledge of the self within the Self (capital 'S') which is the Supreme, without name and form. In the framework of Eckhart, for whom salvation is tied to the *kenotic* actions of God in history, we were always, in a sense, one with the divine. But we were not in the redemptive position to appropriate it.

I have mentioned that Eckhart liked to allude to non-dual NT verses. One such verse is Gal. 2:20. The verse, in its context, has been included in the lectionaries of the established churches for centuries. Perhaps the implications of the passage are readily bypassed. The verse reads: 'I have been crucified with Christ: the life I now live is not my life, but the life which Christ lives in me; and my present bodily life is lived by faith in the Son of God, who loved me and sacrificed himself for me'.[92] Eckhart quotes this verse in abbreviated form, although not often. Twice, he follows it immediately with part of Phil. 1:21: 'For to me life is Christ . . .'.[93] A literal version of the Greek of the non-dual core of Gal. 2:20 can read as follows: '. . . I now live, no longer I . . .'. To draw out the meaning, it might be useful to express it as follows: 'In the follower of Christ, it is Christ who exists'.

Is a form of personal annihilation involved here? If so, does Eckhart subscribe to this? When his perspective is applied to the Galatians passage, it could be said that the soul recovers its 'emptiness' or 'nothingness'. This occurs through the surrender implied in Eckhart's 'releasement'. Within this process, the soul finds its union with God; or rather, the soul reverts via 'emptiness' to that unity for which it was created.[94]

To avoid limiting the concept of mysticism to experiences of feeling, the category of consciousness is best understood as extending beyond experience. McGinn makes this clear when discussing Eckhart's 'indistinct union with God' in terms of intellect as well as love. If and when God gives the gift of God's presence, it is not possible to distinguish knowing from loving.

> There is no apprehension of God as object here;
> rather, the divine presence becomes active in the soul's ground
> of awareness. So too there is no loving God as an object of desire,
> but only a co-presence of infinite divine love.

This new affective state is conscious, that is, present to the subject,
but not yet explicitly known or objectified.
It can become known, but only in an indirect way
as a tendency or drive, not as something capable of conceptualization,
because of its unlimited and unrestricted nature.[95]

McGinn attempts a summary of Eckhart. He sees him as directing people to '. . . become aware of the indistinct union with God always present in the *Grunt* (innermost depth) of the soul'.[96] McGinn continues:

Since God exists 'without a why' (*sunder war umbe*),
the life lived out of an awareness of indistinction from God
is spoken of as a life 'without a why'.
Eckhart spoke of such a mode of life in a number of ways,
including the spontaneity of love:
'He who dwells in the goodness of his nature, dwells in God's love,
and love has no why'. This kind of 'whyless' love
is described as pure, unmixed and perfectly detached.
. . . German Sermon 82 comments on this transcendental mode
of loving by noting that God is Nothing (*niht*),
neither 'this nor that that one can speak about'.
Rather, as Eckhart puts it, 'He is a being above all being.
He is a being without a mode of being,
and therefore the way in which one should love him
is without a why; he is beyond all speech'.
. . . The non-duality of love of God, however,
is not other than the non-duality of intellect
as identical with God in the ground.[97]

Eckhart's tendency to engage in mystical hypothesizing is understandable. In common with countless others, he is working within the competing trajectories of Greek and Judeo-Christian thought. The Christian strand, on its own, is replete with ambiguity. Anything other than imaginative theopoems will carry the risk of vainly trying to objectify the divine. Is Eckhart compelling for this reason?

He is popular today, as never before. It is important to note that his emphasis on the divine presence within the depths of human consciousness is not an easy avenue to 'spirituality', let alone an entrée to ecstasy. The equation of my basic, egoic self with the divine would represent a serious distortion of his message. It is true that salvific grace is everywhere present . . . and yet, without the progressive discipline of the right kind of self-awareness (i.e. self-forgetfulness) and non-attachment, the interior birth of the divine is unlikely to manifest. In relation to Eckhart's advocacy of self-awareness, Richard Woods writes as follows:

Such self-awareness, devoid of images and concepts, is not simply reflexive knowledge. This would intrude the element of self-referential subjectivity . . . .

The God within is identical to the God beyond. There is a double reciprocity at work here – the mutual knowledge and indwelling of God and the soul, and the identity of the divine presence intuited within and in the world beyond.[98]

In the following chapter, I discuss the distinctiveness of Julian. Her non-dual undercurrent connects with aspects of Eckhart and Traherne. In Chapters 4 and 5, I will make some assessment of Ramana's modern version of *Advaita*. His strong non-dualism counterpoints the moderate non-dualism of my three principal writers.

3

Mother Julian of Norwich

Transgressive Saints

1. Hadewijch of Antwerp, from a convent garden, 1233

My mind's clacking mill
grinds and grinds.
Words confound, ward off peace.

I stack wood, beat, mangle, peg clothes.
I moisten dry clay, turn damp earth,
tend beet, onion, turnip.

Silence: my true nature,
where nothing confuses your language, holy Mary,
Mother of us all.

Plum tree skeletons find green flesh.
Spring-time earth, water, sky,
invite surrender: separateness dissolves.
I relinquish speech for seven days,
rest in oneness
underlying sense, thought and word.

What is worth saying may be said without a tongue;
what is worth hearing, may be heard without ears.

I walk our north wall's length,
dwell within mystery near and far,
familiar, yet impossible to understand.
Campions, near the pond, beam pink light.
Sky turns sword-grey; the sea no longer glints
but heaves like a black bruise.

Here in the garden, five nuns, each widowed
to either plague or war. Last night, heavy with child,
a farm girl came to our gate. Mary,

Mother of rich earth, fair and dark sky:
we see your radiance in all things;
we see all things in you.

They say: *Divinity is beyond.*
But I hear of it in a storm's howl,
in the boom-boom of a torrent; today, in the rustling
of leaves shaken by a breeze. I fear the Bishop's censure.
Whether I starve, freeze, or burn at the stake,
I declare my trust: all will be well.

My ducks nod and waddle in my wake,
nuzzle fallow ground.
Here, see us, they say.
Look, you earnest Sister,
hoping to survive the stake,
look at us.
This *soil;*
that *worm.*

Trust belongs to a duck,
a farm child, a robust worker.
How can I find real trust?
I will go out again, confront
the place of my greatest fear
and meditate there.

Help me, Mother,
to forsake attachments
which beguile.
I want to flow with sap
of fidelity to all.

Hadewijch of Antwerp was a theopoet of the early thirteenth century. In my poem *Transgressive Saints* she is placed in a convent, which is not strictly accurate. Hadewijch and her community of Beguines chose an informal structure; they did not pursue the official approval of the Church. But, like a convent, her community was organized to pursue an ascetic and self-sufficient focus. There is no evidence that Julian of Norwich was familiar with the seemingly sensualistic unitive tone in the writings of Hadewijch.[1] But both writers take embodiment seriously, both literally and metaphorically, as a supreme divine gift. Their writings tend to be highly visual, direct and not overburdened with abstract concepts. Predictably, we have very little information about either woman. I intend to highlight the way in which Julian's themes are imbued with a non-dual tone. Along the way, her work will be reviewed in conjunction with that of Eckhart and Traherne.

Although Julian's background seems likely to remain opaque, it is obvious that she was highly educated, especially for a woman in medieval England. We know that wealthy women in Norfolk had access to books, because of the county's proximity to Cambridge. It is not known if she had access to *La Divina Commedia*. Since Dante lived at the same time as Eckhart, this is possible; Julian is thought by medievalists to have been familiar with Eckhart's work. Some would hold that she was influenced by it. Much remains unclear. But we might imagine her enthusiasm for such a passage in the *Commedia* as the following.

> And all are blessed even as their sight descends
> deeper into the truth, wherein rest is
> for every mind. Thus happiness hath root
> in seeing, not in loving, which of sight
> is aftergrowth.[2]

Julian claims that some of the 16 visions were seen with her physical eyes. Others were strong mental impressions, while a third grouping, which she calls 'spiritual', consisted of silent teachings 'in the heart'.

> I desired many times to know in what was our Lord's meaning. And fifteen years after and more, I was answered in spiritual understanding, and it was said: What, do you wish to know your Lord's meaning in this thing? Know it well, love was his meaning. Who reveals it to you? Love. What did he reveal to you? Love. Why does he reveal it to you? For love.[3]

In one of the visions, Julian sees something small and round 'resembling a hazelnut'. The small object enlarges her awareness that each item in creation is significant in its own right. But each item might also convey a message. The nut can therefore speak to Julian of womb-like fruitfulness and of the preservation of life through love's close attention. As with the nut, so with humanity; Julian states that all of us are enclosed or enfolded in love. I once visited her reconstructed cell: A small enclosure, with openings both to the interior of the church and to the exterior world. I doubt that Julian would have regarded her years of confinement as a retreat from life. More likely, she saw them as an opportunity to be attentive to her many visitors and to hone her expanding theopoem.

One of the themes in Julian's work is that of 'enclosure'. This interweaves her pastoral concern. She believes she has experienced the enclosure of divine love. In turn, she has desired to enclose that love so that she might encompass it within her whole personhood. She repeatedly writes that divine love is all-encompassing, implying that it is simultaneously immanent and transcendent. The 'object resembling a hazelnut' occurs in LT 5 of *Showings*. Later in the same chapter, Julian states that:

> ... our good Lord revealed that it is very greatly pleasing to him that a simple soul should come naked, openly and familiarly. For this is the loving yearning of the soul through the touch of the Holy Spirit.[4]

As with Traherne and Eckhart, Julian emphasizes personal experience. If pressed, they will place spiritual experience ahead of received, abstract statements. But since their tendency is non-dual, they are not going to create another dualism, in which conceptualization and experience are opposed to each other.[5] Traherne's non-dualism can be nominated as 'experiential'. Relatively speaking, the non-dualism of Julian and Eckhart can be described as 'more conceptual'. But such labelling is not always helpful. The tendency to categorize our 'ways of belief' is often a precursory move, along the path to excessive dualism.

As to their understanding of the Trinity, all three writers make use of the traditional tripartite approach. But there are variations. The divine is configured as triune and humankind is assumed to be reflective of this. The Father (maker and knower) and the Son (doer and sufferer) and the Spirit (lover and bliss-giver) are reflected in human nature as body, soul and spirit. Julian puts forward two distinctive versions of the Trinity, in addition to an implied reiteration of the tradition.

First, she says that because we bear the image of God, we have the ability to see *truth*, contemplate *wisdom* and delight in *love*. These three abilities of truth, wisdom and love correspond to the 'persons' of the Trinity. Truth corresponds to the Father, wisdom to the Son, and love's manifestation to the Spirit.[6] But Julian does not imply that the three abilities are independent of each other. Although God is triune, neither Father, Son nor Spirit is engaged in any activity which is separate from the activity of the other two.

Second, Julian puts forward a version of the Trinity which is even more distinctive, in that it partially subverts the 'gender' of the Trinity. Her preferred Trinity seems to be that of Father, Mother and 'Good Lord'. This threesome is nonetheless one divinity. Julian also uses the word 'Love' as an implied synonym for the divine. If 'Love' was absent to any degree, evil would fill the void. But 'Love' is not ultimately distressed by evil. This is because the apparent 'opposites' have been (from 'before the foundation of the world') brought together in Christ. To some degree Julian puts forward a theology of co-inherence. The divine is readily 'available' or 'accessible' in Christ. The divine is 'before us' (in front of us, *now*) and within us, yet beyond us. Here then is Julian's non-dual predilection: she brings God and humanity into conjunction.

As with Eckhart, some decades earlier, and with Traherne centuries later, Julian desires not so much to instruct as to awaken us. To this end, the three of them regard the world as replete with signs that point to a *transcensus*. Time itself is viewed as not only *chronos* but *kairos*, the now-moment to 'receive inwardly' (*intus suscipere*) and to make a life-orientating decision. No clear description of non-dualism is provided by either writer; their views might oscillate between various meanings. Although this puzzle will persist, prudence might indicate that they do not mean a literal 'oneness' so much as an inability to enact 'twoness'. By this I mean that they regard other people, and conceivably all other life forms, as elements of their own selfhood. Accordingly, they regard the sufferings of others as their own sufferings, in part. Apparent 'opposites' are deemed, to some extent, to nourish each other in fruitful coincidence.

As mentioned, Julian's non-dualism might be regarded as more conceptual than Traherne's, despite the graphic nature of Julian's imagery. In the first chapter, I cited poems by Traherne in which he objects to an overdrawn subject/object dualism. Eckhart (Chapter 2) markedly reduces the subject/object dualism when 'the birth of the Son takes place in the soul'. This 'birth' implies a 'death' to the egoic self. To put an end to humanity's restless suffering, there must be an *end* to the self (as perceived by itself to be a separate entity). This might paradoxically imply that a personal self did not substantially exist in the first place. But it would seem more likely that Eckhart accepted an initial dualism. Otherwise, how could we freely choose the detachment of *Gelâzenheit*? A primary dualism would seem the natural precursor to Eckhart's insistence on our return to the primordial Oneness of the divine.

Julian's distinctive use of naturalistic female imagery for the divine is widely known. She 'writes womanhood'. She does so in a limited way, but in a way that is striking for a medieval European. By contrast, Eckhart is cautious of the *via positiva*, believing that metaphor piled upon metaphor would contribute to distortion. His *via negativa* is recognition that the 'Godhead beyond God' cannot be described because it is unknowable. But Eckhart's intention is far from reducing the divine to a non-personal, abstract symbol. The point for him, in this regard, is that a spiritual life does not consist of knowledge in the head. Julian and Traherne concur with Eckhart here. A 'consciously lived' life has priority. By this I mean a life that is both aware and ethical. Ideas 'about' God are secondary; they remain important, and they retain an important link to the imagination.

Divine maternity

A phrase from Julian which has entered the Western lexicon occurs in *Showings* (LT 27) and elsewhere: '. . . but all will be well, and every kind of thing will be well'. This and other expressions of hope are grounded in what she believes to be her divinely instigated experience of the depth and breadth of God's love. From this position, she encourages me to love my own embodied self, otherwise my love for the rest of creation will be tainted with my own lack of self-love. Julian repeatedly questions God as to his reasons for allowing sin and suffering. It is in this context of questioning that the consoling words 'all will be well' occur.

Relative to her era, Julian might de-emphasize sin, yet is careful to state that her model of spiritual life includes both Fall and Redemption. She registers surprise that her visions have downplayed the ultimate impact of sin.

> But I did not see sin, for I believe that it has no kind of substance, no share in being, nor can it be recognized except by the pain caused by it. And it seems to me that this pain is something for a time, for it purges and makes us know ourselves and ask for mercy . . . .[7]

Julian proceeds to reiterate that Christ asks me, not to dwell on what might or might not be sinful, but to open myself to his embrace. She wants me to experience full 'enclosure'. She writes: 'And of his great courtesy he puts away all our blame, and regards us with pity and compassion as innocent and guiltless children'.[8] Julian seems to imply that human nature is basically good, if weak. The weakness is an occasion for growth; sin itself can awaken humanity to the original goodness of Creation. In LT 49, Julian writes: '. . . our Lord God in his goodness makes the contrariness, which is in us now, very profitable for us'.[9]

It is important to note that when Julian brings humanity and God into conjunction, she assumes that any human move towards the divine is not a later gift, but part of human nature from the beginning. Here she reveals that her sympathy lies more with humankind's divinization than with any tendency of the Western church to overemphasize human sinfulness.

> To be human, for Julian, is to be already utterly immersed in God's creation *as part of him*. . . . We need do nothing, undertake nothing, venture nothing, except the final recognition of and assent to *what actually is*. . . . Salvation is found in our true created natures; salvation is a restoration, not an innovation – a return to our true and original participation in the Holy Trinity.[10]

Traherne is similar to Julian here; both maintain that the relationship between God and humanity does not begin with sin and end with redemption. There is immense love, within the divine, before sin 'arrives' and 'during sin', as well as in the traditional redemptive acts themselves.

> . . . everything is penetrated, in length and in breadth, in height and in depth without end; and it is all one love. // But now I should say a little more about this penetration, as I understood our Lord to mean: How we are brought back by the motherhood of mercy and grace into our natural place, in which we were created by the motherhood of love, a mother's love that never leaves us.[11]

God's motherhood is not mentioned in Julian's first reflection upon her visions (ST). Years later, her much fuller reflections (LT) develop both her sensibility of identification with Christ and her unusual elaboration of motherhood as a primary attribute of God. Both strands are non-dualistic, to a point. Julian's identification with the crucifixion leads her to identify with Christ's love for the world; she develops confidence in the oneness brought about, as she saw it, by the divine condescension of incarnation. She does not use the words 'interconnected' or 'integrated'. But she does use the word 'wholeness'. And she repeatedly employs the words 'one', 'one-ing' and 'oneness'.

The second part of my poem *Transgressive Saints* concerns a woman who, like Hadewijch of Antwerp, followed an ascetical life without formal 'approval'.

Transgressive Saints

2. Simone Weil at Saint-Marcel d'Ardèche

She bends in opaque light, in heat-blaze;
picks grapes, prunes thoughts and words.
A hare crouches near the vines:
fully attentive, no muscular effort,
no brow-wrinkling concentration.

The vines' silent liturgy: stem, branch,
stalk, leaf. Attend the planet's rhythm, repeat
the Rhône Valley's quiet recitation of pure grape,
nine hours each day.

In borrowed cape and boots, Simone
pursues her life's anomaly: to crave for less,
achieve peace with loss of all sense
of presence. *Truth is conveyed by what's withheld.*

Attend, recite, repeat: stem, stalk, sap.
She picks her way into autumn,
the body's rhythm. Snip this tangle,
snap tendril; shift away from words.
A brace of ravens waddles down a furrow,
lunges at each songbird. Nature's daily work;
truth of world as is.

*I'd rather be an atheist with passion
for Earth than a consoled Christian.*
Give up self-questioning, abandon
the search. Relinquish the mind's
mythographic cast. Accept the void
of letting-be.

*It is not for me to seek, or even to believe
in God. I have only to refuse belief
in gods that are not God.*

Each pilgrim vine is circumscribed yet wayward;
each cluster blazing purple in light,
cold black in shade.
A matter of seeing deeper, penetrating truth.
Only the lived reality has point.

Can trellises entwine the vine?
Then excise all belief: face emptiness.
Expose the mesh of long-held shibboleths;
defy the grid imposed upon
the world's real labour.

Grace Jantzen and Patricia Donohue-White approach Julian's use of divine motherhood
with caution, and not simply because a motherhood ideal can be oppressive. Jantzen
finds that Julian's motifs of divine maternity are integral to a theology which reflects
both personal experience and Church teachings. But the real question, Jantzen asserts,
'. . . is whether Christian theology has any implications for psychology; whether
salvation remains purely theoretical . . . or whether there can be genuine spiritual

healing and fulfillment in our relationship with Christ in this life'.[12] Donohue-White seems to reluctantly endorse the motherhood motifs. She writes:

> Although Julian does not diversify her female images of God
> into sister, midwife, or female lover, she does identify God's maternity
> with God's wisdom; thus she places her theology, knowingly or not,
> squarely within the Sophia tradition with its personification of divine wisdom
> in female form, a form that includes but is not limited to the symbol
> of maternity.[13]

Donohue-White has no doubt that Julian '. . . intentionally counters patriarchal models of a God of wrath and judgment'. Julian does this by her '. . . constant focus on God as love and her portrayal of God's love as all-encompassing, all-sustaining, and all-renewing . . .'.[14] It could be argued that Julian's reduced emphasis on sin downplays human responsibility. But another interpretation could be this: She assumes that putative readers are likely to be disposed towards a spiritually oriented life. Julian writes: 'This, then, was my astonishment, that I saw our Lord God showing no more blame to us than if we were as pure and as holy as the angels in heaven'.[15]

  Julian's references to the motherhood of Christ appear especially in LT Chapters 57 to 63. Christ is our 'mother of mercy in taking our sensuality'.[16] Julian uses the word 'sensuality' in positive ways, to express my created nature and to underline Christ's humanity. Christ achieves for me the personal integration which is necessary for union with God.

> . . . for in our Mother Christ we profit and increase,
> and in mercy he reforms and restores us,
> and by the power of his Passion, his death
> and his Resurrection, he unites us to our substance.[17]

Julian provides a number of vivid examples of Christ's motherhood. Dying on a cross, Christ resembles a woman in labour, imparting life to us as a result of suffering. In LT 60, she writes that:

> . . . all mothers bear us for pain and for death. O, what is that?
> But our true Mother Jesus, he alone bears us for joy and for
> endless life, blessed may he be. So he carries us within him
> in love and travail, until the full time . . . .[18]

Julian invites me to see the Passion of Christ as resembling my own physical birth. As I am squeezed from my mother's womb, so the life of Christ is squeezed out from him, in order for another life to come to birth. Having been 'birthed by Christ', I am also 'a member of Christ', born into the life which lies beyond the confinement of individualistic self-consciousness.

Another example of Christ's motherhood is seen when he nourishes me in the Eucharist, with his own substance, as a woman will nourish her baby from her own body. Again, in LT 60, Julian writes:

The mother can give her child to suck of her milk,
but our precious Mother Jesus can feed us with himself,
and does, most courteously and most tenderly,
with the blessed sacrament, which is the precious food of true life.[19]

Finally, Christ cleans me, as a mother will clean her baby. This seems to mean that Christ welcomes me into his arms, regardless of behaviour. A degree of radicalism is expressed, not only in the thought of Christ as birth-mother, but in Julian's doubt concerning traditional expressions of divine wrath. In LT 46, she describes God as:

... that goodness which cannot be angry, for God is nothing but goodness. ...
For our soul is so wholly united to God, through his own goodness,
that between God and our soul nothing can interpose.[20]

She implies that her outlook is orthodox.[21] Dramatically, however, she can venture a most unorthodox viewpoint.

And I saw no difference between God and our substance,
but, as it were, all God; and still my understanding accepted
that our substance is in God, that is to say, that God is God,
and our substance is a creature in God.
... And the deep wisdom of the Trinity is our Mother,
in whom we are enclosed.[22]

In Middle English, the word 'substance' possibly conveys the idea of 'potential', as well as 'essence'. Whatever her purport, Julian fails to adequately qualify her use of 'substance'. But she manages the puzzlement of her non-dual statements by being clear that on the relative level of ordinary experience, Christians need to continue with the traditional spiritual practices or disciplines. So that, although a Christian might be confident that she or he shares the 'one substance' of God, this absolute level of discourse must be actively balanced by the relative level of discourse. It is possible to construe a third or intermediate level, wherein God's lovers are seen to be living 'in real time', poised between the 'already complete or realized' and the 'not yet' of expectation. Accordingly, in Julian, there is *both* unitive experience and the necessity to engage with the world of differentiation. She saw the believer's interaction with the world as a spontaneous outflow from the non-dual intuition of non-separation.

Julian was perhaps familiar with Anselm's references to the motherhood of Christ. Among Anselm's prayers is a lengthy 'Prayer to St. Paul' in which he praises Paul's mothering of those who had been brought to faith in Christ. Then Anselm switches from addressing Paul and begins to talk to Jesus.

And you, Jesus, are you not also a mother?
Are you not the mother who, like a hen,
gathers her chickens under her wings?
Truly, Lord, you are a mother;
for both they who are in labour
and they who are brought forth
are accepted by you.
You have died more than they, that they may labour to bear.
It is by your death that they have been born,
for if you had not been in labour,
you could not have borne death;
and if you had not died, you would not have brought forth.[23]

According to Sr. Mary Paul it is 'very likely' that Julian knew the Ancrene Riwle of the early thirteenth century.[24] A textbook of the reclusive life, the Riwle uses a mother-child metaphor for the relation of Christ to his followers. After noting the inadequacy of all words involved in the traditional picture-language of the Trinity, Mary Paul suggests that the name 'God the Mother' could be adopted for the 'third person' of the Trinity.

I want to suggest that 'God the Mother' may be the true
and meaningful name of the Third Person of the Trinity,
the Person who is so vague in our theology, the Person whom
we call the Holy Spirit, though these words do not in any way
express the *proprium* of the third Person, for God the Trinity
is Holy, and God the Trinity is Spirit, and each of the three
Persons is Holy and is Spirit. The third Person seems to be the
unnamed member of the Trinity. And it is not a matter of name only,
but of function. The function of a mother is to be a life-giver:
to bring to birth and to nurture. May it be that the whole creation
is being brought to birth in the Holy Spirit?[25]

Such discursiveness conceals the reality that Julian refers more frequently to God as Father than to God as Mother. Kathryn Reinhard can write that 'Julian's motherhood theology doesn't replace a patriarchal God but completes him'. Reinhard continues:

Julian describes God as Father and Mother, together, in a profoundly
holistic way, which does not ignore or negate differences of gender
but relies on difference and particularity in order to make a complete
and creative union. As God's creation and God's children,
we are the place where the particularities of the motherhood
and fatherhood of God come together.[26]

Is this parental dualism subsumed within a clear non-dual conviction? It remains unclear. Julian is concerned with the understanding of those affective ideas which transform us. More mystical as a theologian than systematic, she favours the letters to the Corinthians rather than those to Rome and Galatia. All those who experience Christ's mothering are the recipients of divine secrets. This mystical move has the effect, in Julian, of disclosing God as more intimate than transcendent in the classical sense. Reinhard, for her part, concludes on a non-dual note.

> In the womb of Christ our Mother we are reunited not only
> with God our Father but also with each other. The love of God
> that unites us so completely in the Trinity that we ourselves become
> bearers of the Trinity also unites us to our brothers and sisters.
> Like the hazelnut Julian saw held in God's hand, our relationships
> are bound together in a round, tight wholeness, small and potentially
> unstable, but united everlastingly, because God loves it.[27]

Reinhard brings her imagination to Julian's theopoetics. By contrast, Kerry Dearborn is less engaging; he observes that Julian places the self-giving nature of the divine within metaphors of both Motherhood and Fatherhood. Dearborn views Julian as constructing a somewhat orthodox *via media* between God's Motherly nature and the traditional position. Dearborn is confident:

> She was clearly not attempting to move outside of scripture
> and the church to create her own feminine language for God.
> Her writing reveals that one need not revoke Jesus' normative use
> of 'Father' as found in the Gospels to include also the use of 'Mother'.[28]

But Dearborn concedes that Julian's contribution is distinctive wherever she links motherliness with the crucifixion, the Trinity and the disciple's life 'in Christ'.

> Her visions helped her to formulate theological reflections
> that challenge associations of the cross with a harsh and destructive
> patriarchal God. Her theology also challenges the idea that a motherly
> vision of God is purely subjective and distorts the biblical revelation
> of God. As numerous scholars have noted, there are clearly references
> in scripture to the motherly nature of God, which are all the more
> remarkable in light of the patriarchal cultures in which they were written.[29]

Enfolded by the Infinite

None of the writers at the centre of this study approve of escapist or pietistic religiosity. Transpersonal and communal engagement is always placed ahead of individualistic cultivation. This also applies, emphatically, to Ramana and Panikkar (discussed in Chapters 4 and 5). An authentic spiritual life is a matter of living 'out of' the implications of a sense of (primordial?) Oneness. Among the Christians I discuss, Julian is the most explicit regarding the means by which humanity is 're-established' within Oneness. Julia Lamm offers the following summary of Julian's detailed descriptions.

> Christ gave all that was in him, all that he was and all that he had,
> to the point that there was nothing left but shredded remnants of his flesh,
> which revealed the fullness of his humanity and love. Julian's originating
> revelation is thus essentially a *kenosis* – a self-emptying love,
> an emptying of all that is human in Christ so that nothing remains hidden.[30]

Lamm favours the words 'expose' and 'exposure' as being potentially able to provide an adequate rendering of Julian's Middle English 'shewe'. The word 'shewe' (show) has generally been taken to mean 'reveal' or 'disclose'. The idea of exposure, rather than that of revelation *simpliciter*, adds a fuller purport to the explicit treatment by Julian of the sufferings of Jesus. Lamm continues:

> . . . just as she had seen Christ emptied and had seen everything in him be
> exteriorized, so God will empty Godself through a 'plenteous flowing'. . . . The
> final revelation will be an opening of God's very self and a spilling forth, such
> that what had seemed exterior to God is now immersed in God. . . . Not only
> does revelation occur when God, through *kenosis*, exteriorizes what had been
> interior, but further revelation occurs when God interiorizes us, enfolding and
> enclosing us.[31]

Julian wishes to safeguard God's distinction while also declaring the divine to be ultimately inseparable from created humanity. She balances the absolute level of discourse with the relative level by repeating the two truths: human *destiny* is oneness with God; yet this oneness can be appropriated in the *present moment*. She knows that humanity cannot claim to have 'grasped' God through any belief concerning God. The divine cannot be grasped or understood, because it already creates, grasps and understands *us*.

Julian's non-dual tendency finds a well-known metaphor in 'knitting'. She uses knitting to draw attention to humanity's oneness with God (truth #1) and also to the process by which humanity is realizing oneness (truth #2). We are already 'oned' but yet still on the way to 'oneing'. Christ asks for *trust*. But this includes the horizontal movement of *trust in humanity* as 'enclosed' or 'enfolded' by Christ. The process of achieving unity is particularly inferred in LT 5. 'For until I am substantially united to him, I can never have perfect rest or true happiness, until, that is, I am so attached to him that there can be no created thing between my God and me.'[32] We are 'oned' or united with God through a process of self-emptying on God's part. We in turn participate in the *kenotic* or self-emptying life of God.

> When the simple soul by its will has become nothing for love,
> to have him who is everything, then it is able to receive spiritual
> rest. . . . it is very greatly pleasing to him that a simple soul
> should come naked, openly and familiarly.[33]

Julian's motif of enfoldment was taken up, curiously, by physicist David Bohm in *Wholeness and the Implicate Order*. Whereas, in mechanistic physics, two of the 'foundations' are extension and separation, this is not exactly the case with quantum physics. Bohm proposes the words 'implicate order' to characterize the dictum that 'everything is enfolded into everything'.[34] The 'implicate order' is contrasted with the 'explicate order'. In the latter, physical entities are accorded particular space and time for their *unfolding*, as distinct from Bohm's *enfolding*.

> In the implicate order we have to say that mind enfolds matter in general and therefore body in particular. Similarly, the body enfolds not only the mind but also in some sense the entire material universe.[35]

In the quotation above, it is evident that Bohm believes that relationships (e.g. between matter and consciousness and between body and mind) can be rendered more comprehensible through the interdependence expressed by the words 'implicate order'.

For her part, Julian writes (even in her early text) of a merging or assimilation with God: 'And the soul who thus contemplates is made like to him who is contemplated, and united to him in rest and peace'.[36] In the experience of merging, we become enlightened with what becomes our own light. This light is derived; it is a divine gift. But it does not remain external. Julian's developing non-dualism becomes clearer when she alludes to an organic fusion between our life and that of Christ.

> Our good Lord revealed himself to his creature in various ways, both in heaven and earth; but I saw him take no place except in man's soul. . . . He revealed himself several times reigning, as is said before, but principally in man's soul; he has taken there his resting place and honourable city.[37]

In her essay entitled 'Medieval Medical Views of Woman', Elizabeth Robertson offers this suggestion:

> As far as I know, Julian's emphasis on the sensuality of Christ is distinctive. . . . I suggest that Julian is speaking here not simply of a gender-neutral sensuality, but more specifically of women's sensuality; . . . (this) ultimately resulted in a reassessment of the value of femininity.[38]

Robertson concludes:

> I am inclined to believe that Julian of Norwich was a subtle strategist who sought to undo assumptions about women and to provide . . . a new celebration of femininity through contemplation of Christ's feminine attributes.[39]

In my view, Julian struggles to affirm her true position. I think this becomes clear in the passage quoted earlier, concerning 'substance'. She appears to pay respect to the traditional viewpoint. At the same time, her experience urges her to a theopoetic of qualified non-dualism. Here again is part of the passage:

> And I saw no difference between God and our substance, but, as it were, all God; and still my understanding accepted that our substance is in God, that is to say, that God is God . . . .[40]

The tension is almost palpable. In the next chapter of *Showings* she returns to the non-dual side of the tension. And she heightens it by adding the word 'sensuality'.

> I saw with absolute certainty that our substance is in God, and, moreover, that he is in our sensuality too. The moment our soul was made sensual, at that moment was it destined from all eternity to be the City of God.[41]

In Julian there is no distinct body/soul dualism. By contrast with other Western theologizing, she cannot separate our sensuality from our spirituality. To her, there is apparently no substance called 'soul' which can clearly be separated from our bodiliness. Julian's positive regard for the body is sourced in her acceptance of the great sensual act of the Incarnation. This is the proof, to her, that humanity is inextricably linked to the divine.

Popularity

Julian's non-dual emphasis connects, in my view, with her popularity in recent decades. Her non-reductionist approach to the body, and its relationship to the divine, resonates with today's scepticism regarding 'truths' that seem to be purely propositional in character. For her, as for Eckhart and especially for Traherne, religion is a mode of thinking and acting which includes intuition and feeling. They understood the importance of feeling, where 'feeling' refers, not necessarily to bodily agitations of emotion, but to conscious affective responses. These responses are taken by Julian to constitute part of reason itself. So that, when her extended theopoem highlights 'feelings', her readers understand that she implies a *rational* appreciation of what is *felt*.

The sense of immediacy in Julian's work, plus the sense of *intimacy*, are surely factors in her popularity today. But I think the key to her acclaim is creative tension. She is struggling with tension between her professed adherence to a body of dogma and her actual experience. The latter underlies her theopoetic. To rephrase this in a different way, I think her appeal, and that of Traherne, relies on the 'vastness' which emerges from a contextual 'narrowness'. Julian reports an experience of the 'dropping away' of a confined, separate self. This 'dropping' occurs in the act of uniting with something else. She frames this experience as a vision of *agape*, which is the *kenotic* or self-emptying love underpinning everything. It is transformative love. On her view, the divine in the formless form of Spirit brings everything into conformity to the *agape* of Christ. It is the self-emptying of Spirit which reconciles all humanity to the infinity of beauty, or rather, to the beauty of infinite love. Mysteriously, Spirit conveys both death and life; both are experienced by Julian as *kenotic*.[42]

Three 'mystics' as connected presences

Traherne and Eckhart seem aligned with Julian regarding the *kenotic* life. All three are concerned that I should transcend my confined, self-delusory character by abandoning my rigidly dualistic thought. Wherever transformation is imagined, it is woven between the two truths: Absolute truth and conventional truth. For example, the kingdom of heaven (absolute truth-level) is within each person (conventional truth-level). The kingdom is eschatological (absolute truth-level), yet exists in the present moment (conventional truth-level) as well as in the eschaton (absolute truth-level). Full participation in that which is conveyed by Spirit is not an achievement. It is a reversion to union with the divine. At the same time, the process of awakening to one's true self will continue. Delusions and illusions will still need to fall away.[43]

Julian's Trinity (of Father, Mother and Good Lord) has received attention from the New Zealand medievalist Alexandra Barratt. In 2002, Barratt published an original vignette on Julian's 'our good Lord'. Barratt demonstrates that Julian's title for Spirit ('our good Lord') held a meaning which was specific to Julian's time. It was 'good lordship' which generated harmony; the good lord would represent or in some way assist his citizens or clients in matters which might come before law courts. Barratt then alludes to the unique word *parakeletos* (advocate or intercessor) which is applied four times in John's Gospel to the Spirit. Transliterated into Latin as *paraclitus* and into English as 'paraclete', the word finds a precise parallel (Barratt argues) in the Julianic 'our good Lord', who brings closer together those who were formerly at odds.

Thus the disciple can now cooperate with Spirit's inner activity; narrowness can give way to vastness. The phenomenal self (small-s) will need to be dismantled, just as a wall obscuring a garden might need to be dismantled. The supreme, non-dual Self (capital-S) comes into view. It is notable that the self-subsisting Self (of my appropriation, here, from the sub-continent) is not an acquisition.[44] Julian might perhaps consider that nothing has actually altered. Or, to appropriate Blake's phrase, something has cleansed the doors of perception, from within. A degree of contradiction is probably accepted by Julian, even as a sense of unity is conveyed. She manages the non-dual puzzle by balancing the ultimate or absolute with the conventional or relative. Eckhart, for his part, argues that nothing capable of being 'known' can hold absolute existence. Traherne and Julian do not philosophize to the same extent, but they convey their vivid sense of oneness with the divine. They do this with theopoetic emphasis on the particularity and preciousness of each 'thing'. Although there is a future destiny, they are more concerned that each person should (re)enter union with the divine now and here. Distinctions will be transcended; at the same time, each person will retain a particular wholeness, a singular selfhood.[45]

Does Julian's feminine iconography amount to a change in ways of thinking and writing about the divine? Does she modify the traditional boundaries of expression? Does she advocate 'a feminine God', outside patriarchal tradition? Scarcely. Nor is it reasonable to take a discourse from later centuries and project it onto medieval England. But Julian does aim at a theopoetic expression of the dominant paradigm. That is to say, the divine becomes feminized for her. She does not challenge the hierarchical frame; or rather, her challenge is within the tradition itself and represents her discovery of the tradition's subtle poetic.

Although I have construed her emphasis as non-dual, her blend of passion and equanimity ensures a dualistic undertone of devotional love for God. The divine is 'understood' as both Subjectively and Objectively the One. Today, this might imply the defeat of unconstrained individual autonomy by a passionate surrender to love's constraining communion and community. Included here would be the probable surrender of certain beliefs (such as 'hell' in Julian's case?) and the surrender of any doctrinal system which demands ruthless defence.

To speak of Traherne, Eckhart and Julian in one breath is obviously to court a charge of historical carnage. They cannot be situated together in the narrow, critical sense. In these first three chapters I have chosen to collapse time somewhat and to remember them as connected presences within the holy communion which overflows time. They share a passion to 're-insert' their readers into Spirit. At the same time, they are not oblivious to the reality that knowledge comes through embodiment, 'personhood' develops through relationship, and community is established through open communion. Creative, *kenotic* love is relevant here, as part of the work of *agape* to establish networks of open and just relations. But *agape* is inhibited if we lack information as to the worth of humans and the worth of the non-human creation. Beyond intention and sentiment, rightly informed actions will enrich the life of that which is loved. Mainstream Christian tradition is clear that *agape* must add to the affirmation of creation's worth.[46]

In the first chapter, I suggested that Traherne took the formularies of his tradition and deepened them in a theopoetic way. The same might be said of Julian and Eckhart. They desire to take us back to That from which we came. In their sensibility, 'Jesus' is not reducible to subjective experience, nor is 'Spirit' reducible to soulfulness. They do not confuse 'the spiritual' with aesthetics or with psychology. Their view of Spirit is biblical: It is infinite and ineffable. It transcends the traits of personality, moving in and through the cosmos; indeed, around and within each one of us. We can enjoy real, embodied affinity with Spirit. But the friable, contingent reality of enfleshment is not elided by these writers; they are neither misanthropic nor docetic. They are grateful to have bodies in which to appreciate other bodies, *qua* bodies. For example, Traherne is most attractive to me when he departs from his use of abstract qualities and brings a tighter exuberance to bear.

To fly abroad like activ Bees,
Among the Hedges and the Trees,
To cull the Dew that lies

On evry Blade,
From evry Blossom; til we lade
Our *Minds*, as they their *Thighs*.[47]

I do not wish to infer that Julian, Eckhart and Traherne share an identical idea of embodiment. Nor should internal consistency be assumed. But a non-dual tendency implies a relational world; the experiences to which they bear witness are those which tend towards the interconnection of all things. If a paradigm could be located in their work, it would be a paradigm of *perichoresis*. As stated earlier, this signals the defeat of the paradigm of domination.

But my trio are not early Whiteheadians or nascent process theologians. And their emphasis on the interconnection of all things does not lead to their desertion (for example) of the church's sacramental ministry. Since, on their understanding, God's transcendence has taken embodiment, the divine is figured as fully participating within humanity's 'concrete immediacy'. Julian shares the interest of Eckhart and Traherne in the transformation of humanity, through *kenotic* and *perichoretic* enactment. Where the patriarchal model might tend to become a paradigm of domination and subordination, these writers would tend to undercut it by emphasizing affinity and intimacy.

In view of the elapse of centuries, we remain largely ignorant of their levels of epistemic sophistication. People today are less likely to accept the idea of unmediated experiences of divine presence. And yet, post-secular humanity is not necessarily prepared to reject all forms of 'presence'. When someone asserts an awareness of 'presence', we might feel (with Derrida[48] and others) that they are reporting a mere 'trace' of presence. In other words, we feel that no being, whether an earwig or a rhododendron, can ever be *fully* present to us. Be that as it may, an unmediated experience of God is generally regarded today as unbelievable. Rather, we tend to accept that whatever the nature of our experience, it cannot be regarded as fully separate from our social structures and conditionings.

In the broadest of senses, Julian and Eckhart anticipate Traherne's overt non-dual tone. At a stretch, Traherne might be imagined as anticipating the irreducible plurality of truth. If his non-dualism is nominated as 'experiential' and the non-dualism of Julian and Eckhart is configured as 'more conceptual', this might be convenient but not helpful. Christian non-dual discourse does not lend itself to close definition or neat category. From its beginnings, the Christian tradition is aware of being enveloped by Mystery, both cosmic and immanent. On the other hand, the non-dualisms of the 'East' require detailed elocution.[49] As to Julian, it would be wrong to label her as a non-dualist, *simpliciter*. In the cause of connected or relational theology, she partially collapses the classic Western dualisms of creator/created, spirit/matter and subject/object.

The non-dual tone of my three writers is based (see the Introduction) on the non-dual approach of Jesus himself. They are very conscious that their commitment hinges on the primary teaching of Jesus: 'God is Love'. It seems likely that they view the Trinity as the most profound (and yet most 'simple'?) poem of theology. This is because the manifestation of 'God is Love' requires a threesome: a Lover, a Beloved and the love that passes between them. Julian, Eckhart and Traherne understood themselves to be participating in divine creative action. In a literal way, they seem to have experienced the purport of Acts 17:28: The divine is that in which we '. . . live and move and have our being'.[50]

Is Paul saying, in the Acts passage, that we are grounded in *Being* itself? If he is, there might be Christian warrant for characterizing the divine, not as 'a being', but as the act of Being itself. In addition, is Paul implying that we are inextricably linked to the transpersonal energy of *Consciousness*? If so, there might be warrant for characterizing the divine as the ground of Consciousness. There is possibly a recognizable Pauline resonance between *Brahman* as the ground of Being and *Ātmān* as the ground of Consciousness.[51] The interest, here, is in locating a possible line of concurrence, while at the same time accepting the metaphysical incompatibility of Christianity with Hinduism.

Losing and Finding the Self

Non-dualism is confronting. The traditional Western dualities (such as spirit/matter, God/humanity, self/other . . . and so ad infinitum) are easier to manage. If the divine can be accounted for as *quite separate* from humanity (or, as an absolute projection by humanity), then the divine can readily be ignored. But non-dualism confronts us with potential layers of meaning that require response. The field is tricky to walk across. Clear boundaries are ever more unlikely.

The purpose of this study has been to suggest a degree of consonance between Traherne, Eckhart and Julian in the area of 'spiritual non-dualism'. The word 'spiritual' is far from satisfactory. But I need to make it clear that this book does not enter the mind/body debate, still less the free will/determinism debate. I simply reflect on the reality that Traherne, Eckhart and Julian tend to collapse the assumed objective world into a world beyond form and name. They share an 'internalist' approach. They favour inner transformation, in the direction of unitive consciousness. In other words, they see the purport of *Tat tvam asi*.[1] With no knowledge of *Vedānta*, as far as we know, each writer expresses the implications of the central assertion of *Advaita Vedānta*. This might partly be explained by their familiarity with the great disclosure: 'I Am That I Am' (Ex. 3:14, considered in Chapter 2).

To express the *Vedāntin* assertion in trans-religious terms, an affective realization of the 'I Am That I Am',[2] would yield consequences which parallel the implications of *Tat tvam asi*. We would experience our true nature of oneness with the divine. Our experience would be authentic spiritual experience (*anubhava*) of non-dual knowledge. Beyond all names (or mental phenomena) and forms (or physical phenomena) we would know ourselves to be one with . . . with . . .? An authentic answer to that question, on my understanding, cannot be reached outside the *śūnyatā* or the *kenosis* that constitutes a vision of reality that is non-dual and is both 'empty' and 'full'.

Ramana Maharshi's modern version of *Advaita* reinvigorates classical *Vedānta* as potentially non-sectarian, non-elitist and non-culturally bound. As is the case with Traherne, Eckhart and Julian, Ramana raises questions about the reliability of our ordinary perceptions of reality. But his analogical value lies in his 'strong' non-dualism counterpointing their moderate non-dualism.

Influence of Ramana Maharshi

Ramana's pluralist outlook and sense of presence was an indirect influence on the Hindu–Christian ashrams which now exist in India. Well-known personalities include Abhishiktananda (Henri Le Saux, d.1973) and Bede Griffiths (d.1993). Ramana put forward two movements as being indispensable to spiritual life. The first movement takes us away from over-identification with our bodies, our thoughts and our feelings. Ideally, this first movement is accompanied by a second movement; namely, the experiential realization of the true nature of reality. This experience involves the reception of divine grace. We come to *know* that we are more connected to infinite Awareness (the non-dual, supreme Self) than to the body or mind or senses.

Accordingly, Ramana's teaching can be summarized as the pursuit of one's true identity. The 'method' (such as it is) involves the continuing investigation into *who* is beyond, or deeper than, the outward manifestations. This is the concealed being, the non-dual 'I' behind the layerings of superficial identities. Passing beyond the self (small 's') the aspirant will find a new life in a natural surrender to the Self (capital 'S') which is the One without a second (and the substrate of all that exists).

A question arises: Will my ego permit me to 'go beyond' my ego-identifications? Ramana maintains that I will learn, through stillness, to accept myself as a deeper being than my ego permits. He speaks of silence as the wordless communion behind all thought and action. Indeed, he speaks of Silence as my true nature, through which the One Source discloses itself by grace. Ramana's emphasis on 'self-enquiry' is intended to lead to the direct, immediate realization that my true life is not separable from 'limitless Awareness' itself. Ramana regards the *I Am* (of Ex. 3:14) as another way of characterizing the ultimate Silence. The *I Am*, the Silence, the Self, the Pure Consciousness and the limitless Awareness tend to be treated as synonymous terms.[3] As to the basic motif in Christianity, Ramana can say:

> Real rebirth is dying from the ego into the spirit.
> This is the significance of the crucifixion of Jesus.
> Whenever identification with the body exists,
> a body is always available, whether this or any other one,
> till the body-sense disappears by merging into the source:
> the spirit, or Self. The stone which is projected upwards
> remains in constant motion till it returns to its source, the earth,
> and rests. Headache continues to give trouble,
> till the pre-headache state is regained.[4]

The tendency here is towards the recovery of a pre-existing condition. There is no hackneyed talk of the spiritual 'journey'. Traherne, Eckhart and Julian would tend to agree. Indeed, the idea of a spiritual 'path' holds a self-defeating element. It reflects a dualistic habit of mind and a future-orientation that counts against authentic life. Among spiritual writers, Traherne, Eckhart and Julian are united in focusing on life as it is lived 'now'. Would they favour the word 'Awakening' as applied to the present moment? We cannot be certain. But I wish to restate the obvious: A 'spiritual' concern with one's 'journey' implies a yet-to-be-reached future. It would seem to be anti-Hindu and anti-Christian. The poem below alludes to this point.

Walking in Tamil Nadu

Near the ashram gate, palm trees flow with the wind;
red hibiscus remain open. A large bird sculls across the sky;
the holy mountain burns with archaic value.
Our notion of time dissolves
for just a moment, as in a dream we greet the ancestors
and think the eternal present unremarkable.
We watch the rain, tactile rain,
in demure light. Someone lowers the word *spiritual*
onto the Kaveri River. We watch it drift away
into nothing, into everything. Drenched by hidden sweetness,
we cling less tightly to thought. A large bird dips, floats,
alights next to us. It peers up: *I am here. I am here.*
Beyond arrival, beyond non-arrival, we are already home.
Each thorn, sharp seed, hibiscus: always harshness
at the heart of life, always openness.

Sages such as Ramana tend to keep silent because they know that pivotal spiritual experiences are 'in the moment' and non-transferable. No one can do spiritual work on behalf of another. In the Gospels we read of the healings of people who manifested 'openness to the openness'. But we accept that 'transferred wholeness' cannot persist. The recipients are not so 'whole' after all. They rarely manifest the way of liberation for others.

Śaṅkarā argues against the false distinctions which he sees arising from 'divided time'. In developing non-dualism as a branch of *Vedānta*, Śaṅkarā is responding to what he regards as the Buddha's denial of a genuinely transcendental metaphysics. Alluding to Śaṅkarā's thought, Ramana writes that it cannot accurately be said that we have a goal of knowing spiritual 'truth'. This is because 'the truth' in *Vedānta* is already the ground of all knowing. Salvific knowledge is accorded priority over the desire for spiritual experiences, as such. *Vedānta* and its development in *Advaita Vedānta* is vulnerable to 'Western' queries as to the inherent value of individual persons. If we abide by classical logic we might ask: What happens to my particularity? If that which is 'individual' is absorbed within *Brahman*, just *who is it* that goes about living the compassionate life? Ramana was asked: 'If the Realized and the unrealized alike perceive the world, what is the difference between them?' Ramana replied:

When the Realized Man sees the world
he sees the Self that is the substratum of all that is seen.
Whether the unrealized man sees the world or not,

he is ignorant of his true being, the Self.
Take the example of a film on a cinema screen.
What is there in front of you before the film begins?
Only the screen. On that screen you see the entire show,
and to all appearances the pictures are real. But go and try
to take hold of them and what do you take hold of? . . .
So it is with the Self. That alone exists; the pictures come and go.
If you hold onto the Self, you will not be deceived
by the appearance of the pictures.[5]

Another analogy, which Traherne would have appreciated, runs as follows: 'The divine is like the sun. I am like the sun's reflection on a vast, changing sea. Therefore I am an illusory sun. My reality, my authentic Self, comes from the sun itself'.

The vulnerability, to which I refer above, arises from my 'Western' conditioning as to the value of individualism. Why, for so long, was I wedded to concepts such as 'inherency' and 'separable personalities'? Is Kant to blame? He would likely say that *Vedānta* leads to illusionism. A modern Kantian might that say that *Vedānta* is a rationale for social determinism. And, true enough, rigidly conservative *Vedāntin* ideas have historically provided legitimacy for abuses of power.

Although there is a confluence of diction between aspects of the *Advaita Vedānta* of Ramana and Traherne, Eckhart and Julian, it would be disingenuous to argue for compatibility. Not only do their presuppositions differ, but the multifaceted nature of their implied positions warns against generalized remarks. Yet, to sound general, they all concur on 'the way of interiority' (Eckhart). The conceptual, and even the *sensible*, tends to disappear. What is retained is purportedly pure experience, whether of 'the *Ātmān*' (see the Glossary) or of 'Emptiness' or of 'Spirit'. In Christian terms, 'the way of interiority' is the entrance, more and more deeply, into the ineffable mystery of Spirit. It is an experience, beyond traditional dualistic thought, of a unified field of presence. Subject and object are perceived as inseparable, and not merely as interrelated. In Buddhistic terms, especially in the Mādhyamika school, there is said to be a realization of being-as-emptiness. Being is said to be empty because it cannot be understood in terms of any reference point beyond itself.[6] Switching to Traherne, Eckhart and Julian, salvation is divine action to draw the world back from nothingness into fullness. It is a drawing back from the negative formlessness of nothingness, and a recovery of present-time fullness. The 'way in' to salvation is within: It is within the deepest centre of one's being.[7] Yet it is not separable (on this view) from repeated divine actions of compassion, in history. Laurence Freeman, a Benedictine who leads a community of meditators, states that compassion is the result of mindfulness:

> It limits the sway of evil in the world, and it can undo negative karma – as Jesus 'took away the sins of the world' not by judging the world, but by loving it with the compassion of his mindfulness. . . . Evil is not so much the wilful concentration of our energies on a deliberate wrong. It is rather the tragic foreshortening of consciousness to the key hole of the ego, through which we can only peep into reality.[8]

To repeat: It is unwise to draw firm comparisons between *Advaita Vedānta* and traditional Christian teaching. There is a degree of consonance; there are concurrences of thought and experience. Wolfgang Smith is salutary, by way of reference to the non-dualism of Jacob Boehme (d.1624). Smith writes that '. . . one must remember that there are different kinds of non-dualism, and that even in *Vedānta*, the *advaita* of Śaṅkarā represents but one school, one 'point of view' if you will'.[9] A Christian non-dualist, Smith believes that an easy dismissal of non-dualism as monistic is uninformed. He is clear that '. . . for the Christian, the non-dual or *advaitic* state is realized in the Incarnate Son of God'.[10] Alluding to the unitive emphasis in both *Vedānta* and Buddhism, Smith can say:

> Our union is with the Incarnate Son of God, *and through him*, with God the Father. Now, in this union the creature does not disappear – does not, like the dewdrop, 'slip into the shining sea' – but rather becomes assimilated to the Mystical Body of Christ.[11]

Smith here implies that union with God does not entail the cessation of diversity. He quotes Nicholas of Cusa, as follows: 'In God, identity *is* diversity'. He locates a non-dual statement by Clement of Alexandria: '. . . the Son is neither simply one thing, nor many things as parts, but one thing as all things, whence also he is all things'.[12] All people can potentially realize their 'oneness with God'.[13] This is not the same as literally being transformed into God. Early in these reflections, I cited Traherne's notion of the divine as 'interconnecting Spirit'. This Spirit is not separate from me; we are not two. But neither are we one (numerically). For Smith, then, we approach a reasonable formulation of *how* we can realize our oneness with God when we accept the kind of language that Eckhart and others employed. That is, Realization is accomplished by an activation of the divine Word or Image in our souls. In Chapter 2, this divine activity came into a discussion on Eckhartian *Gelâzenheit*, the letting-be of detachment or releasement. I see Eckhart's non-dual position as a precursor of Julian's less-figured non-dualism. Both of these teachers might be viewed as precursors of Traherne's (sometimes) thorough-going non-dualism.

Charles Taylor and the demise of Western Christian non-duality

It is obvious that a church imbued with a paradigm of domination and subordination will take issue with Eckhartian thought, and with aspects of Julian and Traherne. Within their texts, all three writers find it challenging to pick and choose between what might be *of God* and what might be *of humanity*. They venture a sub-text, and sometimes an explicit text, of the non-duality of being. They do not regard the Ultimate or the One as 'another' in the sense of absolutely 'other'.[14] Taken as a whole, the passages quoted in these reflections amount to careful declarations of mystical union. But the language of 'the One' and of 'Oneness' is fraught: It is forever vulnerable to misuse, not to mention oversimplification. Although I see consonance (and although Ramana's perspective is theopoetically helpful to me), it cannot be assumed that 'the One' means the same thing across the traditions.[15]

One Fruit

Come outside
to my apricot tree,
where galahs have left
but one fruit.

Let me have pleasure
in your pleasure
in its taste.

You have watched bees load their legs
with rosemary pollen;
you have seen spinebills
eat the bees.

Sensory impressions,
fragments of information,
deductions which might feed
an intuition.

To be alive,
to be here this moment.
Loved in the nearness;
drawn to an otherness.

Poetry is not about delivering messages. Nonetheless, writing which carries 'a message' can find wide acceptance.[16] My poem above expresses the potential pleasure of non-dualism; it also hints at my disquiet with individualism. Does contemporary society push people in the direction of excessive individualism? Does it do so under the lure of self-fulfilment? If this is true, one of the consequences might be that values which transcend the individual will be shut out.

No commentator has, in my view, chronicled the 'Western' demise of 'spiritual non-duality' more persuasively than Charles Taylor.[17] Taylor traces the emergence of a self-identifying 'self' to the Enlightenment. The gradual breakdown of social hierarchies and the rise of a sense of egalitarian dignity were two main factors. An ideal developed of inner authenticity. Gradually a personal identification which was *socially derived* came to be considered as feudal. Taylor argues that the authentic self does not fully emerge from one's inner depths, but is 'coaxed out' by other people who are felt to be significant. Self-knowledge, therefore, depends upon the dialogical recognition of others with whom one shares language and hence understandings.[18]

Taylor implies that the greater the dialogical recognition, the greater the individual's transformation. A person's self-images become more positive; they implicitly invoke the truer self as a regulative ideal.[19] As an earlier 'indefiniteness' or lack of authenticity is transcended, communion can be experienced. Taylor laments, in a later book, that 'the culture of authenticity' has sunk from a defensible ideal to the level of an axiom. Few people, he states, can now bring themselves to argue the case for moral positions which might support authenticity.

> By this I mean the view that moral positions are not in any way grounded in reason or in the nature of things but are ultimately just adopted by each of us because we find ourselves drawn to them. On this view, reason can't adjudicate moral disputes.[20]

Reason has trouble in adjudicating disputes because of the predominance of moral subjectivism, which Taylor rejects. He continues as follows.

> The general force of subjectivism in our philosophical world and the power of neutral liberalism intensify the sense that these issues can't and shouldn't be talked about. And then on top of it all, social science seems to be telling us that to understand such phenomena as the contemporary culture of authenticity, we shouldn't have recourse in our explanations to such things as moral ideals but should see it all in terms of, say, recent changes in the mode of production, or new patterns of youth consumption, or the security of affluence.[21]

A self-described Christian humanist, Taylor holds that 'spirit' is an irreducible component of human nature. We define ourselves in terms of a vision of what is pre-eminent to us. Ontologically, such self-definition is unavoidable: We need to articulate that which moves us. This is especially true in relation to the values by which we aspire to live. These will constitute our ultimate 'goods', our pre-eminent vision. Layers of modern assumptions might need to be worked through, in order for us to bring these 'goods' to full consciousness. Taylor notes that 'feeling' ought to be defended as inherent to the spiritual component of humanity. 'Feeling' has irreducible epistemological value. It is closely linked to our views on the nature of reality; it is integral to what we regard as all-important. In a distinctive move, Taylor links a sense of 'who we are' with the process of becoming 'oriented in moral space'.[22] He rejects naturalistic accounts of moral development. Instead, he holds the view that we are *necessarily* oriented with *some sort* of moral framework. We acquire 'languages of moral and spiritual discernment'[23] by means of which we are empowered to discern between our experiences and to make distinctions which constitute acts of understanding. Taylor uses the words 'epistemic gain'[24] to describe our movement, from diverse backgrounds and feelings and intuitions, towards varied patterns of 'qualitative discriminations'.[25] We move towards new ways of seeing, which become the acts of understanding whereby we arrive at a sense of who we are.

The Gospel stories, rather obviously, give us something additional to Taylor's 'epistemic gain'. The disciple who goes out to 'find' her true self will find *that which she already is*. Jesus has a direct interest in lived experience and in finding the right words to depict the underlying meanings of experience. He is not represented as being overly concerned with general abstractions. The theological construction of his parables tends to reveal an absorption with actual *perichoretic* situations, with what William James called 'primary realities', and not with doctrines. Hence, the reported emphasis in the Gospels on discovering *that which we already are*. To venture another language, it might be said that transcendence of the false or delusory self results in the disclosure of the non-dual Self.[26] But I need to be careful, in the pursuit of parallels or congruencies, not to elide words and concepts. Different religious languages are involved. And not only languages *per se*. We are also dealing with attempts to give names to aspects of reality which are 'different'. In view of this, John B. Cobb proposes 'complementary pluralism'. His premise is that '... the totality of what is, is very complex, far exceeding all that we can ever hope to know or think'.[27] Cobb suggests that complementary pluralism might adopt three kinds of 'ultimates'. These are, first, the 'formless' or 'acosmic', such as we find in *Advaita Vedānta* and in Eckhart's 'Godhead beyond God'. Second, the theistic or 'formed', such as Yahweh and Christ. Third, the 'cosmic', such as primal religions and so-called Native traditions.[28] This proposal from Cobb seems to provide a circumspect means of honouring the irreducible plurality of the voices of truth.

Simone Weil and attentiveness

Weil[29] is indebted to Eckhart in her frequent allusions to self-emptying. Her autobiographical *Waiting for God* carries expressions that could be those of Eckhart himself.

> God permitted the existence of things distinct from himself ....
> By this creative act he negated himself, as Christ has told us to negate
> ourselves. God negated himself for our sakes in order to give us
> the possibility of negating ourselves for him. This response, this echo, ...
> is in our power to refuse.[30]

Weil wrote very little about the oppression of women under particular 'interpretations' of the tradition of self-negation. But she might be more conducive to our sensibilities when she discusses 'attention', as in *attention-giving*. She found this in Kierkegaard (d.1855). It is worth quoting him; I have retained his own emphases:

> The immediate person thinks and imagines that when he prays,
> the important thing, the thing he must concentrate upon,
> is that *God should hear what he is praying for*. And yet in the true,
> eternal sense it is just the reverse: the true relation in prayer
> is achieved not when God hears what is prayed for,
> but when *the person praying* continues to pray until
> he is *the one who hears*, who hears what God wills.
> The immediate person, therefore, uses many words
> and therefore makes demands in his prayer;
> the true man of prayer only *attends*.[31]

Weil follows Kierkegaard in her view that attention-giving is a precondition of the *kenotic* lifestyle. She would have preferred that people who are interested in prayer should drop the name *homo sapiens* and rename themselves *homo orans*, meaning the people who *attend*, or pray or focus. Attentiveness without an object is regarded as prayer in its supreme form. Through a choice to focus on the other/Other, the seemingly separate individual transcends the illusion that her ego is dualistic. She will realize experientially that the duality of 'there is me' and 'there are other objects' is an illusion borne of post-Enlightenment reifications of the individual ego.

In the section 'Reflections on the Right Use of School Studies' in *Waiting for God*, Weil writes:

> Attention consists of suspending our thought . . . . Our thought should be in relation to all particular and already formulated thoughts, as a man on a mountain who, as he looks forward, sees also below him, without actually looking at them, a great many forests and plains. Above all our thought should be empty, waiting, not seeking anything, but ready to receive in its naked truth the object that is to penetrate it.[32]

It could be said that 'attention' for Weil is an experience of 'openness to the openness'. To state this less opaquely, 'attention' is a refusal to fasten one's focus upon any particular phenomenon. It involves a withdrawal of a desire for any particular thing. Such openness is unconditional, in the Gadamerian sense of allowing the 'text' to which I attend to disclose itself. Nonetheless, openness will inevitably include my prejudgements, which I will question as I reach fresh interpretations, fresh horizons and fusions of horizons.[33] In the presence of another's 'text', my mind and senses might grasp something of the external details of the other. But, in Gadamer's view, my spirit (*Geist*) can go further and enter something of the totality of the person (who is otherwise 'other'). This other person can then be seen as 'whole' rather than as a collection of separate attributes. In other words, one person can enter into the subject-being of another, and maybe vice versa. One sees that the other *is*, in a sense, one's own self. The world has dramatically ceased to be broken up into 'we's' and 'they's'. Further into *Waiting for God*, Weil can write:

> To give up our imaginary position as the centre, to renounce it,
> not only intellectually but in the imaginative part of our soul,
> that means to awaken to what is real and eternal,
> to see the true light and hear the true silence.
> A transformation then takes place
> at the very roots of our sensibility . . .[34]

We need to be aware, she writes, that the fragmentary is the bearer of infinity.[35] God essentially is unknowable, but God in *fragments* may be known. This is because the fragments are not 'out there' but 'in here'. To the extent that the Real is accessible, it is found within our fragmentary selves. It is 'in here' and not 'out there' waiting to be discovered. We might recall a basic question, posed by sages to disciples: 'What is Reality?' Insofar as there is an agreeable answer, the disciple replies: 'When the mind declines to assume or to generate falsity, *there is Reality*. Thereafter, the teacher (Weil-like) warns that the acceptance of contradiction and incompatibility is preferable to any fantasy of artificial unity.

It is notable that Rowan Williams is respectful of Weil, and yet critical of her chosen life of 'abandonment'. In a book of essays (2007), Williams (as I interpret him) criticizes her tendency to overdetermine the divide between God and humanity. That is to say, she exaggerates the *kenotic* imperative confronting any person who is devoted to truth and to justice. Weil safeguards God's absolute otherness (and human surrender) by downplaying a biblical assumption that in reaching out in love to the created world, we also move nearer to God. Did Weil, in trying to model her life on that of Christ, overstretch her theory and practice of self-abnegation?

The idea that attention-giving will mean the withdrawal of desire for any particular thing is basic to many traditions. Writing within a Christian tradition, Cynthia Bourgeault states that the purpose of prayer is not to 'access' God. Rather, it is to '. . . align spontaneously with Jesus's own continuously creative and enfolding presence through emulating his *kenotic* practice in all life situations'. Noting that ego-driven spiritual ambition 'can wind up in very bad places', Bourgeault says '. . . it is important never to lose sight of the fact that *spiritual ambitiousness and attention of the heart are mutually exclusive categories.* The proud may fall, but it will not be through following the Way of the Heart, for the heart has its inbuilt safeguard: it perceives only in the modality of surrender'.[36]

As to the *kenotic* surrender of Jesus, it appears that he grew to accept that attention to truth and to justice would result in great wrong being done to him. The Gospel of John at first presents a particularly exalted view of Jesus. It gradually emerges that John wishes to coax the reader to move beyond regarding Jesus as an exalted being, merely. Within the text, Jesus moves to the view that he is going to suffer appallingly. The implication is that those who follow Jesus are also destined to suffer.

> Very truly, I tell you, unless a grain of wheat
> falls into the earth and dies,
> it remains just a single grain;
> but if it dies, it bears much fruit. (Jn 12:24, NRSV)

Here then is a picture of *kenotic* life: I am invited to less self-projection, in order to allow more space for 'the other'. This may involve an experience of pure consciousness: '. . . the mind of Christ' (1 Cor. 2:16 REB). Such a notion of transcendence would not find favour with many Buddhists, because of cautiousness concerning the idea of transcendence. There is, however, a Buddhist tradition which takes genuine transcendence seriously, namely, Shin Buddhism, the Japanese 'Pure Land' expression of the Mahāyāna. Shin includes, as an axiom of enlightenment, that an authentic gift of grace is necessary.[37] The relevant Japanese word is *tariki*, the power of Another. Might not there be some accordance, here, with Paul's view that the small-s (or phenomenal) self lacks the motivation to be transformed?[38] Of relevance here is Jn 15: the invitation by Jesus that I should come to terms with my own reality. In the first part of Jn 15:4, there are two closely balanced clauses: 'Abide in me as I abide in you' (NRSV). In his commentary, C. K. Barrett (not regarded as radical) considers these clauses to be saying: 'Let there be mutual indwelling'.[39] Commenting on the overall theme of John 15, Barrett states: 'There is a mutual indwelling of Father, Son, and disciple'.[40] This disciple finds herself dramatically reconciled with 'all reality'. That is to say, she is indwelt by the Source, the Ultimate. The stillness of Jesus' inner being is offered throughout the NT as exemplary. In his stillness lies a potential revelation of the unity of body and spirit and of genuine *gnosis* (Gk: experiential knowledge). The revelation, on this view, is the experience of knowing who one really is. Only then is the disciple ready to engage in unselfconscious self-emptying. The little self has found its place, that is to say, it *has no* ultimate place. It no longer feels threatened by the imaginary total otherness of God or by the delusory total otherness of others.

In the Christian *kenotic* story there are dialectical terms: *Spirit* empties itself in order to become *body*; conversely, *body* empties itself in order to participate in *Spirit*. In traditional language, the Father empties himself in creation and humanity empties itself of divine intimacy as a result of the Fall. In due time, Jesus empties himself in love and is declared to be the Christ. Finally, Spirit empties itself across all humanity, indeed, across all creation. This Spirit potentially ignites individual and collective actions which are said to be those of Jesus extended more widely. Such actions are characterized by love manifesting as surrender; they are *kenotic*. They are also oriented towards the furtherance of community.

Andrei Rublev and Buddhist 'emptiness'

I have proposed Rublev's *The Holy Trinity* as an exemplary illustration of *perichoresis*. Rublev represents the divine as a movement between three figures, seated as part of an open circle. Gone is the Church's patriarchal notion of unity at the expense of community. Gone is the hierarchical Church's tacit sequence of control: First the Father, then the Son, then the Spirit. Rublev's icon is concerned with the flow of love, the circulation of energy within a table setting of equality. The icon, when observed deeply, conveys a strong sense of intimacy. *The Holy Trinity* is quintessentially Byzantine, but painted in Russia. Rublev consciously bypasses any possibility of 'three gods'. He also avoids monism and dualism. A monk within the Byzantine rite of the Russian Orthodox Church, Rublev's integrity of insight was recognized by his contemporaries. He depicts a single divinity with three differentiated aspects. The Father, Son and Spirit (or rather, the three angels of Gen. 18 who are polite stand-ins for the Trinity) are humbly engaged in mutual deferral. There is no power-inclined hierarchy; no stratospheric manipulator of things Earthly. Orthodox understandings favour a double view of *kenosis*. First, God surrenders a degree of divine freedom in creating free humans; second, the life of Jesus liberates human consciousness so that it might be freely, *kenotically* offered back to God.

Negative assessments of the doctrine of the Trinity are widespread. Personally, I once considered the idea of a triune God, with an apparent bias towards masculine power, to be damaging as well as unintelligible.[41] Observing Rublev's icon, I see that I overvalued intelligibility. In front of me is a theo-poem *par excellence*. A hidden voice seems to say: 'See . . . I am the divine! See . . . I am relating to my divine-self in love! And in some shape or form I am ever-present to you as well!'

Whether or not I am reaching a clearer view, I am no longer surprised at Rublev's popularity. He occupies a singular place in a form of art which allows for immediate spiritual communication. His vision is *perichoretic, kenotic* and non-dual. The heightened emphasis which is given to bodiliness, in all the Orthodox Churches (not only the Russian) means that bodily fulfilment is given a higher value than in much of Catholicism. The *kenotic* process paradoxically evolves, wherever a balanced orientation of bodiliness is upheld, into the emergence of fullness. *Kenosis* (as emptying) becomes *plerôma* (fullness). Vacancy is repeatedly brought to fullness. In the foreground of *The Holy Trinity* is a vacant space. A chair is missing, reserved for me. Will I pull up my chair? Seeing the icon deeply, I see that no unbridgeable gap exists between me and the divine. A form of consummation is proffered.

Donald Mitchell has written a dialogical account of the shape of Buddhist *śūnyatā* (emptiness) and Christian *kenosis*. He states that the creation of a true mode of human life cannot be achieved through reason alone, or by human volition alone, but through spiritual realization. Then he asks, in effect: Might not *śūnyatā* and *kenosis*, as the heart of Buddhism and Christianity, represent the way to compassion and love? Do not both traditions point to interior freedom or non-attachment as the way to transformation? Mitchell therefore can align himself with the classical observation that emptiness is simultaneously fullness.[42]

> In the kenosis of Christ, God communicates himself. He is not revealing something other than himself. He 'speaks' himself in his Word. And the essence of this message is love: 'For God so loved the world that he sent his only son' (John 3:16). This love of God for the world that is revealed in the kenosis of the cross, is also found in the kenosis of love at the core of creation . . . .[43]

A traditional Christian point of view adheres to two principal *kenotic* events. First, creation; second, redemption. Mitchell refers to the second *kenotic* event as follows:

> The power of this redemptive kenosis rescues us, it overturns our ordinary mode of being in the world and recovers our original mode of being in the world. In so doing, it recovers our original union with God and unity with others and all creation.[44]

Mitchell engages with the thought of Keiji Nishitani (d.1990) and his predecessor in the Kyoto zenist tradition, Kitaro Nishida (d.1945). He hints that Eckhartian 'nothingness'[45] or 'mystical Void' might have commonalities with Buddhist emptiness, provided that we face a real disparity: The Christian non-dual vision (Mitchell believes) cannot be all-inclusive. There remains a divine transcendence. Discussing Nishida and Nishitani, he writes:

> They see a dynamic identity between Absolute Nothingness
> and the forms of creation. The kenosis of Emptiness,
> seen from the near side by Buddhists, is an emptying out of Emptiness
> as the fullness of the world in an absolute sense
> that leaves nothing transcendent from this world. . . .
> To use Nishitani's terms, the near side is the far side, *samsāra* is Nirvâna,
> Emptiness is forms and forms are Emptiness. In this way,
> Emptiness experienced in Buddhism moves one back to the world of forms
> to find it anew as a fullness of wondrous being.[46]

In this quotation, *samsāra* would seem to hold its primary meaning as the Earth-bound cycle of reincarnation. Although Buddhism, in general, resists speaking of a true self (and distances itself from Hinduism in this regard), Mitchell uses the words 'true self' when writing of the parallels between *śūnyatā* and *kenosis*. As implied above, he notes that neither are achievements of the will. They are, instead, the lived-out expressions of '. . . negation of the ego-self'.[47] He goes on to state that wherever there is 'awakening', there is '. . . a realization of lived compassion, of the compassion of Emptiness lived in the realizer'. Mitchell reiterates a wisdom-saying attributed to the Buddha: 'Who sees the Dharma, he sees me. Who sees me, he sees the Dharma'. He then isolates a major difference between Buddhism and Christianity.

> In Buddhism, one can become a Buddha in the realization of Emptiness.
> But in Christianity, one cannot say that one becomes a Christ in the realization
> of the redemption. Rather, this Christian realization is a participation in Christ's
> redemptive kenosis.[48]

The customary translation of *śūnyatā* as 'emptiness' or 'voidness' is unfortunate if emptiness becomes equated with misapprehensions of 'nothingness'. Is it helpful, in popular 'Christian-Buddhism' to equate the divine with 'Absolute Nothingness'? Perhaps *śūnyatā* is better translated as 'openness', although not in the sense of receptivity to anything whatsoever. I consider that the concept of 'openness' helpfully reflects the open-ended nature of reality itself. It might be understood as the context in which 'experience' is experienced, with spiritual discernment and discrimination. But, is 'openness' a state which one can consciously enter? Maybe not. It would seem more likely that 'openness' is that which is always present, but requires recognition. The broad injunction, within the *Vedāntin* teaching on the Self, is that we should grow beyond our tendency to *obscure* the original 'openness' of our true nature.

Beverly Lanzetta might offer clarification on Eckhartian nothingness.[49] She maintains that implicit in Eckhart is a metaphysical nothingness which '. . . cannot rest at any final and definitive revelation of God'. Lanzetta continues:

> The very mystery of the twofold *kenosis* intrinsic to Christian thought always
> points *beyond itself*, never resting on a final identity. Therefore, the true 'end' of
> the soul is not Trinitarian, Christocentric, or necessarily tradition-centred, but
> the nothingness that is 'neither this nor that'.[50]

Approaching the end of her essay, Lanzetta avers that Eckhart's position at this point is complementary to that of Buddhism.[51] That is to say, she finds in Eckhart '. . . a movement from emptiness . . . to form . . . and from form back to emptiness centred in the inner life of divinity'.[52]

Love's work

False interpretations of *śūnyatā* (emptiness) and *kenosis* (self-emptying) have proved manipulative, especially of women. As a legitimate (and today, ecologically imperative) ascetic practice, the *kenotic* lifestyle put forward by Jesus was one of the reasons for his desertion by his closest friends. Johannes Baptist Metz mentions this in a pointedly modest booklet which hints that the Vatican itself is indifferent towards *kenosis*.

> Poverty of spirit is always betrayed most by those who are closest to it.
> It is the disciples of Christ in the Church who criticize and subvert it
> most savagely. Perhaps this is why Jesus related the parable
> of the wheat grain. Finding in it a lesson for himself,
> he passed it on to his Church, so that it might be remembered
> down through the ages, especially when the poverty
> intrinsic to human existence became repugnant.[53]

This booklet by Metz became popular, despite its theme of Jesus-as-empty and its exhortation that humanity must discover its identity through embracing emptiness. Metz continues:

> It is no accident that poverty of spirit is the first
> of the beatitudes. What is the sorrow of those who mourn,
> the suffering of the persecuted, the self-forgetfulness of the merciful,
> or the humanity of the peacemakers – what are these if not variations
> of spiritual poverty? This spirit is also the mother of the three-fold
> mystery of faith, hope and charity. It is the doorway
> through which we must pass to become authentic human beings.
> Only through poverty of spirit do we draw near to God;
> only through it does God draw near to us.[54]

Metz concludes that an enlightened understanding of love is contingent upon would-be lovers accepting their inner calling to 'hand over'.

> Every stirring of genuine *love* makes us poor. It dominates the whole human person,
> makes absolute claims upon us (cf. Mt 22:37), and thus subverts all extra-human
> assurances of security. The true lover must be unprotected and give of himself or
> herself without reservation . . . .[55]

Did thinking such as this prompt the statement, attributed to Jesus, that I must enter the Kingdom through the needle's eye? If a tiny aperture is meant, this would require an amusing shrinkage, if I am to pass through it. I would need to be markedly *reduced*. This seems to me to be the *kenotic* thrust of Phil. 2: the form of God is characterized as undergoing shrinkage. Paul states that Christ emptied himself (*eauton ekenôse*), taking the form of a servant (*morphên doulou*). But emptiness or *kenosis* becomes manifested as fullness: '. . . in him all the fullness (*plêrôma*) was pleased to dwell' (Col. 1:19). In sum, Christ is represented as the self-emptying form of God. Upon emptying himself, he reflects divine plenitude (*plerôma*) so that humanity might become '. . . sharers in the divine nature (*theias koinônoi phuseôs*)' (2 Pet. 1:4).

> Let the same mind be in you
> that was in Christ Jesus,
> who, though he was in the form of God,
> did not regard equality with God as something to be exploited,
> but emptied himself,
> taking the form of a slave,
> being born in human likeness.
> And being found in human form,
> he humbled himself
> and became obedient to the point of death –
> even death on a cross.
> Therefore God also highly exalted him
> and gave him the name
> that is above every name,
> so that at the name of Jesus
> every knee should bend,
> in heaven and on earth and under the earth,
> and every tongue should confess
> that Jesus Christ is Lord,
> to the glory of God the Father.
> (Phil. 2:5–11, NRSV)

This passage is widely regarded as an early hymn, embedded decades later in what is regarded as Paul's final extant letter. Whatever its origin, Paul conveys the idea that in *kenosis* we can discern an act of divine self-communication. Sebastian Moore has paraphrased the passage in a testamentary manner, as follows:

> Jesus, being in the form of God (as all humans are)
> did not translate this into being for himself (as all humans do).
> On the contrary, he took our humanness on
> in an extraordinary way, its true way,
> a way of total self-dispossession, of freedom from ego

in which (upsetting all our ideas of what befits divinity)
he made manifest the ultimate mystery
that itself is poor, for-all, has no possessions,
makes rank meaningless . . . .[56]

The centrepiece of the Gospel's declaration (the *kerygma*) is the un-Platonic and anti-Gnostic understanding that humanity is not required to ascend to union with the divine; rather, the divine descends to humanity. Unhappily, as the *kerygma* solidified into dogma, *kenosis* came to be used as part of an ideology of oppression. But *kenosis* should not be thought of as self-denial, in the sense of withholding from the self its necessary needs and desires. Paul (and Jesus[57]) is not pursuing a doctrinal position; the language of dying to self is within a discourse of freedom.

As to the whole of Phil. 2, a degree of prejudice against some aspects of Pauline teaching might mitigate against a grasp of the radical nature of his embodied, interpersonal and *transpersonal* ethics. As to Jesus himself, his *nothingness* (from ambiguous origins to near-total rejection as an adult) becomes symbolized by the offensive cross of execution. But as the Buddha's emptiness opened the occasion for his enlightenment, the *kenosis* of Jesus opened the occasion for 'the kingdom'. This is the realm of true children, the unencumbered, the trusting. It is only the children, the ones who become 'as children', who inherit the spiritual effulgence of the divine 'parent'. Adults are invited to die, not only to their self-importance, but to their limitations generally, including a personal sense of exclusiveness, or of separateness from others. But the invitation to die in this sense (the 'true *kenosis*'?) is also an invitation to rise into a life of new communion and renewed community.

Various *kenotic* solutions have been put forward to address the question of how the divine can unite with the human. One appealing avenue of resolution might be to assert that God needs humanity, even though we, and our world, remain contingent. Perhaps God cannot choose to deny God's own character of love. If the expression of this love involves the risk of rejection, the assertion is made that God is genuinely *kenotic*. While God's character is consistent, God is not necessarily unchangeable.

In the absence of any detailed treatment of *kenosis* put forward by Traherne, Eckhart or Julian, I will make use of a text by French philosopher Stanislas Breton (d.2005). In an exposition of Phil. 2, Breton writes that '. . . the final intention of this sublime theatre, by emphasizing a will to love that would renounce all possession, signifies the need to transcend the conceptual schemas of an ontology that has heavily strained the historical representations of faith'. Breton continues:

> This moving image of sacrifice and emptying unfolds schematically to make us aware of the emergence of a sovereign freedom, whose ecstasy of giving requires as preamble the rejection of every richness, of substance or attributes.[58]

That which is divine becomes a slave. In the form of the man Jesus, the slave is '. . . dispersed in the unconditional service of those whom he has come to serve'.[59] The very being of this slave '. . . consists precisely in not being'.[60] At the close of the pericope, the actions of self-emptying are reconfigured as holding sublime consequences. But the actions have been performed by the slave without condition. He has not calculated his chances of a self-serving 'heaven'.

> The Son of Man retains the form of the slave only to render it insupportable and to make the condition of an incomparable joy surge in the forgetfulness of self: that which raises to the dignity of selfhood the disinherited of every kind, who must be able to say: I am what I am. *Agape* is inseparable from this liberating service, which makes of nothingness not only something but someone.[61]

The already existing hymn, which Paul invokes, certainly gives us a story of disruption. Jesus disrupts the 'normal' world and its worldly assumptions and expectations, not least those of the 'worldly religious' who gained from the stratification of society. To use the language of anachronism, both Right and Left are set to be discombobulated. Both the underprivileged and the overlords of Philippi are enticed to a position of faith. Or rather, it is Paul's hope that faith is evoked, on all sides, by the radical metaphor of reversal. The Ultimate One, with the onto-theological accoutrements that antiquity had bequeathed to Philippi, is radicalized. There is a funnelling down, into suffering and into death. And then, the *kerygma* of a new way of being, a new life, is offered within everydayness and within an imagined future. But the future is deemed, already, to have begun. It is an *experienced* future, in the sense of a felt knowledge which is *already* felt. Its basis is the unconditional love of the divine-become-human. Just as Jesus at his baptism is represented as hearing God's voice: 'You are my beloved one; in you, I take great delight', so too, each follower of Jesus is intended to hear an *identical* affirmation. As with Jesus, they are interpenetrated or interpermeated with Spirit, so that they can bear witness: 'Not I live, but Christ lives in me' (Gal. 2:20). I briefly mentioned, in Chapter 2, the trans-identification of this passage.

The disciples of Jesus are represented as reluctant to accept, from the lips of Jesus, that he is about to be divested of life itself. *Kenosis* is not humanity's natural ambiance; the disciples are within the process, along with their developing tradition, of thinking of 'messianism' in terms of power politics and restoration. Their assumptions are antithetical to the developing *kerygma*. Unambiguous arguments and assured foundations, worshipped by religious lovers of certitude, are always likely to trump fresh ideas, such as *kenosis*. For *kenosis* is a precursor to *perichoretic* expressions of mutual indwelling. And these are imprecise. As a way of speaking about possible differentiation within the divine, *kenosis* indicates relationality. We might ask: Does Philippians chapter 2 foreground humanity's incorporation, within divine modes of energy and participation, in the ever-on-going creation?[62] To articulate *kenosis* as a basic standpoint for Christianity[63] is arguably to accept a weakening of the metaphysical foundations of 'Christendom'. It is to follow the implications of *kenoticism* by questioning anything that resembles essentialism. Postmodern apologetics would benefit, as would the current moves to bring theology into more creative interplay with both the Continental and the analytic traditions of philosophy.

How rapidly did large parts of the church degenerate from a *kenotic* community, into a system of mediation designed for the reinforcement of 'certitudes'? A move beyond (any) mediated religion will tend to foreground the non-dual.

Luminous Bodies

Her old VW
      mows the dirt road
            to my shack,

past the noiseless fall
      of frangipani,
            a flash of butterfly

in deep shade.
      We walk in the garden
            of now,

and find an alcove
      of tenderness
            behind the melaleuca.

She listens
      to the hidden life:
            roots drawing nourishment,

sap rising in stems.
      Each twig,
            an inverse tongue;

each leaf and flower
      a wisdom far removed
            from knowledgeable din.

Infrangible desire:
      a thousand cicadas
            throbbing the heat.

Shyly assertive,
      she sings my body;
            I, hers.

We sing
      the joy
            of imperfection,

the caress
      of impermanence.
            Soft tissue,

exquisitely bruised,
      collapses
            into limb-sized folds.

An attempt is made, in my poem above, to juxtapose sensuality with ever-abiding wisdom and truth. The passion which motivates Traherne's work is important to the poem, except that my own work is more anchored in physicality. Desire commonly participates in the conventional truth-level; it highlights the particular or personal form which can manifest the formless. A reviewer has written that my poem can be read '. . . as an expression of the universal need of connection and comfort. It appeals at many levels'.[64] Within the Abrahamic traditions, it might be said that humanity *becomes* what it desires. We continue to become what we are *desiring*.[65]

Derrida and the faith of the 'mystics'

In previous chapters, I have mentioned Kearney, Caputo, Derrida and Vattimo. Each one has paid attention to the *kenotic* emphasis of Phil. 2. Perhaps they have contributed to the 'emptying out' of (possibly) 'unsustainable' metaphysics. I am using the word 'metaphysics' in the ancient sense of an attempt to uncover knowledge of 'reality' in and of itself. This was the way in which Traherne and his predecessors regarded metaphysics. Although aware of some of its limits, they can be presumed to have viewed metaphysics as the pinnacle of philosophy. But, to them, there was something more important than metaphysics; namely, faith. Faith, in the sense of a trust which manifests as love, allowed recognition of the 'end-point' of metaphysics. As to Derridean[66] tropes, I suggest that he desires to reassess the Gospel's *kenotic* theme. Faith seems to be ranked ahead of reason; faith is figured as reason's reason. This is perhaps the purport of the Derridean 'faith as meaningful *event*'. An authentic person is viewed as someone who faces up to faith's *kenotic* nature. That is, faith is always subject to a deconstructionist reconfiguration; it arguably lacks substantive content. There is nothing about the content of faith which can be separated out and 'known'. But Derrida nonetheless maintains that faith is a meaningful event. The 'meaningful' part is *the necessary doubt* which is inseparable from authentic faith. While presuppositions of metaphysics are unacceptable (at least if these purport to claim that descriptions of God can be fully intelligible), the meaningfulness of faith is broadened out, within the vital unknowingness of uncertainty.

Derrida's interest in *kenosis* and *perichoresis* appears to stem from his admiration for Eckhart. This, despite (or because of) the fact that Derrida attempts a theology without an assured object. Such a way of doing theology retains the possibility of the subject, God, as actually *being the subject*, and not the object of human projection. I remain uncertain as to following Derrida in his rejection of the metaphysics of divine presence. Did Derrida, like Eckhart, desire to be faithful to the kind of vision that attempts to adopt God's perspective? To the extent that such might be achievable,[67] it could transpire that postmodern 'excess' is liberational in its intent. Perhaps, in addition, it protects particularity. Perhaps it can also be full of joy.

In order to lessen the duality of 'us' and 'them', Derrida advises an ongoing commitment to see or to feel one's way into the 'other side' of any apparent dualism. A community which respects diversity (and is therefore non-violent?) will acknowledge the inescapable presence of 'the others' as part of its self-definition. Here Derrida approaches Christian teaching on *perichoresis*. The three persons in Rublev's *The Holy Trinity* maintain a separateness. And yet they defer to each other; they cede their separateness and 'interpenetrate'. They are held to share one nature, after all. Rublev is Russian Orthodox by both birth and conviction; he believes that God is One. My point here is this: Derrida seemingly believes that humanity needs to learn the practice of seeing 'the other in oneself and oneself in the other'. Such practice is both meditative and *perichoretic*.[68] Derrida holds that the meaning of 'God', of the Holy Name, must translate into the practice of love without remainder. The kingdom of God is therefore a *when*, and not a *where*. As with faith, so with the divine: God is not so much an entity as an event. Derrida writes of traces, rather than signs, because he considers that 'a trace' might point less ambiguously beyond itself. A sign, on the other hand, might merely convey a largely imaginary memory of pure presence.

Derrida's name might be allied, not only with Eckhart, but with Nāgārjuna (d. ca. 250CE), the Indian founder of Mādhyamika Buddhism. Confuting a contemporary Buddhist concern to establish precise meanings for words, Nāgārjuna pointed to the priority of developing a certain kind of awareness; hence his Middle Way (Mādhyamika). It became basic to the development of Māhayāna Buddhism. Within the Māhayāna, the central concern is not an understanding of what *śūnyatā* (emptiness) might *be*, or how it might *function* within Buddhism. Rather, the central concern is with an emptiness that is actualized or realized. Only in realized emptiness can the full interdependence of the metaphysical dimension and the ethical dimension be found. That is, realized emptiness is not separate or separable from the cultivation and actualization of compassion. As with the Māhayāna, so with non-dual Christianity: there is an articulation of distinctions which must then be brought together, existentially. Traherne, for example, attractively brings distinctions together: the divine and the human, the theological and the existential, the Word as written and the Word as lived experience.[69]

Derrida draws attention to the unstable nature of conceptual meanings. They are unstable because of language-dependency. He re-mints *śūnyatā*, from the thought of Nāgārjuna, to advocate a need for perpetual openness inasmuch as conceptual meanings are never settled; texts and contexts share in the general condition of flux. If we look for a consistently stable essentialist 'core', we have trouble locating it. It is a commonplace that many Christians have historically clung to fixed ideas about substance and identity. Similarly, many Buddhists have perhaps reified *śūnyatā*. But Derrida might be regarded as lending his 'undecidability' to Nāgārjuna's use of *śūnyatā*. This is because emptiness is a way of expressing the exhaustion of all points of view, of all theories whatsoever. It needs to be remembered that undecidability does not mean that a decision cannot be reached. The ethical choices that we constantly feel obliged to make are necessary decisions. We decide them, as we have to, in the face of undecidability. Those who desire to do so are invited (whether by 'calling', by temperament or by cool decision making) to throw off the mooring ropes. The call of *śūnyatā* is the call to slip outside the safe, conceptual harbour. The openness of the ocean draws us. It seduces us to a greater level of creative risk.[70] In the next poem, I aim 'to write' an epiphany of openness. The experience occurs at a rugged locality in Tasmania.

Tasman Peninsula

Climbing a headland which faces a grey swathe
stretching to Antarctica,
I walk the precipice rim
to scan chasm edges,
see a petrel,
bird of husky alto
and straight drop,
dive to a garfish. The petrel's beak points
to nothing except the fish, which in turn
symbolises nothing but itself,
a lesson I resisted,
much as that raptor
resists plummeting to garfish,
an easy talon-catch it wouldn't rise from,
should the ragged up-curvings of its rust wings
prove unequal to a wave's down-curling.
One afternoon, as the heat thrust upward,
I watched the wing-tip touchings of falcons courting,
their aerial spiral
of tip touch,
bank away,
retouch.
Always, an unfixed interplay,
invisible with visible:
turbulence, purple shadow, diverse currents.
I pause to greet momentary things,
nature's ebullient commerce. A stick
transmutes into an insect; in the bay
where we learnt to swim, supported underneath
by arms gently lowering our bodies on the swell,
a fish transmutes into a sponge.
Drawn, almost,
to pass beyond sense, reflective thought,
its structures, definitions,
I loop down to a marsupial lawn.
Casuarinas lean landwards from long habit,
raindrops pearling from their branches.
Small skulls move me,
of themselves,

but signify nothing beyond life, death.
The fly which buzzes over a wombat,
killed on the highway;
an infant wombat, asleep in this pullover,
and the pullover itself;
medicinal oil scent,
thick fur's clamminess;
heave of in-breath
and soft wheeze
of out-breath:
specific material realities,
coherent in their origin and end:
wombat, casuarinas,
petrel, garfish, waves:
not the knowledge
that each belongs to all
and all to each,
but an immediate grasp,
an embrace of wide-armed uselessness,
as when your face strikes a door
left ajar:
experience of the bruising world
and us
immersed in the unnameable
which imbues all praises and laments,
abides in all things,
ever united, ever distinct.
The distant waves dissolve,
re-shape,
dissolve,
barely cover
firmly rooted
lurching kelp.

It is all very well to conclude a piece of writing on a lofty, non-dual note. Do I really 'see' the formless and nameless? Lacking in mindfulness, I am quite capable of confusing the absolute level of truth with the conventional level of truth. Left to myself, I tend to overlook the Gospel-wisdom that 'lowly things' are in fact 'high'.[71] Judith Beveridge has written that my work 'makes a plea for experience . . . *to pass beyond sense, reflective thought, its structures, definitions* . . . into an acceptance of the material world as a place where boundaries can dissolve, to make way for deeper, non-dualistic forms of communion'.[72] Beveridge, in turn, is quoted by Janet Upcher in an *Afterword* to my poetry collection *So Much Light*.[73] Upcher concludes: 'By exploring momentary things, by pushing boundaries to make way for deeper communion, and through observation of seemingly insignificant creatures and natural phenomena, Charlton integrates the physical and the spiritual and shows that genuine transcendence is possible'.[74]

The most 'spiritual' of our senses is probably 'unobstructed vision'. In Mt 6, Jesus is represented as endorsing such vision. The divine must be permitted, by clear sightedness, to declare itself (while remaining incomprehensible). Derrida perhaps follows Emmanuel Levinas (d.1995) in writing that although the divine is beyond all representation, it will inveigle its presence (even if I am an atheist). To examine this notion of the vision of God (this God who might not exist, but who nonetheless will influence me), Levinas uses 'illeity' from the Latin pronoun *ille* (or *illa*), which literally means 'that over there'. The God of dubious existence, signalled by 'illeity', will interrupt me to provide motivation to find the unobstructed vision of *you*. For *you* are 'the other' to whom I bear an ethical responsibility. God (the other beyond all others[75]) underwrites my responsibility to you, even if (claims Levinas) I am an atheist. God is 'that over there'. It is beyond the possibility of a meaningful conjunction, as between it and me. Yet 'illeity' imposes upon me the responsibility to see *you* clearly. This is a theme in Levinas; nuanced, it is also a theme in Gillian Rose (d.1995), whose small book *Love's Work*[76] influenced my writing of the following poem.

To Your Fully Open Eyes

You have emerged from water
    for a dot of time.
Your middle name is Pagan
    – dweller in nature –
a slight exaggeration, since,
    like any urbanite,
you check your hair
    and double-check it looks alright.
You are evolution's intuition;
    a sliver of light
not bound by clothes
    or skin.
You hold exploding stars
    and dust which weeps.

Only yesterday, it seems,
    you stretched across me –
hands upon hands,
    eyes upon eyes,
        mouth upon mouth.
Confluent passions,
    woven in the fabric of the deep,
will reach a oneness
    beyond all purpose.

And so I praise your fully
    open eyes,
the way they dwell alongside
    your thoughts;
the way they live suspended happily
    between hope and
hopelessness, beaming your portion
    of time
into infinity's heart.

I praise these eyes which neither cling
    nor push away,
but exalt in dappled light,
    entertaining no wish
for life to be otherwise,
    knowing themselves inseparable
from the evanescent,
    like a banksia's fragrance,
briefly held
    upon the motion of clean air,
      after rain.

In metaphorical and literal terms, seeing the other's face, as it is, creates the prerequisite for dialogue and hence for love. Recognition (to follow Levinas here) has priority over cognition.[77] Sallie McFague writes of the loving eye '. . . trained in detachment':

This is the eye trained in detachment in order that its attachment
will be objective, based on the reality of the other and not on its own
wishes or fantasies. This is the eye bound to the other as is an apprentice
to a skilled worker, listening to the other as does a foreigner
in a new country. This is the eye that pays attention to the other
so that the connections between knower and known,
like the bond of friendship, will be on the real subject in its real world.[78]

McFague had earlier written of the need within Christianity, as practised in the 'West', to return to the non-dual intimations of the original Christian vision. Reminding us that 'enfleshment' was the radical point of the *kerygma* (declaration; the Gospel announcement), she writes as follows.

Christianity is the religion of the incarnation par excellence. Its earliest and most
persistent doctrines focus on embodiment: from the incarnation (the Word made
flesh) and Christology (Christ was fully human) to the eucharist (this is my body,
this is my blood), the resurrection of the body, and the church (the body of Christ
who is its head).[79]

McFague implies that institutional developments resulted in oppositional thinking. This led to the privileging of a de-incarnated idea of 'spirit'. Clear vision can restore the kerygmatic emphasis on Christianity as '... a religion of the body'.[80] This is a viewpoint with which Traherne might have agreed. It means, for today, that the story of the incarnation of Christ is not a completed story. It is an on-going narrative which is intended to take place through the bodies of Christians. They incarnate, for example, Micah 6:8. This verse can be seen as an ethical summary of the First Testament. It might be paraphrased as follows: 'What does the divine ask of you? Three things: To enact justice, to show mercy, and to have a right understanding of who you really are'. This summary is not an implacable statement, delivered from elsewhere. It is not another three-fold shibboleth with which I can shore up a foundational onto-theology.[81]

Shiva and the Spirit's transformative power

A few centuries before Christianity came to Europe, *Vedāntin* experience was expressed in India in terms of salvific knowledge of the true nature of reality. Christian experience also came to be expressed in terms of salvific knowledge of the truth. The emphasis in both streams of tradition was on 'the knowledge which saves' and not on the transient play of personal experience as such. After all, any experience (whether it leaves us feeling more complete or less complete) is only as valuable as our interpretation of it. And our interpretation is not necessarily connected with any valid understanding. In *Vedānta*, there was (and is) an emphasis on awareness. In Christianity, there was (and is) an emphasis on action. But the world of action involves the dualism of subject and object. It is 'me' who acts in time and space, 'out there'. But the Self (capital 'S') which is basic to *Vedāntin* understandings is not a person. It is the formless and nameless substrate of all that exists. The Self, therefore, is not involved in dualisms.

It should be repeated that Hinduism and Christianity have more in common than meets the eye of any proselytiser. Both religions stand for an awareness that ultimate value lies outside our little or false selves (granted that *Vedānta* does not recognize a false self, except in the most conventional sense). This is a transcendent claim. But both Hinduism and Christianity pursue an 'inward turn' as well. The transcendent which is 'without' can be sought and found 'within'. The *Vedāntin* path is towards Self-realization. The Christian path is towards '... the mind of Christ' (1 Cor. 2:16 REB). In both streams of tradition, that which might be called 'the One' or 'the ultimately Transcendent', chooses immanent manifestation. In the *Vedāntin* system, God has been variously termed *Isa*, or *Isana* or *Isvara*, which each might translate as 'Lord'. As with Christianity, the word 'Lord' need not imply a feudal, authoritarian control, but the pure Awareness which bestows grace.

Let us return to the conjunctions between the modern sage Ramana Maharshi and Traherne, Eckhart and Julian. If I have received 'the knowledge which saves', I will accept my true identity. As salvific knowledge suffuses my mind, it will become purified. Actions will flow, not from my conditioning or from my ego, but from the purity of the Self (or, as the case may be, the Christ). I have stated that Ramana reinvigorates *Advaita Vedānta*. He 'sits loose' on matters which are ceremonial and/or cultic and/or based upon distinctions of caste. He insists that the only valid confirmation of the truth of the nature of reality (as being non-dual) is *anubhava* (authentic personal spiritual experience). Such confirmation, beyond the duality of 'knower' and 'known', is explored in my poem below.

Apology to God

I'm sorry for treating you as disembodied;

I forget that I'm one of your embodiments.

I'm sorry for regarding you as indestructible.

Today I destroyed you

in a person I ignored.

Forgive me for treating you as unborn,

when you are constantly being born.

Excuse these very words.

I forget that you're beyond words.

And excuse me for thinking these thoughts.

I forget that *I Am* is not a thought.

In Christian terms, the sculpture of *Shiva Nataraja*, originating in South India, can be appropriated as *kenotic*. In its familiar form it dates from the tenth century onwards. Shiva's dance is the *ananda tandava*, the cosmic dance of bliss, which includes everything that happens in the cosmos, indeed, everything *that is*. The dance takes place within a circle of fire, continuously lit from the hand of Shiva. Change is perpetual, but the surrendered heart may find equanimity within flux, because out of the dance comes the proffered palm of one of Shiva's hands. This is the *abhaya mudra*, the gesture of the raised hand with the outward palm. It conveys the injunction: Do not fear! It says: Fear not, for the *I Am* is with you! The *abhaya* reassures the surrendered heart. It does this within an ongoing awareness of one's true identity within universal reality. In another of Shiva's four hands is a *damaru*. It is the little drum which emits the OM, which I choose to interpret as the sound of the ultimate *I Am*. The circle of fire and the sound of OM (throughout the cosmos and within the human heart) are simultaneous events.[82]

The play of Shiva, his *lila*, takes place both in the cosmos and in the heart. The very name of the surrendered devotee, looking at the sculpture, can be said to be 'Shiva'. It can also be said to be 'Apasmara', the diminutive person upon whom Shiva dances. This small being is the symbol of our spiritual forgetfulness. But the sculpture captures

Shiva in the dancing attitude of *ananda tandava*, which frees the devotee from dualism's illusion. She or he finds harmony; finds all things in the Self and the Self in all things (BgG 6:29). From the perspective of conventional truth, there is differentiation. There is joy/suffering; life/death; you/me; the innumerable contexts of contingency. I have suggested that the ceaseless flow of energy might find an analogue in the undecidability of Derrida. The flux is necessarily chronic; yet, from the perspective of ultimate truth, Shiva's dance brings the inner and the outer worlds creatively together.

To reiterate: Shiva supports the little flame which sets everything ablaze. But with another hand, Shiva presents us with the *abhaya*, the open hand bestowing peace with the assurance: 'Don't be afraid!' Another hand holds the *damaru*, the small hourglass-shaped drum. With two fingers, Shiva taps the primordial sound, the self-begotten, self-existent sound of OM. Shiva destroys forms and remakes forms.[83] In the dynamic interplay of opposites, no being or thing or process is absolutely destroyed or preserved. Rather, all things are transformed.

To transpose a Christian trope into Shaivism, let us imagine Shiva's activity as *kenotic*. He is broken down, broken up. He empties out, pervading all things. Shiva is at the still point of the inferno, the apex of paradox. Although he might be absolutely characterized as Other, in the empirical world he is not 'other' to anyone or to anything. He can be characterized as *I Am*. In the form of *Nataraja*, he not only manifests eternal energy but bestows personal grace on the devotee. Shiva bursts out in all directions; he is not 'just Oneness' but can be discerned in all events and all entities. He is non-dual in relation to all people, all things. Formless, he bears all forms, holding or manifesting all forms.[84]

Although there are contiguities between *Shiva Nataraja* and the cosmic and personal claims of Christianity, there is no evidence that the main characters of this book had encountered Shaivism. To them, the consciousness of Christ is paramount. The follower of Jesus grows into Christ-consciousness as she or he is established in the knowledge of reality, as it is. In situations of ethical choice, the disciple does not ask: 'What would Jesus do?' Instead she or he asks: 'What should *I* do, within my true humanity?' True human consciousness, in this perspective, turns out to be divine consciousness, since Jesus brings the divine within the ambience of all. I have suggested that the Christian tradition of non-dualism has been ignored, if not opposed. Eckhart's writings were attacked; he was more non-dualistic than officialdom could accept. The non-dual emphasis in Julian and Traherne was not attacked but ignored. But in view of the incompatibility of *Vedāntin* and Christian metaphysics, neither Eckhart nor Julian nor Traherne can be authentically regarded as *Advaitins*.

The thorniest aspect of *Advaita Vedānta* is the declaration that humanity and the Infinite share identity. There is but one indivisible reality; all else is a mental construction of a conventional kind. But the question remains open as to the *form* of identity which is shared by divinity and humanity. The Infinite, by definition, cannot exclude the finite, so that a basic identity of some kind is allowable to Christians. But classical *Advaita Vedānta* asserts more than identity; it declares that individual personhood is absorbed within the infinite Self, thereafter to participate in the supreme bliss. Affinities with *Advaita* are clear when Eckhart attempts to write from

God's perspective. Yet we know that the Self is not necessarily to be equated with God. Hence it is vital, in any debate about *Advaita Vedānta* and Christianity, to acknowledge differing perspectives and the probable incompatibility of key terms.

Although Traherne, Eckhart and Julian make no claim that humanity is divine, they allow a remarkably 'Eastern' participation *within* the divine. This relies upon the progressive departure of the separate, calculating, egoic self. We need not assume that 'supernatural' intervention is required, if by 'supernatural' we mean a power which is 'unearthly' yet interventionist. Rather, the transformation of the egoic self lies within the natural framework of life.[85] It is a transformation of perspective. Within ordinary activities, 'the Spirit itself beareth witness with our spirit, that we are the children of God' (Rom. 8:16, KJV). The point is this: It is not our own spirit which 'beareth witness'. It is the Spirit of the One who is Inexpressible. In the following extract from a poem, I give Spirit the title 'All-Encompasser'.

> You have lost the all-embracing song
> which nurtures the past
> into the future. You have failed
> to see the All-Encompasser:
> One who inhabits the wind,
> without being it; One who dwells
> within the cutting grass, but isn't botanical.[86]

Earlier in this chapter, Andrei Rublev's painting *The Holy Trinity* was presented as a sign of 'inter-permeation'. But for Rublev, as well as for Traherne, Eckhart and Julian, 'inter-permeation' does not negate 'transcendence'. In the Rublev painting, the viewer is encouraged to enter the participatory communication of the three 'persons' who are imagined as comprising the Source of All. But they are seated around a garden table, in front of the home of Abraham and Sarah. Non-dualism brings transcendence within any *perichoretic* activity. Receptivity and connectedness mean the demise of the rationalism of autonomy and aggression. The notion of participatory communication is not only personal, but transpersonal and impersonal. It includes recognition of the interdependence between humanity and social institutions. It can prevent us from shrinking our idea of community down to the size of our immediate comfort zone. The tonal register is one of participation *all-ways*. In terms of the absolute level of truth, the Spirit is the matrix of all that *is*. And the very nature of reality is non-dual. But at the level of conventional truth, where our input is obviously indispensable, we negotiate the 'increase' of non-duality. We bring 'inter-permeation' to every sphere of life. We realize our non-separateness, while retaining conventional distinctions.[87]

A review by Kerry Leves[88] of my book *So Much Light* surprised me by its reference to Ramana Maharshi. Leves seems to have guessed that my poems of moderate non-dualism were influenced by the teachings of the sage[89] of Arunachala. But I do not mention Ramana. And the spaciousness of non-dual awareness is not something that I consistently inhabit. Some days, I feel so influenced by Occidental conditioning that 'strong' non-dualism disturbs me. From the viewpoint of absolute truth, Ramana maintains that both the observer and the object of observation are insubstantial. Further, the very idea that I might be the separate observer of thoroughly external objects is a phenomenon which only arises with the beginning of the 'I-thought'. This 'I-thought' will emerge from the Self (since the Self is held to be the singular, eternal Reality) for as long as I do not realize my unity with the Self.[90] Whenever the 'I-thought' emerges, it promptly identifies itself with *the body* and tends to view the world as made up of *separate bodies*.

Ramana teaches, therefore, the radical reduction of boundaries. To him, the world of discrete individuals is (in terms of absolute truth) a dream world. His emphasis on non-separation led to the following poem.

Languid Day, Heat and Haze

We loll near a headland, meld clammy scents, as couples do
when no rankles surface, none loom, and the moment
finds a mindfulness of flesh.

Wind-thrown trees, all asymmetrical. We climb
to a light-drenched clearing. Frisson of impermanence;
all barriers thin or friable;

no facts to relate, no opinions. Calm passion. Squat banksias
smell like treacle or urine. Thought's endless tape
unravels just a fraction.

An ongoing theme of many traditions is that I do not automatically know who or what I am. Kant mightily reinforced the view that I am, *in essence*, quite unknowable to myself. But at the same time, there is a sense in which I *am* known to myself, self-evidentially. In the early twentieth century, psychotherapy made a de-spiritualized version of the classical question 'Who am I?' fashionable. A range of therapies sought to recover a sense of authentic existence or personal being, often over-individualized. Cut loose from spiritual traditions, psychotherapy attempted to establish that I am, in fact, a *somebody*. But an older wisdom would indicate that from the point of view of absolute truth, I am a *no-body*. That is to say, all the *conditioned* definitions of my identity are inadequate. Worse, they are illusions. And so I need to go deeper, to find in affective, experiential knowledge that I am more connected to infinite Awareness than I am to my body, mind or senses. In Ramana's mode of speech, the 'I-thought' or 'ego sense' prompts me to superimpose false identifications on the non-dual Self (capital 'S').

Although his approach was not necessarily Shaivite, Ramana regarded each person (even before Realization) as a manifestation of Shiva. As well as recommending the question 'Who am I?' (*ko'aham*), Ramana could therefore ask: 'Why not remain as you are?' This question, asked at the level of absolute truth, was intended to uncover inherent nature, draped as it mostly is by relative or empirical nature.[91] Neither question is amenable to a adequate answer from the mind, which will produce yet more thoughts and concepts regarding self-identity. Ramana did not endorse the behaviour of those who might like to repeat 'I am *Brahman*' or 'I am Shiva' or 'I am the Self' in the absence of emotional and spiritual maturity. At the conventional level of truth most of us cling to self-images, beliefs and opinions which we think contribute to our identity. Our awakening, or our movement to undivided awareness, will involve a process. Hence, at the level of conventional truth, Ramana can join with Eckhart, Julian and Traherne in their approval of regular meditative or devotional practices, engagement with scripture, and non-egoic ethical action in the quotidian world. Ramana's emphasis on self-enquiry was balanced by a less abstract endorsement of devotion, as follows:

> Self-enquiry dissolves the ego by looking for it
> and finding it to be non-existent,
> whereas devotion surrenders it;
> therefore both come to the same ego-free goal,
> which is all that is required.[92]

Both ways aim at transcending the boundaries of the individual self, which erroneously considers itself to be separate from others and from the Supreme. The source of the ego, or of 'the I-thought', can be exposed by either path.

> If the mind gradually subsides, it does not matter if other things come and go. In the *Gītā*, Lord Krishna says that the devotee is higher than the yogi and that the means to liberation is *bhakti* (devotion) in the form of inherence in the Self, which is one's own Reality.... (The mind) is immersed in the Self without the uprising of the ego.... Can obsessing thoughts arise without the ego, or can there be illusion apart from such thoughts?[93]

A non-sectarian way of framing *Advaita Vedānta's* strong non-dualism might be to turn one's awareness away from any object and direct it towards awareness 'in itself'. Ramana maintained that in direct experience we can Realize that we *are* infinite Awareness (that is to say, the *Ātman* or the Self) *at the level of absolute truth*, without following any (additional) dogma. At the level of conventional truth, we retain diverse concepts and a phenomenal ego for day-to-day functioning. The ego which Ramana opposed (to employ conditioned, phenomenal language) is the false, illusory self which blocks the realization of our identity with the Self. It is important to recall that neither classical *Advaita Vedānta* nor Ramana's modern version of it can readily employ the language of *two* actual selves. In one of his few writings, Ramana is adamant:

> To say 'I do not know myself' or 'I have known myself' is cause for laughter. What? Are there two selves, one to be known by the other? There is but One, the Truth of the experience of all. The natural and true Reality forever resides in the Heart of all. Not to realize It there and stay in It, but to quarrel: 'It is', 'It is not'; 'It has form', 'It has not form'; 'It is one', 'It is two', 'It is neither', this is the mischief of *maya*. To discern and abide in the ever-present Reality is true attainment.[94]

The implication of such non-dualism can be framed in a universalist perspective, as in the following remark attributed to Ramana by writer and raconteur Paul Brunton in the 1930s.

When a man knows his true Self, for the first time something else arises from the depths of his being and takes possession of him. That something is behind the mind; it is infinite, divine, eternal. Some people call it the Kingdom of Heaven, others call it the soul and others again Nirvana, and Hindus call it Liberation; you may give it what name you wish. When this happens, a man has not really lost himself; rather he has found himself.[95]

It is perhaps the case that the unitive experience of Ramana, Traherne, Eckhart and Julian is the *same* experience, interpreted through very different assumptions, languages and concepts. The assumptions and concepts might be incompatible, but the unitive experience itself might be identical. Ramana's advocacy of 'wakeful sleep' (*jagrat-sushupti*) as a condition of full awareness combined with mental stillness, prompted the following poem.

Restless

Restless as a kite on a loose string,
my mind flits among clouds. Chatter
intrigues, clarifies nothing,

sometimes inspires. Little can be known
by thought, write those who know.
Shorten the agitated thread,
they say, *rein in the kite.*

Let me have insight, not ideas.
Let me know a little truth
and practise stillness.

My mind flits among clouds.
Rein in the kite,
write those who know.
Shorten the agitated thread.

What is the nub of the matter? The renewal of the mind. In Hinduism, this process might be described as becoming subsumed by undivided Consciousness, the infinite basis of all phenomena. The teachers at the centre of this study might have called it the fullness of the One who fills all in all. Or, the undivided Christ. Or, the plenitude of divine Spirit. By whatever name, the suffering world needs truth incarnate. It does not need *a preoccupation* with the absolute-level of truth at the expense of the relative-level of truth. If I am to become a true reflection of the truth of reality, I will need to deal with all that remains conflicted in my inner world.

Non-dual 'Awakening'

The Well

Fatally transgressive,
his poem of divine *I Am*:
the vision too radical,
the experience too vast.
Urged to perform,
he walks alone
to Bethany's well,
watches birds of prey
climb and slow-wheel.
A woman
lowers leather buckets.
He lingers,
blurs convention's code,
and listens.

In telling his story of the Samaritan woman at the well (Jn 4), the Gospel writer has a concealed aim of reminding us that we are beneficiaries of others' work. Tired from travelling, Jesus sits in the well's shade. His apostles leave to go shopping. Jesus then becomes exhausted through a protracted discussion with the woman, resulting in a shift in her sense of alienation. Those who had shunned her are also able to find greater openness.[1] The apostles wander back, and the writer has Jesus remind them: They are reaping the results of more diligent workers. In my glance at the story, in the poem above, I allude to the 'I AM' of Ex. 3.[2] We know that elsewhere in John's Gospel, Jesus is represented as appropriating the divine 'I AM'. We also know that before the Gospels were written, the Epistles of Paul were already declaring the embodiment of the divine.[3]

Awakening to a redefinition of boundaries

The Pauline gospel centres on Christ as the deliverer of humankind.[4] Potential reconciliation between God and the entire material order is put forward, as a result of the embodiment of the divine in Jesus the man, who becomes the Christ.[5] Even material objects are said to come within the ambit of reconciliation. According to Phil. 2, humanity's preconceived ideas of the divine are emptied out, under the sign of the radical openness of Jesus. It would appear that 'the form of God' is emptied out of traditional notions of 'almightiness' and of 'exclusivity'. The experience of non-exclusivity is pertinent to the present study. I have taken non-exclusivity and 'framed it', or part of it, as 'moderate non-dualism'. The motif of non-dualism has helped to structure my forays into Traherne, Eckhart and Julian. All three sought to ground their work in experience as well as in scripture. When they emphasize the *kenotic* obedience of faith, they share common ground in their expressions of connectedness. We might imagine them addressing questions to two competing socioreligious factors. First, to the governing ethos of domination. Second, to the 'counterforce' of domination; namely, excessive individualism. Can we see their expressions of spirituality prefiguring something postmodern[6] and post-secular? They are theopoets who attempt, within different frameworks, to reduce separation by drawing subject and object closer together.

There are degrees of 'awakening' and degrees of integration.[7] A person who is regarded as 'awake', and who attracts followers, might well turn out to be a person who remains undeveloped in certain areas. If I feel I have more 'answers' than you, I am likely to project unreal qualities and values onto you. My experience of apparent 'awakening' would need to be integrated over a period of time, within my community. I would otherwise be at risk of meddling in others' lives. As already stated, some form of union with the divine is traditionally seen as the basis for human *perichoretic* relations. Genuine community is always possible. In some way, we are able to identify with 'the Whole', yet a sense of personal, subjective existence is not lost. Our actions are said to be like God's actions: Creative. In Eckhartian terms, we become what we *are*, a theme taken up by Nietzsche. And who are we? To Eckhart, we are, through Spirit, the continuing incarnation of Christ. We are to go about seeing things from a divine perspective; we are to manifest less of a distinction between 'me' and 'you', less of a distinction between 'me' and the Buddha, 'me' and the Christ, 'me' and Ramana.

Such a perspective resists the traditional claim that the doctrine of the Incarnation relates solely to an absolute event, understood as 'out of time'.[8] What if the Incarnation was imagined along the lines of a creating, circulating expression of embodiment?[9] This might relate to the Thomistic *circuitus spiritualis*. Creativity flares up, dies down, and flares up somewhere else. Expressive acts establish new things. Yet, as always, these new things participate in the general impermanence. But in the diminution of ever-fading productions, the conditions are available which stimulate ever-new creations. It is Spirit which is held (by all three writers under discussion) to 'apply' or 'manifest' the continuing Incarnation. Spirit attracts humanity and stimulates it to remember its true identity. Spirit is the Welcoming Ineffable, transcendently immanent. The transcendence may be more horizontal than vertical. Such thoughts prompted the following poem.

Best Spiritual Practice

Best spiritual practice is to drop the word Best,

the word Spiritual, the word Practice;

is to re-enter your own garden,

find each flower turned

to the light.

To Eckhart, Julian and Traherne, the Spirit is primarily That which stimulates a perception of *who* Jesus is, existentially, and *where* or *in whom* he is manifesting. This might partly be expressed by the phrase 'openness to infinite expansion' which appears in the writing below. I try to say that this kind of recognition is embodied and affective, rather than narrowly cognitive. From the perspective of theopoetics, the truth which might be accessible to 'openness' is deeper than 'facts'. That which constitutes *meaning* can never be reduced to 'facts'. That which could be dubbed 'true truth' has to do with the margins of the experience of sublimity (*Erhabenheit*). In Christian discourses, the Spirit can render the sublime to be accessible to any person, whether or not they are in possession of relevant 'facts'. That is to say, the sublime becomes experienceable (*erfahrbar*). Below, I claim that 'all that matters is embodiment'. It is here that the factual zone can assume its importance. The fact is: I am a body; I have evolved to be 'on the lookout' for another body. I desire bodily contact, desire that my body should be 'transcorporeal' and not fragmented. Perhaps I thereby desire to transcend time and place. But I do not wish for bodily contact only. I desire a deeper 'interactive knowing', for which embodiment is the ground.

On the Rim

In the present dark,
our bodies,
these portable monasteries,
poise on the rim of silence.
Brought here by someone's touch,
our narrowing attention
enters the practice of stillness.
Perhaps a teacher
with the spirit's fullness,
or a disinterested friend,
touched us from a quiet place
where words no longer dominate.
It could have been elders
less concerned

with what they can control
than with openness
to infinite expansion.
Likely as not, they still cavort somewhere,
holding together opposites,
willing to commit themselves to outcomes
of which they can have no inkling,
pleased to bear the unexplained, the vague;
happy to reply *don't know*
to a vital question
and not feel ignorant,
or, not knowing what to do,
remain present
to another who needs presence . . . .
Touched, somewhere,
by one such being
with tinctures of this recognition,
we began to be still,
began to see:
all that matters is embodiment,
these envelopes of sense and soul.
To be faithful to the vision,
to the action:
all that matters
is the felt communion,
unspeakable communion
in the silent depths.
Here's our surrender, beyond all seeking.
Here, the inexhaustible meaning.
It's not separate from the vision,
from the action.
Not separate
from This.

Maximus, classically orthodox, gave currency to the words 'reciprocal interchange'. He wrote that any person, who chose to, could be involved in reciprocal interchange with the divine. Maximus' basis for this view was his moderate non-dualism,[10] garnered (it would appear) from pseudo-Dionysius but given a very different and more directly biblical interpretation.[11] In the view of Lars Thunberg (1995), Maximus believed that 'Nature and grace are not in opposition to each other, for when human nature is truly developed, it is open to divine grace which establishes that relation to God for which human nature is created'.[12]

Maximus and his predecessors wrote of the condition of *theosis*, a word meant to include the notion of bodily exchange as part of the divine's relation to humanity.

Theosis was not purely an abstract relation, because salvation was not abstract. Salvation happened through 'transcorporeal relationality', as a present-moment event.[13] An apparent experience of the divine was not necessarily conceived as exalted or ethereal; it did not have to be 'transcendent' in an abstract and other-worldly sense.[14] Anastasius of Sinai qualified the views on *theosis* put forward by Maximus (his near contemporary), by stating that *theosis* implied 'neither a diminution nor an alteration of (human) nature'.[15]

In consonance with traditional Greek and Latin concerns with ontology, the metaphor of Trinity obviously became 'meaningful' inasmuch as it expressed relational qualities. Christian understandings incorporated the view '... of a Triune God who in transcendent, incarnate, and immanent vulnerability is familiar with suffering and bears cosmic grief'.[16] Such expressions, freed from the implications of remote omnipotence and omniscience, are likely to remain central to Christianity. They potentially redefine the boundaries between 'self' and 'others'. For example, let me suppose that I could regard you, a reader, with a degree of care. And suppose that I knew that you could feel this, bodily. Likewise, let me suppose that you, for your part, look upon me with care and that I feel this, bodily. I penetrate to the depth of *your* heart, so to say. Conversely, you penetrate to the depth of *my* heart. I find myself, my deeper self, *in you*. You find your deeper self, *in me*. Thus, the sense of duality is dispersed.

Within an 'absolute' non-dualism (as within thorough-going *Advaita Vedānta*), the sense of duality is (arguably) dispersed entirely. A rationalistic Christian framework cannot countenance a total dispersal. The fullness (*plerôma*) is held to inhere in Jesus; eventually this fullness is that which 'fills all in all' (Eph. 1:23, NRSV). The angle of vision which Jesus provided is held out to be an angle on the divine nature, which is seen to be both self-emptying and full. A *kenotic* life, lived-out by a follower of Jesus, is held to be incompatible with defensive posturing. Dogmatic statements are likely to be argued in a spirit of inclusiveness (and kept to a minimum). Wherever metaphysics might be required, it will be a metaphysics of attempted explanation and not of certainty.[17] Jesus himself is voided, so to speak; he is emptied out. He does not assert a final identity, but devotes himself to his perception of the Father's will *as itself kenotic*.[18]

Such a *kenotic* picture of the divine dovetails with a redefinition of the boundaries between 'me' and 'you', above. Christ's body is said to be continually reincarnated in our own bodies. The tradition, adhered to by Traherne in common with Eckhart and Julian, has a high regard for embodiment and what it entails. Communion has priority over sacrifice, because communion is 'holy': It is wholesome and wholeness-making. The defeat of fear and the establishment of communion are inseparable from the salvation story. The tradition assumes that Christian communities will manifest *agapeic*, all-embracing reciprocity. This is to be the normal outcome of an experience of God. As within the Godhead, when imagined as triune, relationships are to be experienced as *perichoretic*.[19] Abiding in the divine, God's children will see themselves as interexisting. They are interinvolved because a union with God has been established. This, despite the fact that the surface consciousness might not experience the union.[20]

Raimon Panikkar and pluralism

Panikkar's Christianized interpretation of *Advaita Vedānta* is perhaps a pointer to where Christian non-dualism could be heading. There could be aporetical difficulties, if Panikkar does not sufficiently balance a strong experiential tone (reminiscent of Ramana) with an adequate propositional basis. Although Panikkar (d.2010) did not see himself as a post-modern theologian, it is possible that he blurs distinctions in the service of a universalist vision. For example, he arguably reduces 'meaning' to 'experience' and to the subjective conditions of what he deems to be an appropriate spiritual life. This puzzle, of tipping the balance against propositional content, might not be resolvable.[21] Perhaps Panikkar himself did not regard a resolution as either possible or desirable. His work is likely to grow in worldwide esteem, not least because he 'opened up' spiritual life to the ways in which our imagination discerns the unrestrained flow of Spirit. While not opposed to 'religion', he chose to privilege 'spirituality' because of its ability to cross religious boundaries.

Panikkar believed the divine to be ontologically transcendent, yet also conceived of the divine as emergent possibility. Assuming spiritual and religious development to be part of the evolutionary process, he looked for transpersonal consciousness to arise from personal consciousness. Transpersonally, humanity could participate with God in developing the immanent sphere by means of transcendent values. It is my view that Panikkar added modern cosmology and transpersonal psychology to Ramana's *Advaita Vedānta*. If so, this represents an advance on the anthropocentric consciousness and dualistic metaphysics of much of modernity. Would Eckhart have approved? He might have, wherever the apophatic is informed by the biblically kataphatic.

As implied earlier, a potential difficulty with Panikkar is the status of propositional truth claims. He affirmed the relative value of all religions, while at the same time disavowing relativism. He maintained that any person could experience Otherness whenever they have a direct awareness of their contingency. But, due to an ample and disarming emphasis on relationality, it is possible that obvious sociopolitical problems (such as the tolerance of violence, the oppression of women and all manner of self-serving appeals to divine authority) can potentially be cloaked by naïve optimism. If it is granted that the voices of truth are irreducibly plural, there remains the need for an existential approach that refuses to occlude serious questions in a system of universal, spiritual *laissez-faire*. Panikkar's model is 'intra-religious' rather than 'inter-Faith', since he advocated a move away from exterior understandings of other traditions, in the expectation of a broad emergence of interior experiences. In other words, the designation 'intra-religious' indicates that the best starting point is an exchange of experiences rather than of teachings.

Although Panikkar believed that anyone could experience Otherness, he did not claim that this necessarily equated with experiencing 'God'. He was careful to state that 'It is impossible to experience God as substance and transcendence, and there is no knowledge of the Infinite'.[22] Yet, through our human knowledge of contingency, we could 'touch' the Infinite 'at a point'.[23] Our frailty is therefore the paradoxical place of experiencing the Mystery. 'The Christian expression of this contact is *Incarnation*. A different language would tell us that in the experience of *samsāra* we touch *nirvana*'.[24]

> We cannot experience an exclusively immanent God, which we would confuse with a pantheistic identity. Nor can we experience an exclusively transcendent God, which would be contradictory in itself. Instead, we meet God in *relationship*.[25]

As with many pluralists, Panikkar makes value judgements on the basis of his understanding of an ultimate referent. He writes of the many paths (psychological, traditional and personal) to the experience of divinity.

> God belongs neither to the one nor the other, neither to the good nor the wicked: God transcends all our words and faculties. In this experience of empty transcendence, we experience the void; we encounter emptiness and ultimately silence.[26]

Panikkar held the experience of God to be *subjective genitive*; in other words, it is God's experience. It is '... the experience that *God* has, not of a solipsistic self, but of a Trinitarian and hence relational and participative Being in which we and all creation enter'.[27] The Trinity is the paradigm of relationality; it exemplifies the universal never-ending process of interchange. Between the silent Source ('the Father') and Logos ('the Son') and Pneuma ('the Spirit'), there is harmony of both equality and difference. A little earlier, Panikkar writes: 'God is not an object – either of faith or experience. It is the experience *of* God that occurs within me, in which I participate more or less consciously'.[28]

The principal non-dual passages in John's Gospel were cited in Chapter 2. These are '... the Father is in me and I am in the Father' (Jn 10:38, NRSV) and 'The Father and I are one' (Jn 10:30, NRSV). Panikkar writes that such verses represent 'neither a pantheistic confusion nor a negation of personality'.[29] They are, instead, a declaration of experience. The experience is as follows:

> ... if I do not desire anything for my ego, I am everything and have everything. I am one with the source insofar as I too act as a source by making everything which I have received flow again – just like Jesus.[30]

Colloquial notions of 'the self' and 'the other' are somewhat subverted by Panikkar, as they are, in very different languages, by Traherne, Eckhart and Julian. My (small-s) self will be emptied out, so that my (true) Self will be uncovered as my real nature, with ability to love the other as my-self. I have noted that *perichoresis* literally means 'dance around'.[31] Panikkar uses 'interwoven' to illustrate *perichoresis*.[32] He echoes the metaphor of knitting used by Julian to illustrate two truths that are dear to her. First, humanity is already 'oned' with the divine; second, humanity is still progressing to a full experience of 'oneing'.[33] In the poem below, I have tried to express the invitation to mutual reciprocity.

Dancing with Sophia

She comes to meet me from the inside,
with love not linked to personal desire,
love not drawn to any attribute of mine.
What I thought didn't exist, is nearer than near.
'Who *are* you?' she asks, she asks silently,
as if nothing else matters, as if constantly tripping
over my own thoughts is part of the dance.

The dance of polarities, or rather, of apparent polarities, is potentially in conflict with a post-Enlightenment obsession with classification. Taxonomies, which are frequently hierarchical, can be useful, artificial and delusory all at the same time. On the other hand, theopoetics is most 'unscientific' in its depiction of the divine as neither wholly other (dualism) nor as wholly not-other (monism). Although infinite and hence transcendent, the divine is paradoxically 'delimited' (from the perspective of conventional truth) by the materiality of creation. Indeed, it would appear to be 'delimited' by my personal, material desires. Panikkar puts it as follows: '(God) exists only in its polarity, in its relationship. God is relationship, intimate internal relationship with all'.[34]

Such a move appears likely to offend the heirs of those who were offended by Eckhart's aporetic. But Panikkar nuanced his position by maintaining that reality flowed deeper than truth, in the sense that reality could never be reduced to an abstraction. Beyond relativism, objectivism and separatist doctrinal truth-claims, the divine remained as that Being which could not be grasped in any dimension. The divine could, however, be accessed in mutual reciprocity by means of the symbolic and the mythic. Panikkar nominated his vision as 'cosmotheandric', to express the triadic nature of reality as a combination of the cosmic, the divine and the human. Christ is the embodiment of 'cosmotheandrism'. On the other hand, each person is a Christophany.[35] Mutual reciprocity is expressed by Herman Brood[36] as follows: 'Dear Lord, We accept You as I am'. Such panache might have pleased the three theologians at the centre of this book, as well as Panikkar. In sum, this is because I regard all four of them as advocates of participatory truth (as being 'above' propositional truth). This is highly contestable, but I find it appropriate to align Eckhart, Julian, Traherne and Panikkar more with Ramana than with popular understandings of Christianity.[37]

In Chapter 1 of this study I related Traherne to *Advaita Vedānta*. But if the latter becomes solely concerned with an inward focus, to the detriment of the manifest world, Traherne would disagree. His precise descriptions of the natural world are few, it is true. Yet he leaves no doubt that nature, including the body/mind organism, is to be valued for its own sake:

The Skies in their Magnificence,
The Lively, Lovely Air;
Oh how Divine, how soft, how Sweet, how fair!
The Stars did entertain my Sence,

And all the Works of GOD so Bright and pure,
So Rich and Great did seem,
As if they must endure,
In my Esteem.

A Native Health and Innocence
Within my Bones did grow,
And while my GOD did all his Glories shew,
I felt a Vigour in my Sence
That was all SPIRIT. I within did flow
With Seas of Life, like Wine;
I nothing in the World did know,
But 'twas Divine.

Harsh ragged Objects were concealed,
Oppressions Tears and Cries,
Sins, Griefs, Complaints, Dissentions, Weeping Eys,
Were hid: and only Things reveald,
Which Heav'nly Spirits, and the Angels prize.
The State of Innocence
And Bliss, not Trades and Poverties,
Did fill my Sence.

The Streets were pavd with Golden Stones,
The Boys and Girles were mine,
Oh how did all their Lovly faces shine!
The Sons of Men were Holy Ones.
Joy, Beauty, Welfare did appear to me,
And evry Thing which here I found,
While like an Angel I did see,
Adornd the Ground. [38]

Such an all-encompassing vision has obvious modern resonance; Traherne's theopoetic descendents are many. One such is Andrew Harvey, a meditative activist who seeks to incarnate the Trahernian balance. Harvey writes of 'the direct path' and its complexion of non-dual consciousness.

Plato's philosophers, having seen the illusion of the world return to the world to teach others about it; the Zen master after realizing that 'nothing is real' returns to the 'real' to help others liberate themselves; those who follow the Christ follow him beyond all the temptations of power and false transcendence into the depths of an abandoned self-donation to all beings; those who have taken the bodhisattva vow in Mahāyāna Buddhism pledge themselves to return to the world of pain and constriction forever until every sentient creature is finally liberated. [39]

How can self-donation be effective, for anything? How can non-power, a chosen way of disempowerment, be powerful? The potential answers become clearer if the source of experience, and the impetus for non-dual relationships, carries with it the givenness of intersubjectivity. From such a perspective, self-emptying is the way things *are*. We do not so much 'empty ourselves' as surrender to what is already the case. Or rather, to get away from undue connotations of will power, we *see* something of the reality and are conscious participants in it. If 'reality' is equated with God, then God obviously is beyond comparison; but, *apropos* divine incomprehensibility, Eckhart holds that we participate in the Nothingness of God; we share in the 'Is-ness' of God.[40]

Formal power and authority is reinterpreted, against the grain of the lesser or egoic self's first impulse. Gradually, we integrate the awareness that we are not so much substantial selves as 'relational events'. Our awareness of finitude (and of the self-deceptions of the little self) constrains the desire to claim absolute finality with regard to 'possession' of truth. But when we overlook the limits of language, we tend to reify our concepts and to erect idols. As Panikkar everywhere stresses, we falsely conceive ourselves to be separate selves. Very likely, then, that we should fantasize that God is peculiarly related to 'me and my group'. Any idol, as a conceptual construction of the mind, is commonly seen as a danger to actual faith. Jean-Luc Marion[41] could be consolidating Panikkar's position when he suggests (in an off-handed way) that *Agape* might be a suitable name for 'God'. This is because Marion has a particular concern with the worship of idols within Christianity, such as a reified 'God' as distinct from the true God beyond conception. If I have overconfidence in the concept 'God', I will lack sufficient openness to that which transcends my concept.[42]

Hence the strong emphasis, within Judeo-Christian tradition, that the Word of God lies *beyond* the physical text which talks about God. The Word is regarded as more dissonant and destabilizing than we might at first suspect. Eckhart, Julian and Traherne appear to concur here. Theologians of recent centuries were not the first to attempt to name God as the ever-ungraspable, Unnameable One. More to the point, they did not invent the language which refers to the depths of interbeing or of interpenetration. This is the language of the *perichoretic* experience. It is modelled on the inner life of the Trinity; it expresses a love which is immediate and mutual. It is enacted now, here. Within this love, the expectations of an individualistic ego, intent on establishing itself, are dismantled. Just as the language of substance or essence tends to collapse, the language of separate identity will tend to collapse. In its place will be a deeper awareness of flux, of contingency and of the liberation which the 'kenotic constant' (the life-within-God) both enables and energizes.

Parallel ways of relating

Eckhart's Japanese contemporary, Dōgen Kigen (1200–1253) wrote of the 'original truth' of human identity in terms of non-dual consciousness. On this matter, the two exemplary thinkers are at one. In the sermons of the Meister, the letting-be or releasement of *Gelâzenheit* functions as an overcoming of dualisms in a way that is consonant with Dōgen's non-dualism. But it is common knowledge that Dōgen regarded an experience of 'pure presence' as available to humankind, without mediation (and 'before' interpretation). Part of the puzzle with Eckhart is his ambiguity on this point. Whereas Dōgen held 'ultimate truth' to be available as 'a direct apprehension' (*genjōkōan*), this question remains aporetic in Eckhart. There is a concurrence (of sorts) between Dōgen and the Eckhartian divine birth in the soul (as being 'of the moment' and yet progressive). But Eckhart remains Christian; he will resist a clear, unambiguous ontological identification of humanity with ultimacy.

Schürmann cautions that a Soto Zen interpretation of Eckhart on *Gelâzenheit* does not work. This is because there is a God who authors and enables *Gelâzenheit*.

> . . . God's essential being, releasement, becomes the being of a released man. The disturbing power of Eckhart's theory of releasement consists precisely in the transformation of a psychological or moral concept into an ontological one. Man's way of being turns into God's way of being. The mind can achieve total vacuity of attachment only because God follows the mind on this road and leads it back into the divine 'desert'. The double annihilation of human and divine properties constitutes one and the same conquest of releasement, as being's essential way to be.[43]

Schürmann also warns against assuming that when different authors 'think the ineffable' they are thinking of the *same* ineffable.[44] But Harvey sees the value of Dōgen for meditative practice. He follows Dōgen's way of discovering '. . . your essential self beyond the mind'.

> To discover what Dōgen calls the 'original truth' within us is to know ourselves linked to every other sentient being and thing in the universe. When we plummet deep into our real nature, the boundaries that separate us from the rest of the world start to disappear. The duality of subject and object, I and other, knower and known, starts to dissolve; gradually, we are opened to a bare, naked, transcendental way of knowing that over time becomes a force of clear love that connects us effortlessly, naturally, and transparently to all things.[45]

For Dōgen there can be no substantial or self-existing 'self'. Personal authenticity is only available through the concepts of emptiness and of dependent co-arising. And yet these are not treated as concepts. They are treated as the background through which we can directly experience reality, without having recourse to concepts. How might Eckhart have responded? We cannot know. Yet we remain aware that Eckhart's concern with *Gelâzenheit* does not lead him to the hermetic life.[46] There is a contiguity of interest, here, with Hindu tradition. Prior to the emergence of Dōgen's Buddhism, the Bhagavad Gītā had taught non-attached activity as the way to transcend the duality of self and other, or of subject and object.

> The wise see that there is action in the midst of inaction and inaction in the midst of action. Their consciousness is unified, and every act is done with complete awareness. The awakened sages call a person wise when all his undertakings are free from anxiety about results; all his selfish desires have been consumed in the

fire of knowledge. The wise, ever satisfied, have abandoned all external supports. Their security is unaffected by the results of their action; even while acting, they really do nothing at all.[47]

First, the reader is reminded of the need for action; second, she or he is invited to act without attachment to a goal. To identify with a goal is to be identified with thought. This identification gives rise to a false sense of duality, as between *the mind* with its intention to act with a certain result in view, and *the body* which will perform the action to obtain the result. The context of the passage above is counsel given to the reluctant 'warrior' Arjuna by his old friend Krishna (who at first is not recognized as a divine incarnation). Perhaps a broader context is the author's need to respond to interpretations of *Vedānta* by the yogic schools, some of which favoured withdrawal from community life. The Gītā is regarded by many as one of the later Upanishads, although it is usually found as an insertion in the Mahabharata. In written form, the Upanishads date from the second century BCE; they form part of the large *Vedic* body of literature. The theopoets who produced the *Vedas* (lit. 'Knowledge') chose the indefinite term 'That' to designate the Infinite, which no word or name could attempt to define without implying a limit to the unlimited. Can the Infinite be meaningfully discussed at all? This question troubled the *Vedic* theopoets. By way of answering it, they invoked the deepest experiential dimension of humanity. In Chapter 1, I mentioned the creative move by Arthur Clements in aligning Traherne with the greatest declaration to have emerged from India: *Tat tvam asi*. It is translated below as 'You are That'.

> As bees suck nectar from many a flower
> and make their honey one, so that no drop
> can say, 'I am from this flower or that',
> all creatures, though one, know not they are that One.
> There is nothing that does not come from him.
> Of everything he is the inmost Self.
> He is the truth; he is the Self supreme.
> You are That. . . . You are That.
>
> As the rivers flowing east and west
> merge in the sea and become one with it,
> forgetting they were ever separate streams,
> so do all creatures lose their separateness
> when they merge at last into pure Being.
> There is nothing that does not come from him.
> Of everything he is the inmost Self.
>
> He is the truth; he is the Self supreme.
> You are That. . . . You are That.[48]

The declaration could be taken to mean: 'You are Consciousness'. Or, with an eye to process theology and the 'unfinishedness' of language, we might render it as follows: 'You have a part within the creative principle of the universe'. Literally the Sanskrit is

'That thou art'. And if the resonance of 'thou' is now lost, we might say 'You are It' or 'You are That', as above. The context within the Upanishad is instruction by the sage Uddalaka to his son. The son, Svetaketu, has returned home after 12 years with a guru. But he has returned with intellectual pride instead of Realization. The historic purpose of *Tat tvam asi* could be said to be that of a mantra which helps a disciple to make some sense of an experience of identification, or trans-identification. It is not necessarily intended to serve as a metaphysical equation. As 'the great utterance' of the Upanishads, it implies that 'I' am not the little self or ego of phenomenal or conditioned discourse. I am the *Ātman*: the non-dual 'Self' of unlimited Awareness. But this is a concept; it is not yet a truth which is realized in direct, immediate experience. The *Vedic* theopoets respected concepts, but not as ends in themselves. Buddhistic developments later employed a more nuanced vocabulary, partly in order to set aside overly personalized concepts of a deity or deities. But the conviction remained that Reality was encountered beyond words and concepts.[49]

A little of what this implies is expressed in the writing below. A small tiger snake was part of our garden's beauty for a period of months. It prompted admiration coupled with nervous awareness. The reference to 'the one thing' is from a conversation between Jesus and Martha and Mary, reported in Luke 10. I also had in mind the experience of *tathatā*, the Buddhist 'suchness' or experience of things (purportedly) 'as they really are'. It could be said that 'suchness' expresses in a positive way what 'emptiness' (*śūnyatā*) expresses negatively.

The One Thing

A small snake rests its head
on a wandering geranium leaf.
Tucked up in a bed of greenery,
tattooed by light,
a tremulous blunt nose
and broad head-shield
rest in a dappled place,
a minutely particular
paradise.

The snake eases sideways
to obscurity.

One thing is necessary:
awareness of presence.
No longer *us here* and *snake there*,
but a simple abiding,
beyond the sinewy slippage of language.

Jesus is represented as asserting 'one thing is necessary'. The narrator depicts him as confident that his intuitive insights into reality are accurate. He is not interested in having a title or in being authenticated by external authority in some other way. His authority is self-authenticating.[50] In this regard, Jesus resembles a Hindu *rishi* whose experiential knowledge of Self-realization is so deep that other people intuitively recognize it. Hinduism is powerful at this point: It provides stimulus to Self-realization, the true experience of the *Ātman* as inseparable from the Absolute (*Brahman*). Buddhism, on the other hand, enunciates a parallel experience, that of awakening or enlightenment (*bodhi*). In its very different way, does Christianity partly aim at a reconfiguration of both of the above? Could it have been influenced by both traditions? The Gospel, enunciated by Paul and later narrated in the canonical Gospels, is intended to evoke an ongoing change of personal direction in life. This is what is meant by the Greek word *metanoia*, or openness to conversion. Following a switch in orientation, transformation or progressive 'deification' follows, through active receptivity to grace. To write generally, Hinduism, Buddhism and Christianity, while incompatible at the dogmatic level, are agreed that techniques and methodologies are not to be regarded as ends in themselves. The intention is this: After the relevant authentic experience, whether sudden or progressive, the means and methods fall away.

Wherever a 'mystical' understanding supplements the 'doctrinal' viewpoint of intractable monotheism, the moderately non-dual nature of Christianity becomes clearer. Here, 'non-dual' does not purely mean 'not two'. It means 'not one, not two, but both one and two'. Both the symbol of Trinity and the symbol of *Shiva Nataraja* (conceptually different but contiguous) contain difference and unity. Both symbols draw attention to the divine as relational. There is *kenotic* love, both 'to' and 'from'. There is the 'interwoven' nature of interbeing, as between the apparently inseparable poles of twoness and oneness. The divine is regarded as 'within' and 'without' all things. It is both immanent and transcendent, 'containing' all things and yet 'contained' by no-thing.[51] *Perichoresis* might be also viewed as an image of a completely this-worldly way of relating. Our everyday experience is one of polyphonic unity; we are 'one' with other humans, yet we retain differences.[52]

A Chinese Buddhist text from the late sixth century CE, with the title *Hsin Hsin Ming* (and rendered in English as *On Believing in Mind* and as *On Trust in the Heart*) describes non-dual awakening. A translation by Richard B. Clark begins: 'The Great Way is not difficult for those who have no preferences'. Towards the end, the text runs as follows:

> With a single stroke we are freed from bondage;
> nothing clings to us and we hold to nothing.
> All is empty, clear, self-illuminating,
> with no exertion of the mind's power.
> Here thought, feeling, knowledge, and imagination
> are of no value. In this world of Suchness
> there is neither self nor other-than-self.
> To come directly into harmony with this reality,
> just simply say when doubt arises, 'Not two'.
> In this 'not two' nothing is separate,
> nothing is excluded.

The word 'All' (line three) would seem to carry fuller resonance than the word initially indicates. It is the 'All' of the 'reality' (line eight). But Buddhist non-dualism is not the Christian non-dualism of Eckhart, Julian or Traherne. As used above, the 'All' is more akin to an immanentist or naturalistic use of the 'All'. It does not include a non-corporeal Creator. The injunction is to place ourselves where we might actualize the 'suchness' of the matter: We are not separate from 'the All'. The references to 'not two' do not necessarily imply an undifferentiated monism. As with *Advaita Vedānta*, 'not two' does not equate with 'just One'. A single 'One' would exclude its opposite, namely, 'Manyness'. It would oppose the plural 'Many' and therefore be dualistic. On the other hand, non-duality (on this view) embraces both unity and multiplicity. But the *Advaitin* viewpoint differs markedly from Buddhism, because the latter cannot readily speak of any substantive, non-corporeal *I Am*. For both the *Advaitin* and the Christian, humanity exists at the level of the eternal-absolute before it exists at the level of the contingent-temporal. Wakefulness might therefore be seen as a return to an original state of 'abidance'. The apostle John, for example, writes expansively of abiding in non-dual awareness of the Christ within. In such a sphere of understanding, the Hindu and the Christian can readily concur that non-dual wisdom supplements regular cognitive processes.[53]

'I am nothing; I am everything'

Wakefulness, for Traherne, includes an awareness that religion can potentially express an original human *goodness*. As borne out in the excerpts from his poems in Chapter 1, Traherne represents himself as having found an equality of 'self' and 'other'. But his experience includes both unity and duality. Traherne's tradition had for many centuries maintained that a first step in reaching wakefulness, relatively free of distracting thought, was to develop a meditative discipline of some kind. Accordingly, Traherne accepts the importance of devotion, which implies a dualism between the object of devotion and the devotee.[54] As in the Hindu *bhakti* tradition, devotion was seen as an important factor in breaking open and dispersing the power of the egoic self. The goal would not be to eliminate the ego, but to bring to awareness its delusory manifestations. Traherne's poems, as I have quoted them, exult in a unitive experience. Then he returns to his devotions, in which he is 'no-thing'. Is this what constitutes so-called mystical experience? Is it constituted by an oscillation between the poles of union and separation; 'everything' and 'no-thing'?[55] One of Eckhart's dramatic passages on 'nothingness' (*niht*) is contained in 'A Sermon on the Just Man and Justice'. Since it is not a Latin but a German sermon, it is unlikely that Traherne knew it.

> Therefore, if you want to live and want your works to live, you must be dead to all things and you must have become nothing. It is characteristic of the creatures that they make something out of something, but it is characteristic of God that He makes something out of nothing. Therefore, if God is to make anything in you or with you, you must beforehand have become nothing.[56]

Eckhart's use of 'nothing' or 'nothingness' (MHG: *niht*; L: *nihil*) to characterize 'the self' of all creatures might imply that he agrees with Buddhist rejection of 'essentialism'. But his emphasis on the 'nothingness' of creatures is part of his theological project; God is also 'no-thing' but of such an order that God can express an infinite array of other 'no-things' which are contingent. There is a sense in which Eckhart retains the idea of a genuine self, since he places its origin (as a Real Idea, so to say) within the mind of the Infinite, from whose perspective nothing can be separate. The many forms of Hinduism, and the diversities within the Judeo-Christian tradition, would scarcely be conceivable without some form of genuine self, at the conventional truth-level. This is because whenever 'self-transcendence' is alluded to, in the sense of transcending the false or delusory self, there must surely be some kind of self-appropriation. A degree of self-knowledge or 'self-situating' is required, which implies the necessity of a self that is sufficiently real to be *capable* of appropriation, transformation and continuity.[57] For its part, Buddhism cannot accept any concept of the self that might imply self-existence or inherent self-sufficiency. If the total non-substantiality of the self (Skt: *anātman*; Pali: *anatta*) is asserted, this would appear to separate Buddhism from the other main religions. It is my view that claims by Westernized Buddhists that the self has no substance whatsoever should be nuanced. They are speaking at the absolute truth-level and disclosing a tendency to bypass the relative truth-level.[58]

According to Simone Weil[59] and to countless writers before her, the main barrier to meditative experience and to transformation is not 'sin' but distraction. Indeed, distraction is regarded as the major hindrance to an integrated experience of 'reality' itself. Weil broadly follows the patristics in asserting that perfect attention is tantamount to the vision of God. Transposed to Hinduism, perfect attention effectively equates with full participation in the non-dual Self. Gradually, through a meditative discipline, we yield to the 'is-ness'[60] of the moment. This surrender, to the way things are, is important for Traherne, Julian and Eckhart.

They are theopoets inasmuch as they wish to bring vivid, rhythmical imagery to intimations of the divine in the world and the world in the divine. Our own theopoetic imaginations, like theirs, can add to understandings of traditional concepts. These understandings are not, in themselves, necessarily at fault. They are part of the languages of theology and serve poetic functions.[61] Such a view is disagreeable to those who cannot face the complexity, both of truth and of every effort to locate it. The practice of faith is inherently risky[62] and theopoets will tend to configure the divine as unknowable in essential ways. This does not imply that the divine is inaccessible. On the basic tenet of Christianity, God is approachable to humanity through the human Jesus, who is subsequently reimaged as Jesus the Christ. Such a teaching requires poetics, signs, symbols and relational discourses. Together, poetry and relationality speak of the particular and the universal; they have to do with communication as the foundation of community.

'Where our skin stops, our bodies do not stop'

Traherne, Eckhart and Julian passionately desire to coax their readers to a life of communion and wholeness. Inseparable from this desire is the conviction that self-emptying (*kenosis*) is involved. Within mainstream Christian teachings, the false or phenomenal self is encouraged to participate in a kind of death; this is prefigured in baptism and viewed as a necessary condition for inner resurrection. The false self is held to be continuously making way for the gradual transformation of the entire human family.

In *Vedānta*, the metaphysics is different but the language of public discourse can be similar. Humanity is exhorted to abide in the non-dual Self. It should remain clear, however, that this infinite Self is not discussed in classical *Vedānta* in relation to the existence of a false self. And Ramana Maharshi, although an *Advaitin* with a progressive, universalist message, follows Śhaṅkara in not attributing absolute existence to any lesser or false self.[63] This is not to say that he trivialized the self of conventional language and ordinary life. I have suggested that Ramana represents a telling counterpoint to the qualified non-dualism of my three European theologians. For Ramana, there is a sense in which God is the affective immediacy of the Self, uncovered in our innermost dimension. Accordingly, our true nature is one of non-dual affinity with the divine. It is our forgetfulness of this 'heart truth' which accounts for our deviations from the divine will. Thomas A. Forsthoefel interprets Ramana as follows:

> We are the Self already. We know this in some relevant sense although, owing to misplaced, habituated identifications, it has escaped our active attention.... Grace ... should not be construed as something external to the subject. Instead, it is the divine operating within and outside the individual soul to usher in ultimate self-revelation.... The appropriate response to the incessant presence of grace is surrender, a term which Ramana repeats frequently.[64]

Conceptually, the metaphysic behind the perspective of Ramana is what I have called 'strong' non-dualism. Forsthoefel continues his interpretation as follows: 'The Self, beyond form and particularization, effulgent and blissful, is our deepest truth, and we need only to go inward and access it'.[65] This metaphysic is closely linked to an epistemology of spiritual experience which could be called 'internalist' (and universalist). That is to say, it tends to regard certain basic beliefs as self-justifying and self-authenticating.

Within such an epistemology, Ramana can represent authentic spiritual experience (*anubhava*) as an experience of interiority involving direct or immediate awareness of that which is already the case. This is the kind of non-dualism which relies on a minimal and eventually 'non-abstract' metaphysic. The experience naturally flows from the surrender of the false self (which, in any case, has no ultimate existence). This surrender does not 'earn' anything. A transformative remembering of *Satchitānanda* (Being-Consciousness-Bliss) takes place. A person 'knows' herself to be the Self.[66] Can the Self be accorded an epistemological equivalence to the divine Source, as historically conceived in the 'West'?[67] Can the Self be equated with 'God' as presented in the work of Eckhart? Such questions do not admit of clear answers.

The verses below, from the First Epistle of John, also express resistance to the domination of abstract metaphysics.[68] There is a profusion of verbs. Perhaps the verbs follow a trajectory of ongoing awareness.

> Something which has existed since the beginning,
> which we have heard,
> which we have seen with our own eyes,
> which we have watched
> and touched with our own hands,
> the Word of life –
> this is our theme.
> That life was made visible;
> we saw it and are giving our testimony,
> declaring to you the eternal life,
> which was present to the Father
> and has been revealed to us.
> We are declaring to you
> what we have seen and heard,
> so that you may share our life.
> (1 Jn 1:1–3, NJB)

Awareness has been matched in these verses by receptivity. There is also a degree of confidence which some readers might experience as unpleasant dogmatism. But positive, personal events (especially when deemed to be epiphanies) are likely to generate both confidence and trust. The focus of the confidence might later *de*-generate into an idol. Jean-Luc Marion has written of the distinction between an idol and an icon.[69] Any concept can be reified, of course, to the extent of becoming a fixed mental position; in other words, an idol. By contrast, an icon can confer a genuine sense of satisfaction or ease or rest.[70]

I have implied that Traherne is an iconic poet. Through his stress on boundlessness, on 'Felicitie', on passion for divine truths and for Earth's wonders, he breathlessly seeks to enlarge and to synthesize what we might feel and know. In his poetry and in *Centuries* the kind of knowledge which concerns him is *felt* knowledge. Although discursively inclined, he seems to be sceptical about statements of 'truth' or 'being' which are based solely on cognition. Perhaps his inherited Christian symbolic structure is not so much to be analysed, as 'responded to'. Open-heartedness is required. As with Ramana, so with Traherne, an implied question lurks: Since I am neither my body, nor my mind, nor my senses, who am I? The question is helpful, not if it merely produces a string of negations, but when it progressively uncovers the non-dual 'I' behind the layerings of superficial identities.

These reflections have stressed that *kenosis* and *kenotic* action (cf. *śūnyatā*: emptiness, or the word I prefer: Openness) will function in opposition to individualism. Subjective experience moves towards intersubjective experience. Both Hinduism and Christianity accept that a sacred cosmology interpenetrates the empirical, scientific cosmology.[71] Both religions aim at waking us up. Wakefulness connotes the experience that a true transcendence is not separate from an authentic immanence.[72] The word 'experience', here, corresponds with *Erfahrung* or experience understood as a process of broadening or of self-transformation, rather than with *Erlebnis*, which connotes more of the Buddhist idea of contingent experience.

Traherne does not accept the possibility of deep spiritual experience (*Erfahrung*) without a positive, non-dual manifestation within the world. Truth is valid to the extent that it is *lived truth*.[73] Eckhart and Julian concur, although they write within a meditative stream which differs from that of Traherne. Eckhart's '. . . you must have become nothing' passage, cited earlier, does not hang suspended, without antecedent or long-term consequence. In this connection, John Milbank can write:

> Going 'inward' to attain contemplative unity is not, for Eckhart, the final goal – as it never is, for all authentic Christian mystics. To the contrary, the attainment of perfect detachment, or a kind of refusal to let contingent circumstances alter one's fundamental abiding mood of openness to God, is a way of allowing the divine love to come to constant new birth in one's soul, and so of proceeding ecstatically outward toward others. The 'emptied' soul is also the fertile soul, the soul open to performing God's will as its own and so of acting creatively, which means precisely to act without egotism . . . .[74]

In quest of a qualified, 'spiritually applicable' non-dualism, each of the three Christians does unusual things with language. Traherne, closer to our sensibility than the other two, is nonetheless part of a hierarchical institution, in which the liturgy is saturated with monarchical imagery: God is King or Lord, reigning like the top Feudalist, tweaking history for the sake of his subjects. Yet, so intense was Traherne's sense of realized Presence that the God of his poems is more of a lyrical lover than a dominator.[75]

Denise Inge, as we saw, regards Traherne as a theologian of desire. Perhaps the least egoic expression of desire is an active compassion, where compassion is detached in the Eckhartian sense. Such compassion is the fruit of awakening. We are drawn to it, or drawn *by* it. Some of us might name it 'Sophia'. Eckhart does not favour 'Sophia' as a name; he writes (instead?) of 'Sacred Presence' and 'My Essence'. In his Foreword to Reiner Schürmann's interpretation of Eckhart, David Appelbaum writes of non-duality under the sign of Sophia.

> The transformative flash of Sophia is a cosmic event that is recorded jointly in God and in a human being. This is the brilliant height of Eckhart's realization. We – humanity and God – are co-workers in a universe subject to a nameless transforming force, emanating from the unmanifest and disclosing to God and humans alike that which is.[76]

The Eckhartian puzzle remains. He seems to suggest a shared ontology between God and humanity. A tentative 'solution' (mentioned in Chapter 2) is that Eckhart be assessed as a theopoet given occasionally to hyperbolic rhetoric. For example, in Eckhart's non-dual interpretation of the birth of 'the Son' in our souls, there is a sense in which humanity becomes the realization of divine presence. This is because the birth is 'back into God'. Richard Woods writes as follows:

> Having become fully manifest in both image and likeness in humankind through the *birth of the Word* in time and place, the indwelling Triune God retracts the universe into itself through the birth of the soul back into God – Eckhart's great theme of *breakthrough*.[77]

Breaking through boundaries is a feature with Traherne. The first verse of *My Spirit* concludes with the non-dual mystery of the poet's 'Essence'. This is '. . . Not shut up here, but evry Where'. Transcending boundaries is also the theme of other poems, such as *Goodnesse*. My poem *Sister Spider*[78] attempts a parallel capaciousness: '. . . where our skin stops, / our bodies do not stop'. Traherne filters such awareness through a Christian narrative, positing 'being One' as the sign of divine openness. His theopoetic imagination leads him to combine feeling with thought in an attempt to glimpse fragments of infinity's meaning. The first verse of *Goodnesse* includes two of his favourite words: 'Bliss' and 'Esteem'. Both in his prose and poetry he uses 'right Esteem' and 'rightly Esteem'. The idea is to see something 'as it is'. Through 'right Esteem' I will become an 'enlarged Soul', seeing the artificiality of boundaries. It is not the case that particularity is ignored. Rather, the focus is on holistic non-duality. As ever, a balance needs to be kept between absolute and relative discourses. While a eucalypt seed is potentially a eucalypt tree, prerequisites need to be fulfilled. A prerequisite for awakening is Eckhart's releasement or non-attachment, plus discernment and discrimination.

Although I construe Traherne, Eckhart and Julian as theopoets of 'being One', I hope to have indicated that each one has a singularity of tone. In Traherne, the divine unfolds itself through bodies; Our bodies are graced to be God-substance, expressed as form. Julian has a different but converging outlook. She holds that when we see with spiritual vision, we see each other as infinitely loved. Seeing this, we assist each other to bring an eternal vision to actual, daily experience. Traherne magnifies the unifying mystery as follows:

> Are not all His Treasures yours, and yours His? Is not your very Soul and Body His; Is not His Life and Felicity Yours: Is not His Desire yours? . . . Do you extend your Will like Him, and you shall be Great as He is, and concerned and Happy in all these. . . . Verily if ever you would enjoy God, you must enjoy His Goodness. . . . And when you do so, you are the Universal Heir of God and All Things. GOD is yours and the Whole World. You are His, and you are all; Or in all, and with all.[79]

In such a virtuosic fusion of matter/spirit, Traherne manifests his conviction that 'infinite Worth shut up in the Limits of a Material Being, is the only way to a Real Infinity'.[80] I have implied that his medieval predecessors follow a similar trajectory towards oneness with the divine. Eckhart, controversially, appears to move this oneness towards a union of indistinction, wherein God's nature of indistinction seems to fully draw the distinct human creature 'back in'. But all three writers maintain a basic, twofold view of this mystical union. First, they accept a primordial or preexisting union. Second, they accept the need for a salvific return to union.

Rublev's icon of the Trinity and the sculpture of Shiva Nataraja were mentioned as visual theopoems. Dynamically, they illustrate the necessary balance of transcendence with immanence. An icon is an abnormal artwork because it brings the perspective of the *invisible* to the fore. We are not dealing with strictly logical arguments; the icon is meant to be *sensibly* understood. To the viewer who 'sees the invisible seeing her', the transcendent world is penetrating the ordinary world. The immanent and the transcendent are combining to bring transformation. Another way of writing this would be to say that within the 'heart' of the engaged viewer of the sculpture or the icon, immanence has transcended itself. The 'heart' has apprehended the reality which *always was*: There is no such thing as a separate, single being. The context will normally be inner stillness (Gk: *hesychia*; L: *quietas*). Such 'heart stillness' might be called the ground of participation with the Unnameable Mystery. On such an understanding, the divine merges with humanity so that humanity can merge with the divine.

If I share Rublev's intuition that the divine is triadic, this is not the same as declaring an absolute postulate of onto-theology. I can keep tri-unity as a lively image of engagement, interdependency and interconnectedness. On such a view, the *I Am* does not exist without the *May You Be*. There is no *I Am* without *You Are*. In addition, the *You Are* of you allows the *I Am* of me and vice versa. This does not suggest that human nature is reducible to an unchanging essence. I am not alluding to *passé* essentialism. Mine is a theopoetic perspective which devolves from the *perichoretic* and *kenotic* ground of relational theology.[81]

A recognition of the relationship between the 'I' of the divine Mother/Father and the 'I' of the daughter/son means surrendering a personal sense of individualism. This is because the recognition of divine/human inseparability is the recognition of divine consciousness as the Selfhood of all. The personal sense of self is subsumed in the vision of the *I Am*. Traherne, Julian and Eckhart share the vision of one divine 'I', of one unbounded Selfhood in which we participate. Their prayer is that humanity should awaken to this Presence. But Ramana takes this conceptually further, in the direction of no differentiation whatsoever. He is an *Advaitin* who adheres to a classically *Vedāntin* application of *Tat tvam asi*. Yet it remains a source of fascination, to people such as myself, that his teaching resonates with words attributed to Jesus. A disciple approached Ramana and asked: 'Of the devotees, who is the greatest?' Here is Ramana's reply:

He who gives himself up to the Self that is God is the most excellent devotee. Giving one's self up to God means remaining constantly in the Self without giving room for the rise of any thoughts other than the thought of the Self. Whatever burdens are thrown on God, He bears them. Since the supreme power of God makes all things move, why should we, without submitting ourselves to it, constantly worry ourselves with thoughts as to what should be done and how, and what should not be done and how not? We know that the train carries all loads, so after getting on it why should we carry our small luggage on our head to our discomfort, instead of putting it down in the train and feeling at ease?[82]

A potential puzzle within the three Christian writers is this: Although no *I Am* is ultimately separate from any other *I Am*, each *I Am* carries its particular identity. There is differentiation, but also unity. The symbol of tri-unity alludes to interacting, cooperative being/Being. It hints at the accountability of one person for the next person and of one community for the next. In the largest sense, it is 'eco-relevant'. From the transpersonal to the cosmic, there is one differentiated All, intricately interwoven. Here, the word 'All' is not used in a purely immanentist or naturalistic sense. It is used to indicate the totality of reality, as *inclusive* of a divine creator. It would appear that Traherne, Eckhart and Julian risked an intuition that 'the All' might create itself from the inside, as it were. It might well be that they favoured the creation of a shared spiritual sensibility, within a latent respect for religious differences.

A Way Forward

Today's interpenetration of religions can result in vapid syncretism. It can also bring the deepest truths of reality to the fore. For example, there is currently a turn towards non-dualism. This is occurring across a range of religious traditions. It is not, of course, a 'turn' so much as a *re*-turn.

Wherever the goal is to move away from duality, there is also a need to attend to particularity. Non-dualism requires an awareness that duality is the necessary background for 'awakening'. Here is a personal example: If my mind is flowing with negative thoughts, a realization of the duality of 'me' and 'thinking' is a first step in discovering my true identity beyond the mechanics of the mind. This book has sought to point in the direction of spiritual knowledge and spiritual experience of the non-dual kind.

To repeat the main point: I maintain that Eckhart, Julian and Traherne inscribe a movement *away from* a dualism of the divine and the human *towards* a moderate non-dualism. If we can speak of three main types of 'spiritual' non-dualism (as described by Loy, *ad loc.*), then the position of my three theologians would correlate, in a qualified way, to the third type; namely, the non-difference of subject and object. There is less emphasis on a personal sense of self and a greater recognition of one infinite Selfhood. The purport of the great declaration *I Am* (*ad loc*) undergoes expansion. Since they are Christians, my main characters regard Christ as the exemplar of this Selfhood, or of this divine Consciousness. At the absolute level of truth, this Consciousness is viewed as the Selfhood of all being. At the conventional level of truth, this same Consciousness is regarded as gradually unfolding, as people grow in the experiential knowledge of the One whose love attracts the natural surrender of heart and mind.

This book, therefore, treats Eckhart, Julian and Traherne as theologians whose work tended to run counter to the prevailing ethos. In veering towards a non-dual model of divine-human relations, they understood 'wakefulness' as undivided, practical abidance in 'the inner Christ'. Hence their desire was to embody the divine, rather than to talk about deferred happiness in heaven. In a way, it might be said that all three created cogent starting points in the *all-ways* present struggle to transform dehumanized situations. Moreover, they based their 'critical liberational hermeneutics' (not to put it too absurdly) on what they presented as experiential knowledge of biblical texts.

To be open-hearted is not the same as being intellectually wishy-washy or emotionally uncommitted. The Latin word for heart is *cor*, which gave us the word 'courage'. In praising the open-heartedness of Eckhart, Julian and Traherne, I bear in mind that the heart is a metaphor for the courage to pursue wholeness. There could be dire consequences, in medieval Europe, for writing in a non-dual register. And in England in the seventeenth century, Traherne's non-dual poems were not gestures of nascent Romanticism. They were a high road to being misunderstood and marginalized.

I have described the three theologians as 'theopoets'. It is important to add that their artistry was not the expression of individualism. Their commitment impelled a fusion of theology with a 'faith-hermeneutic'. That is to say, they understood the fullness of humanity as participation in the divine.[1]

Accordingly, they inscribed the reduction of boundaries between the divine and the human and between what is 'you' and what is 'me'. And they wished to elevate their readers beyond second-hand experience, into something actually realized, in the immediate Now and Here.

Since they share a qualified non-dualism of subject and object, Eckhart, Julian and Traherne also share a concern for unitive spiritual experience. In this regard, I have mentioned the concepts of *kenosis* and *perichoresis*. Both these concepts are meant to result in practical outcomes. For example, a Christian will find herself to be not so much a follower of Jesus, as a duplicator of the consciousness of Jesus. She will become the Christ figure itself.

The perichoretic metaphor, of mutual 'dancing around in a circle', speaks of participation in reciprocal relations. None of us can find our true identity solely within ourselves. We need an activated or realized sense of interdependence. I have touched upon the 'strong' non-dualism of Ramana Maharshi, whose advocacy of 'the inner way' has aided the blurring of cultural and religious boundaries in the modern era. I speculate that Eckhart, Julian and Traherne would have found spiritual affinity with Ramana, even while retaining a largely incompatible metaphysics. Ramana's strong non-dualism serves to counterpoint the moderate non-dualism of the three Western theopoets.

Ramana relativizes the cultural accretions of classical *Advaita Vedānta* in order to present a universalist vision of liberation. He asserts that anyone can begin to leave the realm of conditioning, and through divine (ultimately non-dual) grace re-enter the unconditioned Consciousness. We can therefore become established in the non-dual Self (capital 'S') or the *Ātmān*, the infinite principle of Reality behind all life. Ramana's tradition calls this liberated condition 'Self-realization'. It might also be called participation in limitless Awareness. The apostle Paul, on different presuppositions regarding salvation, calls it the reception of '. . . the mind of Christ' (1 Cor. 2:16 REB). It is open to anyone to begin to receive Christ's enlightened mind. In Ramana's tradition, Self-realization relates, not to the subjective, individual 'I' of common understanding, but to 'the heart' or 'the inner I' which is obscured by the ordinary but ultimately illusory 'ego identifications' of conventional living. The non-dual, infinite Self (capital 'S') is of course formless and nameless. It is not a possible object of consciousness. Hence the way to 'locate' it is through direct, immediate experience, without objectifying it. This is why Forsthoefel can give his exemplary study of *Advaita* the title 'Knowing Beyond Knowledge'.[2]

I have construed Traherne's overtly non-dual poems (see Chapter 1) as bringing together conceptual and experiential truth in a vision of transformation. But of course all of my leading characters are concerned with experience and transformation. Neither of them discusses the varieties of non-dualism; they do not wish to impart cognitive sophistication, but to awaken people. Yet Traherne is somewhat different in that he begins with imaginative recreations of the non-dualism of childhood, rather than beginning with theology. It might be said that he held imaginative truth in tension with conceptual truth and experiential truth in tension with both. I briefly hypothesized that Traherne, Eckhart and Julian might have favoured a form of panentheism. Speaking generally, panentheism argues that the divine works in and through a fully connected universe, and yet, is not limited thereby. In the case of these three writers, such an 'inter-weave' of subject and object implies a moderate non-dualism. The paradox appears to be as follows: Within unitive experience there is not necessarily a loss of personal differentiation. The experience occurs within a world of immanence and choice.

Central to Eckhart (see Chapter 2) was his use of *Gelâzenheit* ('letting-be' or 'releasement'). This was taken to involve the non-dual 'awakening' which served as the theme of Chapter 5. We are encouraged to awaken to a form of consciousness without an object. Eckhart was a sage and therefore reluctant to over-conceptualize the divine. Instead, he desired to present an integration of mind and heart within the awareness that 'God is my being, but I am not the being of God'. As with Julian (see Chapter 3) and Traherne, he implied that it is possible to pass beyond thought and image and to enter an experience of inseparability from God. Projections which might have to do with 'reward' (heaven) or 'punishment' (hell) have little relevance in this kind of theology. Instead, the focus is on a lessening of division and a growing realization of wholeness. The inclination that we are 'inter-involved' can be stirred 'within'. This might be labelled 'interiority'. But, as Traherne reminds us, 'interiority' should not be separated from 'true apprehension'. He insists: 'Tis not the Object, but the Light / That maketh Heaven; Tis a Purer Sight. / Felicitie / Appears to none but them that purely see'.[3]

In Eckhartian terms, the little spark (*Vünkelîn*) or little castle (*Bürgelin*) resonates with the 'I Am'[4] of Exodus 3:14. It is this transcendent 'I Am', the creator-God, who models the non-attachment of *Gelâzenheit* and empowers humanity to also become non-attached creators. We are meant, therefore, to be so transformed that we live 'without a why' (*sunder war umbe*) in union with the One 'without a why'. The One who is 'without a why' continually creates the 'I am-ness' which we are.

But when Eckhart writes about union with the transcendent One, he tends towards ambiguity and paradox. He does not deny the particularity of persons; neither does Julian nor Traherne. Perhaps they advance what today could be termed a bio-spiritual oneness, after the manner of the statement attributed to Jesus: 'The Father and I are one'.[5] Such a union with the One is deemed to be available in human experience, through dynamic, *perichoretic* relationality. Did these theopoets anticipate what is now called a process-relational understanding of God? Such hypothesizing would include a redefinition of the traditional 'omni' descriptors of God. Insofar as these 'omni' words have implied an abstract immutability in the divine, they would be reconfigured as enhancing the creaturely freedom of the daughters and sons of the divine. In Eckhart's opinion, these heirs of the divine are all 'words of God'.

The legacy of Traherne, Eckhart, Julian and Ramana can be characterized in terms of 'non-separation'. Nothing exists independently; at the absolute level of truth, that which might appear solid or personal is really transparent and impersonal. The emphasis on unitive reality, or unitive consciousness, brings Ramana into proximity with the three Christians. In terms of *Advaita Vedānta*, the authentic 'I Am' (Skt: *aham asmi*) resonates in the depths of the heart (conceived as 'the organ of apperception'). Arising from the pure Consciousness, the 'I Am' is expressive of the eternal, non-dual Self. And so, at the level of absolute truth, my 'I Am' is not separate from your 'I Am'. At the level of relative or conventional truth, our phenomenal, functional selves continue, but they need to know and to experience that they are not substantially real. Progressive abidance in the non-dual Self is the same as abiding in the Supreme One, or *Brahman*. It is a return to undivided awareness of our permeation by the divine. The various identities which the ego assumes in daily life will fall away. They are seen for what they are: Constructions that are ultimately false.

Eckhartian language converges here, inasmuch as the Meister believes that the individual self, with its sense of separateness, falls away as it learns to participate in the divine. The 'separated self' or ego[6] is 'natural', producing the day-to-day functioning sense of 'I-ness'. But in the light of ultimate reality, this 'I' is insubstantial. The parallel with *Advaita Vedānta* is notable. The little or insubstantial 'I' is to be distinguished from the true, eternal Self, which is ultimately One and which waits to be 'uncovered' as the undercurrent of our real nature.

In a discussion of non-duality in the Bhagavad Gītā, Loy writes: '. . . to experience God is to forget oneself to the extent that one becomes aware of a consciousness pervading everywhere and everything. . . . The sense of "holiness" (Otto's "the numinous") is not something added onto the phenomenal world . . . but is an inherent characteristic of "my" self-luminous mind, although realized only when its true nature is experienced'.[7] Loy is a Buddhist and might therefore confine the absolute level of truth to ordinary life. But those who believe in a transcendent realm are not thereby entitled to neglect the world of ordinary life. A premature retreat into a discourse of absolute truth can leave an individual's emotional, social and/or ethical immaturity unaddressed. This is all too convenient for many of us. We retain aspirations or pretensions, arising from the so-called little or false self, to be 'spiritual' while remaining unintegrated.

Perhaps the absolute truth-level is best construed as having salvific precedence over the conventional truth-level, without being in competition with it. Traherne, for example, carries an ultimate discourse through his poems and meditations; at the same time, he practices and teaches on the relative or conventional level. His emphasis on immanence has the effect, at times, of humanizing the divine, despite his plethora of abstract and sometimes regally oriented diction. He does not dissolve the paradoxes of existence by prelapsarian fantasy. That is to say, despite the recapitulation of his childhood's sense of tranquil oneness with the divine, Traherne does not wish to leave his readers there. He desires that we should see ordinariness with fresh eyes and attend to the moment.

It needs to be noted that when Traherne, Eckhart and Julian write non-dualistically, they presuppose the experience of baptism 'into Christ' (Gal. 3:27 NRSV). This identification with Christ, through baptism, contains both non-dualism and dualism. The dualistic element is present in the 'vertical' relation to the transcendent God who (on this reckoning) 'endorses' baptism. The non-dual element is present in the 'horizontal' relation of interior identification with Christ. Julian passionately blurs the two dimensions. We are held by the arms of the Christ-Mother; we are projected into the all-encompassing love of the Trinity itself.

This non-dual element resonates, to some extent, with the *Advaitin* emphasis of Ramana on the all-embracing, absolutely unitive nature of the Self (capital 'S'). It might be said that transcendence is safeguarded in both traditions. In Christianity, the divine cannot be grasped or understood (because it already creates, grasps and understands *us*). In *Advaita Vedānta*, the ultimate truth cannot be grasped or understood (because it is beyond name and form and we are all inseparable from it). Both traditions manage the non-dual puzzle by giving precedence to the absolute truth-level of discourse *as well as* artfully balancing it with the relative truth-level.

From the perspective of moderate non-dualism, spiritual life can be both personal and impersonal. It is impersonal to the degree that the indivisibility of the divine Presence is recognized. Implicit to such a perspective is an expanding sense of the divine awareness behind the non-dualism of Jesus. To switch to the language of *Advaita*, it could perhaps be said that Traherne, Eckhart and Julian are practitioners (with Ramana) of *abheda bhakti* (devotion without difference). That is to say, they practice non-dual devotion while at the same time teaching scripture, prayer, meditation and a body-honouring asceticism. To continue the analogy with Ramana,[8] it is notable that he also favours these activities for those of us on 'the path'. They assist us to remain imaginatively open to the grace which permeates all things. Thus Ramana balances his impersonalist language with the language of personalism.

If the three great Christian teachers were alive in today's post-secular world, what might their contribution look like? Let me suggest the following. They would align themselves with the holistic implications of a theology of immanence. Integrating scripture with reason, they would be sceptical concerning efforts to 'improve' the world which are driven by the ego and by projection. They would 'dis-identify' with the other-excluding ways of the world. Their theopoems would be provisional and exploratory. And their participation in the ongoing incarnation of Spirit would be interrogative and vulnerable to circumstance and to experience.

I have sought to present Traherne, Eckhart and Julian as theopoets of 'being One' who desire our awakening. The *conditio sine qua non* is participation in the divine.

All three advance the view that humanity participates with the divine in the world's transformation. All three are engaged with the world, by the paradoxical means of authentic non-attachment. Eckhart, in particular, advocates releasement or non-attachment as potentially the deepest way to engage with all creation. Engagement emerges, in each writer, through their reweavings of 'feeling' with 'thought' and of spirituality with theology. Their written legacy reveals their self-understanding as agents of Love's transforming narrative, evoking surrender to the immanence of transcendence.

Glossary

Absolute truth-level: When obliged to be pragmatic, various religious systems make use of 'the doctrine of two truths'. The absolute or ultimate truth-level is generally held to contain within it the conventional truth-level. Within this book the 'self' (small 's') of ordinary, conventional understanding is represented as being subsumed within (or encompassed by) the non-dual 'Self' (capital 'S') which is nameless and formless.

Advaita: Literally 'not two'. In various Western texts, advaita is erroneously treated as 'monism'. It needs to be understood that advaita is not so much an idea as an experience, somewhat beyond reason (perhaps). A committed advaitin will not usually concern herself with definitional issues, preferring to dwell within paradox and taciturnity.

Advaita Vedānta: The school of thought which regards the essence of Hinduism to be non-dualism. Whether or not a person enters the experience of their ultimate identity with Brahman (the Absolute Reality), the knowledge of Brahman is declared to be accessible to all beings.

Aham: The embodied self; the 'I'. The Hindu 'I Am' (aham asmi) and the Judeo-Christian 'I Am' are of great importance in their respective cosmologies, theopoems and ethical understandings.

Anubhava: Authentic spiritual experience. Within progressive advaitin understandings, anubhava provides the confirmation of the truth of non-dualism. By implication, personal experience is capable (within certain safeguards) of being elevated above doctrines, above the authority of teachers, and above the merely written words of sacred texts.

Ātmā Siddhi: Self-realization; in other words, the continuous, experiential knowledge of the inseparability of Brahman and the Ātman. This condition is also described as dwelling permanently within pure Consciousness. See Awakening and see Ātman.

Ātmā Vichara: Enquiry into the non-dual, infinite, unnameable Self. For convenience, the present book sometimes alludes to the true self, as against the false or little self. It should be noted that Advaita Vedānta repudiates the very notion of 'two selves'.

Ātman: Denotes the soul in its deepest, unnameable and formless centre. I have chosen to use 'Ātman' for the supreme non-dual 'Self'. I also allude to 'the Self' as 'limitless Awareness'. Other writers use 'Brahman' (the Absolute) to denote the 'Self'. It is not always accurate to equate the 'Self' with Western notions of 'God'.

Awakening: This book employs the word 'awakening' in the sense of a 're-discovery' of the infinite but ever-present Source. When it discusses Advaita Vedānta, the book relates 'awakening' to the Ātman (or the Self with a capital 'S'). Various things might be implied by 'awakening'. For example, the abandonment of Modernism's idolatry of autonomous reason. Another example would be the letting go of Fundamentalism wherever it sanctions the idolatry of sacred texts and the primacy of individualistic moralism over communal and societal transformation.

Brahman: The Absolute; the Infinite. Some writers use 'Brahman' to denote the supreme non-dual Self, whereas I have used 'Ātman' for this purpose. Spiritual teachers often state that Brahman can become an experiential truth, such that the Infinite is seen and felt to inhere in everything. If Brahman (as a concept) is designed to express Objective

Spirit, then Ātmān (as a concept) is designed to express Subjective Spirit. In Advaita Vedānta, all things are permeated by Brahman; it is ultimately inseparable from the Ātmān. Followers of Śaṅkarā have for many centuries aided the reduction of the ego with a meditation along these lines: 'I am not the body. I am not the senses. I am not the mind. I am the unceasing perfection of Brahman experienced as I, the witness of thought-forms.'

Consciousness: The word means two different things in this book. First, heightened awareness in the common Western sense. Second (usually with a capital 'C'), the traditional Eastern sense of the substance of all things, or infinite Mind. From within his non-dual, unconditioned Consciousness (or Realization, as I have used the word), Jesus can be represented as saying '*I* and the Mother/Father are one; *I* am the truth; *I* am the life; *I* am the resurrection', etc.

Conventional truth-level: This is 'one half' of the dualism which is often known as 'the doctrine of the two truths'. See Absolute truth-level.

Divine Transcendence: For present purposes, that which enables ethical transcendence in the heart, mind and communal life of any creature who 'hears' the divine 'voice'. The little (or small 's') self can thereby become decentred.

Dualism: Simplistically, the philosophical view that the cosmos consists of two entities or aspects: Matter and consciousness. At the personal level, as long as a body-mind organism is retained by 'me', a dualism applies between 'me' as the observing object and 'you' as the observed object. This book assumes the usefulness of such a duality, while suggesting that our minds provide us with a false view as to the separateness of our body-mind organism. See Non-dualism.

Gelâzenheit: The letting be of detachment or releasement which forms a key part of Eckhartian thought. 'Releasement' countermands Eigenschaft (which today we might call 'the ego'). Eckhart maintains that the inner work of abegescheidenheit ('cutting loose') is necessary, if humanity is to recognize its true identity.

Kenosis: Self-emptying; also, for present purposes, the emptying out of received positions and 'objective' idolatries. Open-hearted and open-minded people tend to lead a *kenotic* life. Their way of relating to Earth tends to be *perichoretic*. Boundaries (of tradition, of dogma, of temperament) become redefined in a natural pursuit of reciprocity and of holy/holistic communion. Philippians chapter 2 puts forward kenosis as the paradigm of divine activity. See *Perichoresis* and *Śūnyatā*.

Non-dualism: This book regards 'spiritual non-dualism' (for want of a better phrase) as a basic tenet of Western tradition which is often overlooked. The divine and the human are discussed as moderately non-dual (or not separate and not separable). That is to say, Eckhart, Julian and Traherne treat the Subject (e.g. the divine) and the Object (e.g. the human) as inseparable, within the paradox that the divine remains transcendent. A Jew or Christian or Muslim can be non-dualist without necessarily compromising the belief that the divine is independent of creation. See Dualism.

Panentheism: The concept that the divine works in and through our fully-connected universe, yet is not limited thereby. The present author regards a panentheistic model of the relation of the divine to the universe as having the capacity to embrace theopoems which spring from incompatible cosmologies.

Pantheism: The concept that the divine possesses a fully immanent dimension (and therefore lacks any transcendent dimension). Hinduism has often been erroneously dismissed as pantheistic by other religious groupings which assume superiority. The coherence of Hindu cosmologies and ontologies might well be at odds with the metaphysics of other systems of religious thought. It is not necessarily the case that, within Hinduism, divine transcendence (and salvific grace) is immersed in a sea of immanence.

Perichoresis: Literally, 'dancing around'. Describes a network (or 'inter-permeation') of entities, wherein each entity nonetheless remains 'itself'. *Perichoretic* actions, based upon spiritual surrender, will be vital in the survival of humanity (not to mention the entire biota of Earth). See *Kenosis* and *Śūnyatā*.

Postmodernism: Simplistically speaking, if Modernism stands for an over-inflated reliance on autonomous reason, Postmodernism stands for the irreducible plurality of the voices of truth. It can therefore denote the reinvitation of spiritual traditions to participate in humanity's future.

Process Theology: The earliest Christian traditions regard the divine as ever-relational and ever-dynamic. The divine is characterized (in both its nature and its activity) as 'love' (1 Jn 4:8). This love unfolds or is successive. Most versions of latter-day process theology are indebted to Alfred North Whitehead. Their discourse is about a God who is absolutely related to cosmic evolution.

Sacred Texts: A truthful understanding of a sacred text is not intuitive, or objective, or subjective. It is *interpretive*. A sacred text does not 'speak' to us, in the absence of our interpretation. Just as no religious tradition can be said to 'possess' the divine, no tradition can be said to 'possess' truth or the truths of interpretation.

Satchitānanda: A triadic expression which attempts to be suggestive of the essence of Brahman or the Supreme, with Sat as indivisible or pure Being, Cit (here transposed as Chit) as Consciousness or Absolute Intelligence and Ānanda as Bliss. Christians have adopted the triadic word as expressive of the Trinitarian mystery.

The self (small 's'): The self can be an object of experience, as well as being a subject of experience. But the non-dual 'Self' (capital S) is such that it cannot be known by our normally available means of knowledge. The Self (capital S) is sometimes referred to as the one Being.

The Self (capital 'S'): See Ātmān.

Spirit: When used with a capital letter, denotes the transcendent and immanent Divine, disclosed as Agape/Love. It authors and energizes relationality, in aspects that might simultaneously be impersonal, transpersonal and personal.

Śūnyatā: Often translated as 'Emptiness' to signify that all things are empty of independent existence (but exist in a state of interdependency). As with non-dualism, it is more profitable to experience śūnyatā (as the mutual participation of all things) rather than attempt a definition. The various Hinduisms tend to avoid the word, because of dogmatically 'strong' definitions emerging from some Buddhist schools. This book makes use of the association of śūnyatā with kenosis.

The Trinity: This concept finds endless concurrence in various religious traditions and in diverse cultures. From an orthodox Christian perspective, the Trinity cannot literally be triadic, because the three 'persons' are constitutively related. Nor, in relation to humanity, is the Trinity the ultimate Other. Warped understandings of the Trinity are to be found wherever poetry is in retreat and the role of metaphor is ignored. The author regards the idea of the Trinity as a radical theopoem which tends to subvert some traditional notions of monotheism.

Turīya: A fourth state of consciousness, put forward as deeper (and yet more 'natural') than the impermanent states of waking, dreaming and deep sleep.

Vedānta: The 'end' or consummation of the Vedas, the sacred books of the Hindus.

Notes

Introduction

1 Quotation from: *The Way of Transfiguration: Religious Imagination as Theopoiesis*, S. R. Hopper (R. M. Keiser & T. Stoneburner, eds) Westminster/John Knox Press, Louisville, KY, 1992.

2 The current literature on theopoetics ranges from the self-referential and solipsistic to the more helpful and sometimes theo-centred. Appraisals include: a number of articles in *Cross Currents 60:1* (2010), *passim*; Callid Keefe-Parry, 'Theopoetics: Process and Perspective', in *Christianity and Literature 58:4* (2009), pp. 579–601; Matt Guynn, 'Theopoetics: That the dead may become gardeners again', in *Cross Currents 56:1* (2006), pp. 98–109; Scott Holland, 'Theology is a kind of writing: The emergence of theopoetic', in *Cross Currents 47:3* (1997), pp. 317–31.

3 The distinctions of Western dualism are helpful, to a degree. Historically, they have been emphasized to the point where they harden into separations. Classic dualities include: subject/object, God/humanity, spirit/matter, one/many, inside/outside, cause/effect, good/evil, heaven/hell, freewill/determinism, knower/known, self/other, mind/body. A common assumption has been that of regarding 'mind' as distinct from 'matter'. But dualities can fade; it is no longer generally thought that 'mind' has nothing in common with 'matter'. By the same token, religious people no longer uniformly consider that anything resembling a materialist account of thinking is subversive to the idea of a soul.

4 Denys Turner directly assesses the Eckhartian aporetic concerning non-dualism (see Chapter 2 of the present study).

5 David Loy, who expounds non-dualism from within a Buddhist commitment, distinguishes three main types. These are: '... the negation of dualistic thinking, the non-plurality of the world, and the non-difference of subject and object'. Traherne, Eckhart and Julian support an experience of the divine in which the distinction between subject and object is somewhat collapsed. Therefore Loy's third type of non-dualism is the type most applicable to the three Christians. See Loy's *Nonduality: A Study in Comparative Philosophy*, Yale University Press, New Haven, CT, 1988, pp. 17 and 25f.

6 See Glossary. Perichoresis (characterized in an original way by Charles Williams as 'coinherence') finds an indigenous African parallel in *Ubuntu*, wherein our identity arises from within community.

7 Such experience might be better conveyed in German than in English, which lacks the purport of difference as between *Erfahrung* or the ongoing process of experience which includes broadening of perspective and a consequent self-transformation, and *Erlebnis*, which connotes experience in a contingent, impermanent sense (cf. the Buddhist understanding of contingent experience).

8 Traherne follows Sir Philip Sidney (d.1586) who follows Horace (d. 8 BCE) in believing that poetry should either delight or educate: '*aut delectare aut prodesse est*'.

9 The words 'limitless Awareness' are used in view of their resonance with the *Ātmān* or the non-dual 'Self' (capital 'S') associated with the philosophical system of *Vedānta*. Other writers prefer to use *Brahman* to denote the 'Self' and *Ātmān* as the soul, in its deepest aspect or centre. For present purposes, the 'Self' (capital 'S') connotes the limitless, ever-aware, innermost principle of life, often discussed as *Satchitānanda* (Being-Consciousness-Bliss). Accordingly, references to this 'Self' have no connection with modern proclivities such as individual self-esteem or self-enhancement. Christian equivalents of the *Vedāntin* 'abidance in the Self' might be 'abidance in the Spirit' or 'abidance in the divine Word'. Detailed arguments for and against such parallels are beyond the scope of this study.

10 To them 'sin' seems primarily to be an erroneous way of identifying 'who we are'. Ergo, sin is enacted in ways that have no positive content.

11 Debates concerning the phenomenal or individual self and the non-dual Self (capital 'S') obviously took place in India many centuries before Eckhart et al. But *Vedānta,* as the philosophical substrate of Hinduism, is concerned with absolute truth and does not venture into the conditioned language of dualism, as between the phenomenal self and the Self (capital 'S'). Within later *Advaita Vedānta,* an apparent bifurcation between the *Ātmān* and the phenomenal self need not always imply that the latter is of little consequence. On the contrary, the *Ātmān* or Self (capital 'S') is potentially manifested in and through the (small 's') self. Clive Hamilton, in pithy asides on Hindu philosophy, writes as follows: 'Finding the universal Self, the ultimate subject, is the secret door to the citadel. This is the most profound discovery of the *Upanishads*. . . . To understand the identity of the subtle essence (*Brahman*) and the universal Self (*Atman*) is the purpose of life, as captured in the emblematic principle of Hindu philosophy *Thou art that*'. Hamilton later writes: 'When Jesus said that the meek shall inherit the Earth, he meant that only those who transcend their identification with the ego-self in the phenomenon will find the path to the universal Self in the noumenon,'. See Hamilton, C., *The Freedom Paradox: Towards a Post-Secular Ethics,* Allen & Unwin, Crows Nest, NSW, 2008, pp. 139 and 312.

12 Less problems attend a commonplace acceptance that the entity known as 'the self' (small 's') is largely created by the needy, desire-filled and sometimes joyful external world.

13 Most notably: 'The Father and I are one' (Jn 10:30 NRSV).

14 As per Acts 17:28, the One within whom we 'live and move and have our being' (NRSV).

15 Henri Le Saux (a.k.a. Swami Abhishiktananda) who is of tangential relevance to parts of the present study, could write: 'All that the Christ said or thought about himself, is true of every man. It is the theologians who – to escape being burnt, the devouring fire – have projected (rejected) into a divine *loka* (sphere) the true mystery of the Self'. Quotation from: *Swami Abhishiktananda: His Life Told through his Letters* (J. Stuart, ed.), ISPCK, Delhi, p. 287. Bruno Barnhart, in *The Future of Wisdom* (Continuum, NY, 2007, p. 113), offers the idea that Eckhart's unitive vision anticipates the views of Abhishiktananda.

16 For an essay which flags this likelihood within a discussion of the work of Hélène Cixous, see Krista E. Hughes, 'Intimate Mysteries: The Apophatics of Sensible Love', in *Apophatic Bodies: Negative Theology, Incarnation, and Relationality* (C. Boesel & C. Keller, eds), Fordham University Press, NY, 2010, pp. 349–66.

17   Daniel F. Stramara writes: 'Their relationships are not static but "revolve around"
     one another. . . . The Persons whirl "about" each other and inside of each other.
     The depiction is one of mutual admiration, each Person "falling all over" the other,
     glorying in the other. In a sense, the Persons are continually "falling in love"'.
     Quotations from: 'Gregory of Nyssa's Terminology for Trinitarian Perichoresis',
     Vigiliae Christianae 52:3 (August 1998) Brill Publishers, Leiden.

18   The word 'interpermeation' might be more helpful than 'interpenetration'.

19   It could be said, in defence of the Trinitarian idea, that such a symbolic structure was
     originally imagined in order to forestall the possibility of a rival symbolic structure,
     such as that of an *unconnected* or isolated Being. (I am told that within one system
     of Amer-Indian religion, God is understood to speak only four words: 'Come dance
     with me'.)

20   The quotation is from Kearney's *The God Who May Be*, Indiana University Press,
     Bloomington, IN, 2001, p. 109.

21   Cf. Catherine Keller: 'Jesus was always deconstructing the operative absolutes, the do's,
     dont's, and I believe's. To deconstruct is not to destroy but to expose our constructed
     presumptions'. See C. Keller, *On the Mystery: Discerning Divinity in Process,* Fortress
     Press, Minneapolis, MN, 2008, p. 138.

22   Some of my statements will tend to oversimplify the question of duality versus
     non-duality, given that there are varieties of both. There are ontological categories
     and sub-categories of monism, dualism, pluralism and non-dualism, an analysis of
     which is beyond my scope. But, see footnote 5 regarding David Loy's three main
     types of non-dualism. And cf. the following remarks by Taitetsu Unno. 'Non-duality
     is not the opposite of duality, nor is it a simplistic negation of duality. Non-duality
     affirms duality from a higher standpoint. It is not an abstract concept but lived
     reality. But the difficulty is in understanding it, because we have here a double
     exposure, so to speak, of duality and non-duality'. See Unno's *River of Fire, River of
     Water: An Introduction to the Pure Land Tradition of Shin Buddhism,* Doubleday,
     New York, NY, 1998, p. 132.

23   Within such a perspective, this might be seen as tantamount to a person manifesting
     'as heaven itself'. A rendering of one of the *Mahānārāyana Ups.* expresses it as follows:
     'Heaven is within the inner chamber, the glorious place which is entered by those who
     renounce themselves' (12:4).

24   Quotations from the texts of Traherne, Eckhart and Julian, with attendant
     commentaries, are intended to bear out my assertion of their desire.

Chapter 1

1   Traherne would have endorsed the following viewpoint of S. J. Jean-Pierre de
     Caussade, who was born in 1675, the year following Traherne's death: 'God's activity
     runs through the universe. . . . The actions of created beings are veils which hide the
     profound mysteries of the workings of God'. (Quotations from: *Abandonment to
     Divine Providence,* Image/Doubleday, NY, 1975, pp. 25f and 36.) But Traherne goes
     further and vests all things with value for their own sake.

2   See Chapters 2 and 3 of this study.

3   *Thomas Traherne: Poems, Centuries and Three Thanksgivings*, ed. A. Ridler, Oxford University Press, London, 1966, pp. 27 and 30. Hereinafter 'Ridler'.

4   A. F. Bellette, *Profitable Wonders: An Essay on Thomas Traherne*, unpublished manuscript, 1983, p. 83.

5   Ibid.

6   Ridler, p. 27f.

7   Ibid, p. 28.

8   Bellette, p. 86f.

9   In broad terms, Traherne's body of work can be read as a reaffirmation of the Christian-Platonist position that to 'know God' is to 'know' the inner rationality of all being. Likewise, 'to know' the inner rationality of being is to know God as the perfect One in which all rationality participates.

10 Ridler, p. 29.

11 Ibid.

12 A. L. Clements, *The Mystical Poetry of Thomas Traherne*, Harvard University Press, Cambridge, MA, 1969, p. 192.

13 Ridler, p. 53.

14 Quotation from *Centuries 2:76* in H. M. Margoliouth (ed.), *Thomas Traherne: Centuries, Poems, and Thanksgivings*, Oxford University Press, London, 1958, vol. 1, p. 94. Hereinafter '*Centuries*'.

15 Bellette, p. 83.

16 Ibid.

17 As with Jonathan Edwards in New England in the following century, Traherne represents himself as a humanist as well as a Christian: knowledge is grounded in sensory perception, as well as in biblical revelation. Both men advocated 'a sense of the heart' as an addition to the five senses in John Locke's famous treatise. Traherne implies, for example, that the heart's sense of beauty is superior to a mere opinion or a conception concerning beauty. Perhaps Traherne and Edwards shared a quirkiness which later found expression in the view of C. S. Peirce (d.1914) that our viewpoint on any one thing is identical with our viewpoint on the sensible effects of that thing.

18 Bellette, p. 4.

19 Ibid., p. 21.

20 *Centuries 3:26*, p. 125f.

21 Ibid., *3:11*, p. 117.

22 Ibid.

23 Alluded to in the next chapter.

24 *Centuries 2:76*, p. 94.

25 He is clearly not a narrow materialist. (A hypothetical question might be asked here: If 'spirituality' somehow 'went missing' in the world, and if a narrow materialism predominated, could poetry still be written?)

26 *Centuries 1:1*, p. 3.

27 Cf. the poems *The Circulation* (especially v.3) and *Amendment* and *The Demonstration*.

28 Eph. 1:10, cf. Col. 1:20, NRSV.

29 For example, Louis L. Martz, *The Poetry of Meditation: A Study in English Religious Literature of the Seventeenth Century*, Yale University Press, revised edition, 1962.

30 *Centuries 3:2*, p. 110.

31 Ibid., p. 111.

32   It is well accepted that Neoplatonism is an enduring issue for Western theology. My three authors arguably seek to counter Neoplatonic thought, wherever this tends towards (or presumes) dualism.

33   *Centuries 3:23*, p. 123f.

34   Clements, p. 22.

35   Perhaps *Tat tvam asi* is better rendered, today, as 'You are That!' or 'You are It!' An interpreter of the life and teachings of Ramana Maharshi writes as follows: 'What is the truth? It is that there is nothing besides the one spirit. In that there are no distinctions, even as in the honey collected by the bees there are no distinctions as *This is the honey of this flower; that is the honey of that flower*, and as in the ocean there is no dividing line between the waters of one river and those of another.... The Self is not somewhere in a remote region, unknown and unrealized; [in the *Chāndogya Upanishad*] Uddalaka points at his son, Svetaketu, and proclaims *That thou art*'. (Quoted from T. M. P. Mahadevan, *Ramana Maharshi and his Philosophy of Existence*, Sri Ramanasramam, Tiruvannamalai, Tamil Nadu, 2010, p. 102f.)

36   Clements, p. 23.

37   Ibid.

38   Ibid., p. 108.

39   Ridler, p. 12f.

40   Clements, p. 70.

41   Ridler, p. 14.

42   In Chapters 2 and 4 respectively.

43   Ridler, p. 13f.

44   Clements' words, p. 128.

45   Ridler, p. 14.

46   By the same token, theopoets perhaps tend to overlook the fact that abstract ideas can engage the imagination just as much as 'concrete particulars'.

47   Ridler, p. 53, v. 3.

48   Clements' words, p. 162.

49   Ibid., p. 165.

50   Generally speaking, spiritual traditions (later regarded as 'mystical') have tended to configure their goal as one of unitive experience. Chapters 4 and 5 of the present study have relevance here.

51   Ridler, p. 67.

52   The twentieth-century diary of Henri Le Saux (a.k.a. Swami Abhishiktananda) includes many patristic-like injunctions to inwardness. Dom Henri writes: 'The first task of the human being is to enter within, and himself to encounter himself. If anyone has not met himself, how could he meet God? You do not meet yourself apart from God. You do not meet God apart from yourself.... The God adored by one who has not met himself in the nude is an idol'. Quotation from: *Ascent to the Depth of the Heart* (R. Panikkar, ed.) ISPCK, Delhi, 1998, p. 78.

53   *Centuries 2:80*, p. 96f.

54   Quoted by D. Moran, in *The Irish Mind* (R. Kearney, ed.), Wolfhound, Dublin, 1985, p. 99.

55   Such as, for example, Mark Johnston, who writes of the divine as 'the Highest One' and puts forward a form of process panentheism. He believes that history discloses the Highest One, the source of all existence (M. Johnston, *Saving God: Religion after Idolatry*, Princeton University Press, Princeton, NJ, 2009).

56   Lines 47–51 of *Thoughts IV*, Margoliouth, vol. 2, p. 181.

57 In 'Traherne, Husserl, and a Unitary Act of Consciousness' in *Re-Reading Thomas Traherne: A Collection of New Critical Essays*, Jacob Blevins (ed.), Arizona Centre for Medieval and Renaissance Studies, Tempe, AZ, 2007, p. 203. See also: J. J. Balakier, *Thomas Traherne and the Felicities of the Mind,* Cambria Press, NY, 2010.

58 The other three states of the *Ātmān* (where *Ātmān* might refer to the 'hidden person of the heart') are normal wakefulness, sleep with dreams, and deep, dreamless sleep. More commonly, the *Ātmān* (or the non-dual, supreme 'Self') refers directly to the governing principle or substrate of life and sensation. Whatever the nuances of usage, the *Ātmān* is regarded as ultimately at one with *Brahman.*

59 J. J. Balakier in Blevins (ed.), *Re-Reading Thomas Traherne*, p. 206.

60 Ibid.

61 Ibid., pp. 205 and 207.

62 Ridler, p. 62.

63 Ibid., p. 29.

64 M. R. Miles, *Rereading Historical Theology,* Cascade Books, Eugene, OR, 2008, p. 49f.

65 *Centuries 4:21*, p. 180.

66 Ibid., *3:63*, p. 147.

67 Ibid., *3:60*, p. 145.

68 L. L. Martz, *The Paradise Within,* Yale University Press, New Haven, CT, 1964, p. 92.

69 In her *Showings* (LT, Ch. 27) Julian declares: '. . . I did not see sin'.

70 Ridler, p. 35f.

71 Lines 1–6, Margoliouth, vol. 2, p. 146.

72 Ibid, p. 182.

73 Ibid., line 88.

74 Ibid., line 97.

75 Ibid., lines 95–102.

76 The book of Sirach (Ecclesiasticus) speaks of the necessity of reciprocal responses. 'She will reveal herself; once you hold her, do not let her go. For in the end you will find rest in her and she will take the form of joy for you' (Sir. 6:27–8, NJB).

77 S. Stewart, *The Expanded Voice: The Art of Thomas Traherne,* Huntington Library and Art Gallery, San Marino, CA, 1970, p. 205.

78 Ibid., p. 214.

79 K. W. Salter, *Thomas Traherne: Mystic and Poet,* Edward Arnold, London, 1964, p. 64f.

80 Ibid., p. 65.

81 Ibid., p. 66.

82 *Śūnyatā* literally means 'voidness' or 'emptiness', implying non-substantiality. Accordingly, *śūnyatā* cannot be conceptualized or objectified, or else it becomes 'something' which one conceives and represents (as '*śūnyatā*'). I favour the word 'openness' as a possible rendering of the Skt. Chapter 4 includes a discussion of parallels between *śūnyatā* and *kenosis.*

83 *Centuries 1:29*, p. 15.

84 In an early essay, David J. Tacey writes the following: 'We are creatures of two worlds, of this world and an otherworld. The conflict between the separate demands of these worlds is what defines and constitutes our human experience'. Tacey goes on to characterize the conflict as between Logos and Eros. He then proceeds: 'The "solution" which dismisses Logos, or which dresses up the erotic gods as "spirit", is no solution at all, but represents a mere regression to an archaic "unity" which excludes contemporary consciousness and all the great gains that have been made by the human spirit under the tutelage of a Father God'. Quotation from: 'Spirit, Nature

and Popular Ecology: An Archetypal Critique of the New Paganism, *Quadrant*, July–August 1992, pp. 67–70. Tacey has since published expositions of contemporary consciousness.

85 It can be assumed that Traherne was acquainted with the writings of Sir Thomas Browne (d.1682). Browne's book *Religio Medici* ('Religion of a Physician') speaks of the 'two books from whence I collect my Divinity'. These are the book of scripture and the book of 'Nature'. Browne states that '... those that never saw Him in the one, have discovered Him in the other' (*Religio Medici 1:16*).

86 *Centuries 1:30*, p. 15.
87 Ibid., *1:21*, p. 11.
88 Ibid., *1:29*, p. 15.
89 Ibid., *1:30*.
90 Ridler, p. 6.
91 *Centuries 3:3*, p. 111.
92 Ridler, p. 7.
93 Ibid., p. 6.
94 Ibid.
95 *Centuries 4:70*, p. 205.
96 Ibid., *2:81*, p. 97.
97 Ibid., *3:3*, p. 111.
98 Ridler, p. 8.
99 Ibid., p. 7.
100 Ibid.
101 Ibid., p. 8.
102 D. Inge, *Wanting Like a God: Desire and Freedom in Thomas Traherne*, SCM Press, London, 2009.
103 Ibid., p. 264.
104 Ibid., p. 263.
105 Ibid., p. 246.
106 Ibid., p. 262.
107 Ibid., p. 179f.
108 Ibid., p. 196.
109 Ibid., p. 197.
110 Ibid., p. 200.
111 Ibid.
112 The following *caveat* is assumed: A person is constrained by finite relatedness, whereas God is not.
113 Alison Kershaw, *The Poetic of the Cosmic Christ in Thomas Traherne's The Kingdom of God*, PhD thesis, University of Western Australia, 2005. Kershaw finds Christology to be 'deeply embedded' (p. 14) in Traherne's work. This had not generally been acknowledged.
114 Ibid., p. 2.
115 Ibid., p. 7.
116 Ibid., p. 8.
117 *Centuries 1:3*, p. 3f.
118 Kershaw, p. 288.
119 Ibid., p. 17.
120 Alan Gould, 'The Poet of Sudden Cloudbreak: A Commentary on Thomas Traherne', *Quadrant*, March 2008.

121 Ridler, p. 18.
122 *Centuries 1:1*, p. 3.
123 Ibid.
124 *Centuries 3:2*, p. 110f.
125 Ibid., *4:48*, p. 193.
126 Ibid., *1:17*, p. 9.
127 Stewart, p. 154.
128 Ridler, p. 75.
129 Margoliouth, vol. 2, p. 274.
130 Ibid., p. 275.
131 Bellette, 1983.
132 Ibid., p. 172.
133 Ibid., p. 173.
134 Ibid., p. 174.
135 Margoliouth, vol. 2, p. 283.
136 Stewart, p. 138.
137 Bellette, p. 130.

Chapter 2

1 From *Sermon 70*, in M. O'C. Walshe, trans. & ed., *Meister Eckhart: Sermons and Treatises*, Watkins/Element Books, London, 1979, vol. 2, p. 174. (This sermon is #67 in the 11-volume critical German edition.)
2 From *Sermon 13*, in Walshe, ibid., vol. 1, p. 110. (This sermon is #5 in the critical German edition.)
3 Schürmann (1941–93) in *Wandering Joy: Meister Eckhart's Mystical Philosophy* (Forward by David Appelbaum), Lindisfarne Books, Great Barrington, MA, 2001, p. xviii.
4 As related by the apostle in 2 Cor. 12:1–7.
5 Cf. Jesus, in the desert following his baptism. He is represented as relinquishing; as finding release from the extraneous; as entering the 'emptiness' or perhaps 'the Eckhartian nothingness'.
6 From *Sermon 53*, in E. Colledge & B. McGinn, trans. & ed., *Meister Eckhart: The Essential Sermons, Commentaries, Treatises and Defense*, Paulist Press, New York, 1981, p. 203.
7 Eckhart's MHG term is *durchbruch* (or, in the Latin sermons *reditus*) for 'breakthrough' and/or 'return'.
8 *Meister Eckhart: An Asian Perspective*, H.-S. Keel, Peeters Press, Leuven, Belgium, 2007, p. 176.
9 Colledge & McGinn, p. 285.
10 Ibid., p. 288.
11 In connection with the Martha/Mary story of Lk. 10, Beverly Lanzetta suggests that Eckhart's stated preference for the active life '... may be seen to be a Western mystical version of the "*samsāra* is *nirvāna*" of the Buddhist world'. (*Samsāra* here connotes conditioned reality; *nirvāna* connotes Boundless Openness.) Quotation from: B. J. Lanzetta, 'Three Categories of Nothingness in Eckhart', *The Journal of Religion 72:2* (April 1992), The University of Chicago Press, Chicago, IL, p. 268. In Chapter 4, I make use of Lanzetta's article vis-à-vis Eckhartian nothingness.

12 Ibid., p. 290.
13 From *Sermon 6*, in Colledge & McGinn, p. 187.
14 From the treatise *On Detachment,* in Colledge & McGinn, p. 288.
15 Ibid., p. 200.
16 Ibid., p. 202f.
17 J. D. Caputo, *The Weakness of God: A Theology of the Event,* Indiana University Press, Bloomington, IN, 2006, p. 172.
18 Ruth Burrows writes: 'Only too easily we substitute the "spiritual life" or the "contemplative life" for God. Without realizing it we are intent on a self-culture'. Quotation from: R. Burrows, *To Believe in Jesus,* Sheed and Ward, London, 1978, p. 94. Elsewhere, Burrows writes: 'By faith we *die*. It means renouncing myself as my own base, my own centre, my own end. It means . . . death to the ego'. Quotation from her *Guidelines for Mystical Prayer,* Sheed and Ward, London, 1976, p. 59.
19 'For the soul that is privileged to be in communion with the Spirit becomes all light, all face, all eye, and there is no part of her that is not full of the spiritual eyes of light. As fire, the very light of fire, is alike all over, having in it no first or last, or greater or less, so also the soul that is perfectly irradiated by the unspeakable beauty of the light of Christ, becomes all eye, all light, all face, all glory, all spirit, being made so by Christ, who drives and guides and carries and bears her, and graces her thus with spiritual beauty'. Quotation from: 'Homily I' (of Pseudo-Macarius) in *An Anthology of Christian Mysticism* (H. Egan, ed.), The Liturgical Press, Collegeville, MN, 1996, pp. 83f.
20 Reading Eckhart, Julian and Traherne closely, I have the impression that neither writer is particularly interested in petitionary prayer, with the clear exception of Julian's requests to God that she might enter into something of the suffering love of Christ. I feel that each of these three writers accepts that prayer functions, not to change the divine will, but to release divine qualities and purposes into human consciousness. But my feeling could be a projection on my part.
21 Elsewhere in this book, I have used the words 'limitless Awareness' to characterize the *Ātmān*.
22 There is no precise equation between the lesser or false self (of long-established conventional, conditioned or empirical speech) and the ego of modernist characterization. The contexts for the respective usages would seem to be incompatible, inasmuch as Freud put forward a (then) unconventional, idiosyncratic and perhaps unnatural use of 'ego'. Nonetheless, 'ego' can serve, on the understanding that through the practice of mindfulness and self-compassion this 'ego' can become an object of awareness.
23 From B. McGinn, ed., with F. Tobin & E. Borgstadt, *Meister Eckhart: Teacher and Preacher,* Paulist Press, New York, 1986, p. 267.
24 Ibid., p. 268.
25 'Losing the Self: Detachment in Meister Eckhart and Its Significance for Buddhist-Christian Dialogue', C. Radler, *Buddhist-Christian Studies 26*, University of Hawai'i Press, 2006.
26 See, for example, Paul Rorem's essay 'Negative Theologies and the Cross', in *Harvard Theological Review 101:3–4, 2008,* pp. 451–64. Rorem does not mention the rather obvious point that the apophatic would seem to be best approached as a way of refining the language(s) of kataphatic or positive theology. Vladimir Lossky (1957; 2005) writes of the combination of kataphatic and apophatic theologies, whereby '. . . knowledge is transformed into ignorance, the theology of concepts into

contemplation, dogmas into experience of ineffable mysteries'. (V. Lossky, *The Mystical Theology of the Eastern Church,* James Clark and Co., Cambridge, England, 1957; 2005, p. 238.)

27 Radler, 'Losing the Self', p. 114.
28 D. Soelle, *The Silent Cry: Mysticism and Resistance,* Fortress Press, Minneapolis, MN, 2001, p. 60.
29 Ibid.
30 Ibid., p. 61.
31 And yet, according to Eckhart, there is a sense in which the word *indistinction* is valid. Writing from God's point of view, as it were, Eckhart uses a language of identification or indistinction to figure humanity's return or reversion to God. Does Eckhart actually suggest an ontological identity between God and humanity? This is the area of Eckhart's potential aporia.
32 I sense that he abhors the alternative, where *power* has the last word.
33 Even the crucial *abegescheidenheit* (the letting-be or detachment discussed earlier in this chapter) can be viewed as developing out of Eckhart's doctrine of divine birth in the soul.
34 From *Sermon 2* in *Meister Eckhart: Selected Writings,* ed. & trans. O. Davies, Penguin, London, 1994, p. 112f. (This sermon is #38 in the critical German edition.)
35 P. Sherrard, *Human Image: World Image,* Golgonooza, Ipswich, England, 1992, p. 164.
36 C. Smith, *The Way of Paradox: Spiritual Life as Taught by Meister Eckhart,* Darton, Longman and Todd, London, 1987, p. 82f.
37 Ibid., p. 84.
38 Commenting on Feuerbach's atheism, Denys Turner states: 'You have only to reverse subject and predicate – turn God, the subject for theology, into the "divine" as predicate of the human – and the alienated truths of theology become truths repossessed in humanism ...'. See Turner's *Faith, Reason and the Existence of God,* Cambridge University Press, 2004, p. 229.
39 C. Smith, p. 86.
40 Ibid.
41 Cited in *Meister Eckhart: Teacher and Preacher,* p. 256.
42 Ibid., p. 257.
43 Ibid., p. 123f.
44 B. McGinn, *The Mystical Thought of Meister Eckhart,* Crossroad, New York, 2001, p. 113.
45 See his *Meister Eckhart: Mystical Theologian,* SPCK, London, 1991, p. 180 and *passim.*
46 Quotation from: *Faith, Reason and the Existence of God,* Cambridge University Press, Cambridge, England, 2004, p. 99.
47 See Turner's *The Darkness of God: Negativity in Christian Mysticism,* Cambridge University Press, Cambridge, England, 1995, p. 138ff. Eckhart's use of *abegescheidenheit* and *Gelâzenheit* is preceded by Marguerite's use of *l'aneántissement*: the annihilation of that which prevents me from becoming who I truly am.
48 Ibid., p. 156.
49 In *Julian of Norwich: Showings,* LT Ch. 54. Trans. E. Colledge & J. Walsh, Paulist Press, Mahwah, NJ, 1978.
50 Turner, p. 160.
51 Ibid., p. 162.
52 Paul Rorem reminds us: historically there has been a multiplicity of negative theologies. Furthermore: 'It is a misconstrual of negative theology to regard the

apophatic as a free-floating epistemological principle for individuals, isolated from the cataphatic, from its biblical origins, and from liturgical communities of faith'. Quotation from Rorem's 'Negative Theologies and the Cross', p. 452.

53 Ridler, p. 6.

54 A question which might concern theists is as follows: How can we best (re)incarnate 'inter-being' within an over-individualized culture? If 'inter-being' is to be manifested, 'interlocution' is required. This carries the risk of the conversation slipping sideways into relativism. A second question might be: How can 'spiritual humanism' best be articulated, in a way that is theistic (yet declines to freight theism with every atrocity that has resulted from it)?

55 They could well have cited an aphorism from Pseudo-Dionysius: 'There is no kind of thing which God is, and there is no kind of thing which God is not'.

56 Without *śūnyatā* (or the Western equivalent, purity of heart), might not all our putative concerns with 'spirituality' be distorted by projections?

57 Surrender is not necessarily to be equated with submission. The former involves a conscious choice, whereas the latter might not.

58 In Buddhist terms, surrender is often understood as yielding to *śūnyatā* (emptiness; or what David Loy calls 'ungroundedness'). Loy understands surrender as disclosing 'ungroundedness' to be the source of spirituality. It is also 'something' formless, transcending the self. Unusually (in my readings of Buddhist expositors) Loy does not shy away from a notion of transcendence, albeit one that excludes a higher or inherent reality. Loy's non-dualism points in a somewhat different direction from the use of non-dualism in my reflections. See the Notes to my Introduction for Loy's description of three main types of non-dualism. In addition to the book quoted there, see also Loy's *Lack and Transcendence: The Problem of Death and Life in Psychotherapy, Existentialism, and Buddhism* (Humanity Books, Amherst, NY, 1996).

59 Margoliouth, vol. 2, p. 196f.; italics in the original.

60 Cited in *Meister Eckhart: Teacher and Preacher*, p. 298.

61 In *The Mystical Thought . . .*, p. 47.

62 From *Sermon 83*, Colledge & McGinn, p. 208.

63 In *The Mystical Thought . . .*, p. 99.

64 Ibid., p. 149.

65 An Eckhartian-style aphorism from the tradition of *Advaita Vedānta* is as follows: 'I am one eye in the big Eye of Consciousness'. I discuss *Advaita Vedānta* in Chapters 4 and 5 of these reflections.

66 From *Sermon 57*, Walshe, vol. 2, p. 87. (This sermon is #12 in the critical German edition.)

67 From *Sermon 7*, Walshe, vol. 1, p. 65. (This sermon is #76 in the critical German edition.)

68 McGinn, p. 149.

69 See *Meister Eckhart on Divine Knowledge* (1st edn 1977), C. F. Kelley, Dharma Café Books, Cobb, CA, 2009, p. 149.

70 Ibid.

71 Ibid., p. 64.

72 Colledge & McGinn, p. 187.

73 Kelley, p. 154.

74 Ibid., p. 49.

75 Ibid., p. 163.

76   Ibid., p. 68.
77   Ibid., p. 168.
78   Ibid.
79   Ibid., p. xviii f.
80   Phil. 3:13, NRSV.
81   Ibid., p. 108.
82   Ibid., p. 120f.
83   Transliterated, the Hebrew is: *Eheieh asher Eheieh.* If the second *Eheieh* is taken as
     a reflection or manifestation of the first *Eheieh,* then it might appear that a dualism
     is presupposed, as between a single element and the manifestation of that element.
     In Christian thought, a possible dualism is more evident, as when the 'Father' or
     unmanifested Reality finds manifestation in the 'Son'.
84   The *I Am (aham asi)* was perhaps already a pivotal expression within Hinduism.
     In a cosmology wherein everything perpetually dissolves and is remade, only the
     I Am can be regarded as abiding forever. In Hindu understandings, the primordial
     I Am is found (or rather, refound) within the affective experience of Realization of
     the non-dual 'Self'. Since polarity would appear to be necessary for an experience *of*
     something, the experience of *I Am* need not necessarily be viewed as either monistic
     or dualistic. For present purposes, I am tending to equate the *I Am* with the *Ātmān*
     (the 'Self').
85   The Gospel of John conveys a picture of Jesus as entering such a deep experience of
     Spirit that he discovers himself to be, beyond regular names and forms, a participant
     in the *I Am.* So-called mystics have long enjoined that we should faithfully attend to
     such a consciousness of *I Am* for ourselves. Far from engendering self-preoccupation,
     this attention-giving is held to result in an experiential sense of inseparability from
     the divine and from all creatures.
86   Praying before the icons, the Orthodox worshipper salutes the departed saints as
     '... guests come to the sacramental feast, as in Christ all live and are not separated'. This
     is the view of the inestimable writer Nikolai Gogol (d.1852). See his *Meditations on the
     Divine Liturgy*, Holy Trinity Monastery Press, Jordanville, NY, 1952 & 1985, p. 20.
87   Kearney adds that the divine '... seems to say something like this: *I am who may be if
     you continue to keep my word and struggle for the coming of justice*' (p. 37f.)
88   Ibid., p. 121.
89   Ibid.
90   *Advaita* has proved to be the most influential of the various *Vedāntic* schools. *Advaita*
     puts forward the view that the universe is indivisibly a unity and therefore non-dual.
     Within such a view of reality, the divine is frequently conceived as neither totally
     identical with the rest of reality, nor individually separate from it. Initially expressed
     in the *Upanishads* (and in the explanatory text *Mandukya Karika*), *Advaita* was
     given extensive exposition by Śaṅkara (d. ca. 820). A standard treatise on *Advaita* is
     attributed to him. It is *The Crown Gem of Discrimination* (Skt. *Vivekachudamani*).
91   Ramana Maharshi followed the tradition of Śaṅkara in repeatedly referring to the
     false identification of the 'I' with the body, mind or senses. For example: 'The real Self
     is the infinite "I". That "I" is perfection. It is eternal. It has no origin and no end. The
     other "I" is born and also dies. It is impermanent'. Quotation from: *Be As You Are:
     The Teachings of Sri Ramana Maharshi* (D. Godman, ed.), Penguin/Arkana, London,
     1985, p. 74.
92   Gal. 2:20, REB.

93 REB.
94 Various writers have linked surrender and union with that aspect of evolution which might be moving us forward towards higher consciousness and deeper communion. The following quotation is from Barbara Fiand. 'Self-surrender and subsequent union for the sake of greater complexity has been the evolutionary story of the universe from its beginning. . . . We might say that, in us, this cosmic love story of union toward greater consciousness longs to express itself in total awareness, in a universal, all embracive *yes* that allows for full realization'. Fiand, B., *Awe-Filled Wonder: The Interface of Science and Spirituality*, Paulist Press, Mahwah, NJ, 2008, p. 29. For an interdisciplinary study which assiduously connects a kenotic Christology with evolution, see Claire Deane-Drummond's *Christ and Evolution: Wonder and Wisdom*, SCM Press, London, 2009. A theodramatic framework allows Deane-Drummond to engage with evolutionary change from a participant's viewpoint and to bring Christology and science into proximity.
95 B. McGinn, 'Mystical Consciousness: A Modest Proposal', in *Spiritus 1, 2008*, Baltimore, MD, p. 51.
96 Ibid., p. 54.
97 Ibid.
98 R. J. Woods, *Meister Eckhart: Master of Mystics*, Continuum, London, 2011, pp. 188 and 189.

Chapter 3

1 Cf. Hadewijch's spirit which '. . . sinks with frenzy in [the abyss] of Love's fruition'. Quotation from: *Hadewijch: The Complete Works,* trans. & intro. by Mother Columba Hart, Paulist Press, Mahwah, NJ, 1980, p. 244.
2 *Paradiso*, canto 28.
3 *Julian of Norwich: Showings,* LT 86. Trans. E. Colledge & J. Walsh, Paulist Press, Mahwah, New Jersey, 1978, p. 342. Hereinafter referred to as LT.
4 Ibid., p. 184.
5 Since my own prejudice tends to favour *experience* over *conceptualization*, I need to be careful not to push the two apart. A fundamental opposition of 'experience' and 'doctrine' is hardly likely to prove coherent for any recognizable spiritual tradition.
6 I suggest that Eckhart, Julian and Traherne might regard the Trinity less as a normative teaching than as a suggestive interpretation; that they consider the Trinity, not so much as a *theologoumenon* but as a theopoem to be experienced.
7 LT 27, p. 225.
8 LT 28, p. 227.
9 LT 49, p. 265.
10 John Swanson, writing in *Julian: Woman of our Day,* edited by Robert Llewelyn, Darton, Longman and Todd, London, 1985, p. 79f.
11 LT 59 and 60, p. 297.
12 G. M. Jantzen, *Julian of Norwich: Mystic and Theologian,* Wipf & Stock, Eugene, OR, 2000 edn, p. 124.
13 P. Donohue-White, 'Reading Divine Maternity in Julian of Norwich', in *Spiritus 5,* 2005, Baltimore, MD, p. 25.

14 Ibid.
15 LT 50, p. 266.
16 LT 58, p. 294.
17 Ibid.
18 LT 60, p. 298.
19 Ibid.
20 LT 46, p. 259.
21 ST 1–2 and 33 but especially LT 33.
22 LT 54, p. 285.
23 *The Prayers and Meditations of Saint Anselm*, trans. Sr. Benedicta Ward, 1973, p. 153.
24 Sr. Mary Paul, *All Shall Be Well: Julian of Norwich and the Compassion of God*, SLG Press, Convent of the Incarnation, Oxford, 1976, p. 26.
25 Ibid., p. 31.
26 K. L. Reinhard, 'Joy to the Father, Bliss to the Son: Unity and the Motherhood Theology of Julian of Norwich', in *Anglican Theological Review 89:4*, 2007, Evanston, IL, p. 644.
27 Ibid., p. 645.
28 K. Dearborn, 'The Crucified Christ as the Motherly God: The Theology of Julian of Norwich', in *Scottish Journal of Theology 55:3*, 2002, Cambridge University Press, pp. 283 and 298.
29 Ibid., p. 297.
30 J. A. Lamm, 'Revelation as Exposure in Julian of Norwich's *Showings*', in *Spiritus 5*, 2005, Baltimore, MD, p. 60.
31 Ibid., p. 61.
32 *Showings*, p. 183.
33 Ibid., p. 184.
34 D. Bohm, *Wholeness and the Implicate Order*, Routledge & Kegan Paul, London, 1983, p. 177.
35 Ibid., p. 209.
36 ST, p. 164.
37 LT, 81, p. 336f.
38 Essay in L. Lomperis & S. Stanbury, eds, *Feminist Approaches to the Body in Medieval Literature*, University of Pennsylvania Press, PA, 1993, p. 157.
39 Ibid., p. 161.
40 *Showings*, LT 54, p. 285.
41 From the Clifton Wolters translation, *Julian of Norwich: Revelations of Divine Love*, Penguin, Harmondsworth, 1966, LT 55, p. 159.
42 Apparent 'opposites' are relevant to a discussion about *Shiva Nataraja* in Chapter 4 of these reflections.
43 Such a 'falling away' will include the languages of theology. These always need to be sceptical about any pretensions to 'objectivity'. A *kenotic* commitment will not elevate ontological claims to the point of reification. A question might arise: As my personal experience becomes more 'impersonal', and my way of relating to the other/Other becomes less self-conscious, how much will I still recognize difference? Will I reach the place (or the space) where neither party to the relation becomes a subject or an object?
44 Within the *Upanishadic* traditions, the non-dual, supreme 'Self' (the *Ātmān)* is often (but not always) equated with *Brahman* (the Absolute) from which it is ultimately

inseparable. The 'Self' is never a synonym for the modern, so-called empirical self (small 's'). The 'Self' is not something to be literally discovered or journeyed towards. In one of the main senses of its usage, it is *what we are* beneath the veil of ignorance.

45 Cf. Catherine Keller's observation: 'We move through particular relations to particular things to glimpse the unseen interrelatedness of all things – and always back to the particular'. Quotation from: C. Keller, *From a Broken Web: Separation, Sexism and Self,* Beacon Press, Boston, MA, 1986, p. 158.

46 Cf. Charles Taylor's phrase 'a divine affirmation of the human' which helped my orientation here. See his *Sources of the Self: the Making of the Modern Identity,* Harvard University Press, Cambridge, MA, 1989, p. 521.

47 Quotation from: *Walking* (Margoliouth, vol. 2, p. 135f.; italics in the original)

48 The next chapter includes 'a poet's version' of an aspect of Derrida's work.

49 This is not to imply that *Advaita Vedānta*, for example, is devoid of mystery. The next two chapters will allude to the *Vedāntin* declaration of 'the self within the Self'. If we *are* the Self (the *Ātman*) we are of course inseparable from the ultimate mystery.

50 NRSV.

51 Traditional Indian usage regards 'Consciousness' (capital 'C') as the substance of all things, or as infinite Mind, and not as 'awareness' in the colloquial Western sense.

Chapter 4

1 *That thou art!* (literal Skt.). My preference might be: *You are That!*

2 A caveat regarding this rendering of the Hebrew was mentioned in Chapter 2.

3 The non-dual 'Self' (the *Ātman*) or innermost principle of humanity was briefly mentioned in relation to Eckhart's 'true nature' (see Chapter 2). Further reference will be made (in the present chapter and in the next) to the 'Self' in relation to *Advaita Vedānta.*

4 Cited in D. Godman, ed., *Be As You Are: The Teachings of Sri Ramana Maharshi,* Penguin/Arkana, London, 1985, p. 196.

5 Cited in A. Osborne, ed., *The Teachings of Ramana Maharshi*, Rider/Century Hutchinson, London, 1987, p. 192.

6 Cf. A description by Jack Kornfield: 'Emptiness refers to the underlying non-separation of life and the fertile ground of energy that gives rise to all forms of life. Our world and sense of self is a play of patterns. Any identity we can grasp is transient, tentative'. *A Path with Heart,* Bantam, NY, 1993, p. 200.

7 Cf. Henri Le Saux (Swami Abhishiktananda) who writes: 'As long as I distinguish the *within* from myself who seeks the within, I am not within. He who seeks and that which is sought vanish in the last stage, and there is nothing left but pure light, undivided, self-luminous'. Quotation from: *Ascent to the Depth of the Heart* (R. Panikkar, ed.) ISPCK, Delhi, 1998, p. 146. For the latter decades of his life, Abhishiktananda was both *Advaitin* and Christian. He managed this tension by emphasizing that our experience of the divine is 'meant' to transcend doctrinal or conceptual incompatibilities. Parts of the present reflections attempt to express my agreement with this perspective. There are obvious problems. The aim of the *Advaitin* is to move beyond personal identity and to be immersed in the pure Consciousness or the Infinite One. This involves the transcendence of *namarupa* (the world of *names*

or mental phenomena and *forms* or physical phenomena). A Christian might rightly feel defensive, here, about the status of the phenomenal world and about the Western privileging of objective theological claims over against the transient nature of our experiences.

8   L. Freeman, *Common Ground: Letters to a World Community of Meditators*, Continuum, NY, 1999, p. 35f.

9   W. Smith, *Christian Gnosis: From St. Paul to Meister Eckhart*, Sophia Perennis, San Rafael, CA, 2008, p. 147. For a helpful explanation of the unsatisfactory consequences of translating '*advaita*' as 'non-duality' then proceeding to regard non-duality in an abstract manner, cut loose from experience, see Raimon Panikkar's *The Rhythm of Being*, Orbis Books, NY, 2010, pp. 216–24.

10   Ibid., p. 145.

11   Ibid.

12   Ibid., p. 183.

13   Ibid., p. 218.

14   And they regard their neighbours as neither 'other' nor 'the same'.

15   In classical Hinduism, for example, the One is generally held to be indefinable and 'attributeless'. It is not necessarily to be conflated with any theistic expression. But, whatever the gradings of conceptual thought, it is regrettable that in both *Vedāntin* and Christian life, the experience of *I Am* quickly became subsumed by moralism, ritual and abstract formulae. Intuition and spontaneity, it seems, are doomed to be taken over by *namarupa* ('name and form'). The signs and symbols, and their elaborations, were intended merely as pointers to that which is beyond name and form. In effect, Eckhart and to a lesser extent Traherne and Julian, aspired to peel away the outer 'names and forms' on the onion of truth (*satyam*).

16   I am thinking, for example, of novels and essays by Marilynne Robinson (b.1943).

17   See *Sources of the Self*, mentioned earlier.

18   Ibid., p. 31f.

19   Ibid., p. 43.

20   C. Taylor, *The Ethics of Authenticity*, Harvard University Press, Cambridge, MA, 1991, p. 17.

21   Ibid., p. 21.

22   *Sources of the Self*, p. 28.

23   Ibid., p. 35.

24   Ibid., p. 72.

25   Ibid., p. 77.

26   But although the eternal non-dual 'Self' has a share in transcendence, it is not necessarily (within its own tradition) equated with 'the All and the One'. Nor is this 'Self' always equated with the pure Consciousness, although perhaps it might be regarded as 'root-Consciousness', of which Consciousness is a reflection. Can it be said that Eckhart's 'our true nature' precisely parallels the 'Self' of the *Upanishadic* traditions? There are different conceptual systems here; even so, in both systems the 'primordial true nature' becomes evident when a person develops (or reverts to) a transmuted consciousness.

27   J. B. Cobb, *Transforming Christianity and the World*, Orbis Books, NY, 1999, p. 135. (I might add that pluralism is sometimes erroneously confused with cultural effeteness and/or moral relativism.)

28   Ibid., p. 74.

29   Simone Weil (d.1943, aged 34) features in section two of the poem *Transgressive Saints*, utilized in Chapter 3.

30   1973 [1951] p. 145.

31   *Journals* [1958] p. 97.

32   1973 [1951], p. 111f.

33   As to the art of theology, Gadamer implies that no sensible theologizing can exclude multi-dimensional conversations and such experiences as might lead to the rewriting of one's preconceived positions. This is not to say that personal experience is an adequate basis for either theology or spirituality. As to the plastic arts, and to poetry, Gadamer says that they serve far more than a symbolic role. Their playful and festive character can transport the participant (the reader of a poem, for example) out of ordinary time into 'fulfilled' time. In reaching fresh understandings (via a poem, say) we bring our prejudgements with us. We need to acknowledge that the tradition within which we 'sit' will generate our prejudgements, *and also* and that these judgements do not always distort our understandings. In his philosophical hermeneutics, Gadamer represents a break from subjectivism. As I understand him, he holds that art, for instance, is *not* merely a matter of taste. See Hans-Georg Gadamer, *Truth and Method,* Continuum, NY, 1989: 2nd revised edition; this edition 2004.

34   1973 [1951], p. 159.

35   *The Need for Roots*, 1978 [1952], pp. 120–1.

36   C. Bourgeault, '*Centering Prayer and Attention of the Heart*', *Crosscurrents 59:1,* March 2009, p. 25f, emphasis hers.

37   But of course the Shin gift of grace, and the response of trust, needs to be understood as occurring within a different cosmological context than (e.g.) a Christian one.

38   Some Buddhists have difficulty accepting that Christianity construes itself as a religion of transformative experience, and not primarily as a religion of faith in something handed down from elsewhere. In my experience, Christians generally construe themselves as discoverers of that which is *really* real, not on someone else's say-so, but within lived experience. Such an inner epiphany is taken to imply transformation, generally speaking, into the capacity to love all other beings.

39   Barrett, 1978, p. 474.

40   Ibid., p. 473.

41   I now understand that my reactivity was less against 'divine love relations' than against an idealization of power which can perhaps lie, poorly concealed, beneath 'Christian' projections of divine omnipotence, and so on

42   Mitchell employs a traditional Christian metaphysic and ontology. He has declared himself to be a convert to Christianity from a background in Soto Zen.

43   D. W. Mitchell, *Spirituality and Emptiness: The Dynamics of Spiritual Life in Buddhism and Christianity,* Paulist Press, NY, 1991, p. 65.

44   Ibid., p. 71

45   Eckhartian 'nothingness' (*niht* or *nihil*) has differing applications, as between God and God's creatures, as mentioned in Chapter 2 of the present study.

46   Ibid., pp. 23 and 24.

47   Ibid., p. 58.

48   Ibid., p. 59.

49   In B. J. Lanzetta, 'Three Categories of Nothingness in Eckhart', *The Journal of Religion 72:2,* April 1992, The University of Chicago Press, Chicago, IL, pp. 248–68. (Apropos the Martha/Mary story in Lk. 10, the Lanzetta article is also noted in Chapter 2.)

50 Ibid., p. 263.

51 Ibid., p. 267.

52 In Lanzetta's reading of Eckhart the trope of not resting in purported finalities has resonance with my current interpretation of theological propositions. Do they not culminate in further questions? Are they not therefore capable of being viewed as modes of transcendence? Cf. Hans-Georg Gadamer: 'All that is asked is that we remain open to the meaning of the other person or text. . . . *The hermeneutical task becomes of itself a questioning of things* and is always in part so defined. . . . It is the tyranny of hidden prejudices that makes us deaf to what speaks to us in tradition. . . . And there is one prejudice of the Enlightenment that defines its essence: the fundamental prejudice of the Enlightenment is the prejudice against prejudice itself, which denies tradition its power'. Quotations from: *Truth and Method*, Continuum, NY, 1989: 2nd revised edition; this edition 2004, p. 271ff. (italics in the original).

53 J. B. Metz, *Poverty of Spirit*, Paulist Press, NY, 1998, p. 43.

54 Ibid., p. 21.

55 Ibid., p. 43.

56 S. Moore, *Jesus the Liberator of Desire*, Crossroad, NY, 1989, p. 42.

57 Cf. Statements of a *kenotic* nature attributed to Jesus, such as Lk. 14:26–7 and Mt. 16:24.

58 S. Breton, *The Word and the Cross*, Fordham University Press, NY, 2002, p. 90.

59 Ibid., p. 94.

60 Ibid., p. 96.

61 Ibid., p. 99.

62 *Kenosis* does not relate only to the divine movement towards humanity. Those who follow Christ will adopt *kenotic* attitudes; a range of NT passages relating to the service of Christ enjoin his servants to divest themselves, as per Eckhart's releasement (see Chapter 2). Cf. 'Think of us in this way, as servants of Christ and stewards of God's mysteries' (1 Cor. 4:1 NRSV). Divine *kenosis* is enframed within every encouragement to embody active sharing and compassion. It is understood that it is given to humanity to actualize the divine in concrete ways.

63 As, for example, in the work of Gianni Vattimo, one of whose stated aims is to de-foundationalize Christianity in pursuit of its original impetus of faith and love. As is the case with Thomas Altizer, Vattimo holds that Christianity legitimizes secularisation and the 'end of religion' understood as cultic reification.

64 David Kelly, writing in the Australian literary journal *Famous Reporter*, number 40, Dec. 2009, pp. 158–62.

65 Cf. A statement of longing attributed to Jesus: 'With desire I have desired . . .'. (Lk. 22:15).

66 I wish to emphasize that my comments regarding Derrida are tentative glosses, relevant because Derrida argues that apparent dualities are 'conditions of possibility'.

67 That is to say, without the reification which might approach a form of totalitarian thinking.

68 In my view, twentieth century literary theorists tended to embrace Derrida somewhat uncritically. On the other hand, biblical scholars initially trivialized his originality and significance, and indeed, trivialized the potential value of his 'post-religion spirituality'. Or so it seemed to me. But Derrida was reminding them, in French baroque profusion, that their faith did not consist in the correspondence between propositions and things. There had never been such a 'thing' as 'objective

knowledge'. There was only ever the response of faith to Christ's *kerygma*. This *kerygma* was not a peculiar selection of metaphysical statements but a declaration that the future of humanity depended on activating the commandment of love, in Derrida's case the post-metaphysical truth of love. But it remains love; love in its only true sense of *practicing* love. Derrida agrees with Kierkegaard (and Dostoyevsky) here. On this view, other forms within 'Christendom' tend to be sub-Christian. If they do not feature a community of people who are practicing the truth of love, they are anti-Christian.

69   The Māhayāna has been far more stringent than Christianity in pointing to the irrelevance of abstract notions in the experience of awakening to one's true self. If I desire to move beyond my false, delusory self, how on earth are musings about cause and effect, truth, essence and substance, *when treated abstractly*, going to advance my desire?

70   The aphorism '*One goes, and one IS*' attempts to express the matter. As the vision of the *I Am (aham asmi)* is revealed, the sense of a personal self diminishes. In the symbolic world of *Vedānta*, it is said that there is but one infinite Selfhood, one infinite 'I'. And from an ultimate perspective, the phrase *Tat tvam asi* comes in. As mentioned, it can be translated as 'You are It!' but is often rendered as 'This thou art!' The relation between 'I' and 'thou' can be said to be neither dualistic nor monistic. Rather, the 'thou' can be said to permit or to allow the 'I' and the 'I' can be thought of as allowing the 'thou'. Continual, unobstructed vision is implied; we would cease to indulge opinions or slavishly adhere to concepts. We would not report a vision; the vision would declare itself. The one true 'I' would announce itself in the experience of *I Am*.

71   In every milieu, the question of interpretation will be basic. A follower of Gadamer here, I accept that genuine reflection is hermeneutical and bound to involve constant, imaginative conversation.

72   Judith Beveridge (2003), reviewing James Charlton's *Luminous Bodies* in *The Write Stuff*, vol. 7, accessed 6 December 2011, <www.the-write-stuff.com.au/archives/vol-7/james_charlton/review_beveridge.html>.

73   Pardalote Press, Hobart, 2007.

74   Ibid., p. 71f.

75   But 'otherness', particularly with reference to the divine, can be emphasized so strongly as to effectively place this 'other' beyond all possibility of any relation to *anything*. Hence the desire, from the early Christian centuries onwards, to configure the divine in perichoretic terms. I mentioned, in Chapter 1, a conception of God as 'interconnecting Spirit'. Traherne would everywhere seem to approve of such words.

76   Published by Vintage, London, 1997.

77   However, the Levinasian preoccupation with alterity does not, in my view, take adequate account of the legitimate needs and desires of persons.

78   S. McFague, *Super, Natural Christians: How We Should Love Nature*, Fortress Press, Minneapolis, MN, 1997, p. 116.

79   S. McFague, *The Body of God: An Ecological Theology*, Fortress Press, Minneapolis, MN, 1993, p. 14.

80   Ibid.

81   By onto-theology I mean a representational attempt at 'writing God'. It is notable how far foundational or metaphysical ways of doing theology have moved beyond an assumed sense of the givenness of reality. Following Kant, we know that we do not

understand or perceive empirical objects in a pre-given, realistic way. Whatever we perceive, think, and understand does not arise as a given. It is constructed through our syntactic, semantic and ethnographic backgrounds. We do not so much perceive reality as conceive it: We are knowing subjects. Hence the necessary reappraisal of traditional metaphysics (and ontology). By the same token, I am not suggesting that Heidegger's critique of onto-theology constitutes an adequate critique of any particular theology, still less of any form of theism.

82 Cf. Henri Le Saux (Swami Abhishiktananda) who writes: 'OM is the only *japa* (repetitive prayer) that does not distract. Every other word is *phantasma*, whether it be Christian or Hindu. It settles on a thought, no matter how insubstantial it may be. OM is not something thought. It is 'beheld', breathed with my *prana*, beaten out by my heart, seen in what the eyes see, the ears hear, the body touches, the nostrils smell, etc. OM is the unuttered name of the *ātman* and therefore of the *Brahman* who is beyond and before the *aham*'. Quotation from: *Ascent to the Depth of the Heart* (R. Panikkar, ed.), ISPCK, Delhi, 1998, p. 312.

83 There is death (cruciform-like?) and rebirth (resurrection-like?)

84 Within the symbolic structures of both Shaivism and Christianity, my primary ignorance is held to be my tendency to identify myself with my body, or with my mind, or with my emotions. But Shiva's fire, regarded as the fire of my own true Self, will burn up the false self, destroying the sense of separation and the false identifications. (The foregoing sentence is cast in terms of conventional truth. *Vedānta* deals with absolute truth; it does not allude to a 'false self'.) I will thereby awaken to the *I Am*. The knowingness of the *I Am* (of my appropriation, within lived experience) is held to be the core of the pure Consciousness.

85 This might qualify as akin to Vattimo's 'weak theology', aligned with processive and panentheistic ways of configuring the divine, as against 'strong theology' with its metaphysically assured pronouncements. The poem *Tasman Peninsula*, quoted earlier, might be a clearer example of 'weak theology'.

86 Another instance of 'weak theology'? The extract is from *Truganini's Soliloquy* in my collection *So Much Light* (2007), p. 48f.

87 It can scarcely be overemphasized that Eckhart, Julian and Traherne are 'mystics' *and* activists. Their advocacy of 'the inner life' should not be construed as passive. Although 'mystical' they are known to have lived active, outwardly engaged lives.

88 In the literary quarterly *Overland*, no. 194, Autumn 2009, p. 90f. Other reviewers who have touched on my poetry's non-dual aspect include Geoff Page (in *Australian Book Review*, May 2002, p. 37f., and likewise on ABC Radio National's 'The Book Show', 26 March 2008); Philip Harvey (in *Eureka Street*, July–August 2002, p. 50f.); Anuraag Sharma (in *Famous Reporter*, no. 28, December 2003, pp. 115–17); Anne Kellas (in *Famous Reporter*, no. 25, July 2002, pp. 190–2); James Norcliffe (in *Island*, no. 113, Winter 2008, pp. 52–4); Sheelagh Wegman (in *Tasmanian Anglican*, April 2008, p. 13); David Kelly (in *Famous Reporter*, no. 40, December 2009, pp. 158–62) and Margaret Bradstock (in *Five Bells*, 15:1, Summer 2007–8, pp. 58–60). In similar vein, Janet Upcher mentions non-dualism in her *Afterword* to my collection *So Much Light* (2007). In a cover-blurb, Amanda Lohrey describes my earlier book *Luminous Bodies* (2001) as follows: 'Charlton's poems are poems-of-spirit and poems of a clearly seen material world: a "true" materialism which grows out of a non-dualistic vision'.

89 Combining something of both Christian and Hindu understandings, I would regard a sage as someone who has realized Oneness with the Spirit of Life that is the Self of all.

90 Hence Ramana's tradition understands the experiential knowledge of the non-dual Self as devoid of both 'I' and 'mine'. Existentially, it is held to be True Seeing, devoid of illusion and delusion.

91 The *Vedāntic* approach of *advaitins* has traditionally attracted criticism from some *Shaivites*. The form of enquiry in *Advaita Vedānta* is said to be so austere that it fosters a 'disembodied' attitude. One might imagine certain Christians chiming in, with additional and ill-based criticisms of a supposed idolatry and pantheism.

92 Cited in Osborne, 1987, p. 160.

93 Tape recording of Ramana, cited in A. Osborne, *The Collected Works of Ramana Maharshi*, Weiser, York Beach, ME, 1997, p. 38. This particular book was sincerely assembled, but with less than authoritative understandings of either Sanskrit or Tamil. It is now regarded, at the bookshop at Ramana's ashram, as having been superceded by *The Collected Works of Sri Ramana Maharshi*, Sri Ramanasramam, Tiruvannamalai, Tamil Nadu, 2009.

94 Extract from Ramana Maharshi's *Reality in Forty Verses*, published in *The Collected Works of Sri Ramana Maharshi*, p. 120 (noted above).

95 Cited in A. Osborne, *Ramana Maharshi and the Path of Self-Knowledge,* Rider and Company, London, 1954, p. 20f.

Chapter 5

1 *pari passu*, the Johannine writer endorses the equal apostolate of women and men.

2 The reported statements of Jesus regarding 'I am . . .' (*ego eimi*), seem to branch out from the Johannine prologue and its multiple use of the verb 'to be' (*einai*).

3 Laurel C. Schneider explores what it might mean to speak of an embodied God, in *Beyond Monotheism: A Theology of Multiplicity*, Routledge, London, 2008. She holds that divine unity is best configured through an acceptance of multiplicity, viz, that the Incarnation is concerned with necessarily multiple and mutable bodies. Referring to the story of the woman at the well (pp. 117–20) Schneider relates the water to movement, to the kind of fluidity that might augment habitually static views of God.

4 In 2009 a major study of the 'heart' of *Romans* affirmed a less individualistic and more participatory reading of the apostle than is often allowed. Douglas A. Campbell's book, *The Deliverance of God: An Apocalyptic Rereading of Justification in Paul* (Eerdmans, Grand Rapids, MI.) argues that Ro. 5–8 is central to the Pauline account of deliverance and sanctification. Campbell writes: 'Paul's account of sanctification *is* the gospel' (p. 934).

5 Cf. Col. 1:19–20 NRSV: 'For in him all the fullness of God was pleased to dwell, and through him God was pleased to reconcile to himself all things, whether on earth or in heaven, by making peace through the blood of his cross'.

6 This is not to imply that postmodernism is a singular intellectual entity.

7 I assume the following: If we are taken to one horizon of 'awakening', another horizon will open up before us. In other words, at the level of conventional truth, our spiritual evolution cannot be said to reach an end point.

8 Cf. Jens Zimmermann, who writes: 'Theology must shed any pretensions to timeless, absolute knowledge and will do itself a great favor by abandoning a scientific model of unmediated, naked truth. Instead theology should embrace a hermeneutical model

of self-understanding in which truth is not naked but clothed in the self-giving otherness of God, who offers himself in the incarnation for our contemplation and emulation. The incarnation provides what postmodern ethical philosophy seeks: it embodies radical transcendence in history and time with a human face, and it offers a social subjectivity as persons in relation'. Quotation from: J. Zimmermann, *Recovering Theological Hermeneutics: An Incarnational-Trinitarian Theory of Interpretation*, Baker Academic, Grand Rapids, MI, 2004, p. 318.

9   As, indeed, the body goes about its work of creating. Bodies obviously are continually circulating, absorbing and disseminating, prompting this thought: Does not all creativity perpetually *circulate*?

10 I am grateful to Dr. Cullan Joyce for explaining that perichoresis is employed by Maximus and other patristics as a kind of synonym for non-duality. (Pseudo-Dionysius is well-known to have provided a version of divine relations which is compatible with non-dualistic interpretations. His work is outside the range of these reflections.)

11 Maximus brings the apophatic recognition of unknowable transcendence directly back to earth, that is, to his trust in the divine incarnation of Jesus who becomes the Christ. See, for example, 'Chapters on Knowledge' in *Maximus the Confessor: Selected Writings*, G. C. Berthold, (d. & trans., Paulist Press, New York, NY, 1985, pp. 127–79.

12 L. Thunberg, *Microcosm and Mediator: The Theological Anthropology of Maximus the Confessor*, Open Court, Chicago, IL, 1995, 2nd edn, p. 433f.

13 The importance, to Eckhart, of the lived experience of truth was discussed in Chapter 2 (where, as elsewhere, I have co-opted the word Realization). Julian and Traherne 'enact' their apparent experience of immediacy within their prose and poetry; they theorize less than Eckhart, although all three writers are capable of issuing injunctions to the hearer or reader to enter direct (unmediated?) experience of the 'matter in hand' (cf. the Buddhist 'Great Matter').

14 The putative indivisibility of 'pure' transcendence and immanence has been briefly canvassed in Chapter 2 and *passim*.

15 The quotation is sourced from *Byzantine Philosophy* by Basil Tatakis (N. J. Moutafakis, trans. & intro.) Hackett Publishing Co., Indianapolis, IN, 2003 [1949], p. 67.

16 These words are those of Gloria L. Schaab. See her *The Creative Suffering of the Triune God*, Oxford University Press, NY, 2007, p. 194. Schaab unpacks the Trinitarian motif as follows: 'By sharing the suffering of the beloved creation, the Triune God demonstrates that suffering itself is not redemptive and salvific. Rather, it is the love, the creativity, and the infinite possibility within the Divine that are redemptive through continuous creativity, unconditional presence, and freely offered grace' (ibid., p. 195).

17 Jean-Luc Marion, whose concern with 'Christian idolaters' is mentioned in these reflections, is one of many theo-philosophers who attempt to '. . . do theology without reinscribing it in metaphysics' (Horner, p. 74). Indeed, he '. . . claims to overcome metaphysics by way of theology' (ibid.). See Robyn Horner's *Jean-Luc Marion: A Theo-logical Introduction*, Ashgate Publishing Ltd., Aldershot, HANTS, 2005. See also Kevin Hart (ed.), *Counter Experiences: Reading Jean-Luc Marion*, University of Notre Dame Press, Notre Dame, IN, 2007.

18 I discuss the *kenotic* hymn of Phil. 2 in Chapter 4. As to the claim that Christ reflects the divine fullness (*plerôma*) and conveys it to his Church, see Eph. 1:17–23; 3:14–19; Col. 1:19–20; 2:8–10.

19 Cf. Catherine LaCugna (1952–97) who writes: '. . . God and the creature . . . meet
    as persons in communion. . . . A relational ontology focuses on personhood,
    relationship, and communion as the modality of all existence'. Quotation from:
    C. M. LaCugna, *God for Us: The Trinity and Christian Life*, Harper Collins, San
    Francisco, CA, 1991, p. 250.
20 Cf. Jn 15.
21 The word 'puzzle' could be preferable to 'aporia' because of the latter's traditional
    connotation vis-à-vis a processive discourse coming up against an aporia which
    eventually shows the process to have structural problems. The puzzlement with
    Panikkar might be of a lesser order, and might relate to the necessary ambiguity of his
    attempt to reconcile corporeality with transcendent subjectivity.
22 R. Panikkar, *The Experience of God: Icons of the Mystery*, Fortress Press, Minneapolis,
    MN, 2006, p. 136.
23 Ibid., p. 142.
24 Ibid., p. 136.
25 Ibid. Basically, Panikkar understands the structure of Reality to be triadic: It is
    comprised of the Divine, the Human and the Cosmic. These three participate in
    'radical relativity'; that is to say, they are dependent on each other. This dependence is
    described by Panikkar as 'interindependence'. See Panikkar's exposition of his main
    ideas in *The Rhythm of Being*.
26 Panikkar, 2006, p. 134.
27 Ibid., p. 140.
28 Ibid., p. 137.
29 *Christophany: The Fullness of Man*, Orbis Books, NY, 2004, p. 115.
30 Ibid., p. 116.
31 In the Introduction to this book.
32 Panikkar, 2006, p. 139.
33 Since humankind first gained the leisure to listen to campfire stories, perhaps it has
    often been the theopoets who have stimulated others towards a return to strands of
    filiation, to 'interweave'; indeed, to 'oneing'.
34 Panikkar, 2006, p. 63.
35 Panikkar, 2004, *passim*.
36 Dutch musician/visual artist (1946–2001).
37 A major study of Panikkar's religious pluralism, under the title *The Interreligious
    Vision of Raimon Panikkar*, is forthcoming. Its author is Dr. Gerard Hall, Associate
    Professor of the Australian Catholic University's School of Theology. Hall describes
    how Panikkar elevates the subjective religious experience to a high level of
    importance in cross-cultural religious understandings. He then explores and critiques
    Panikkar's expectation of a fresh revelatory experience which might underwrite, so to
    speak, a necessary shift in spiritual and religio-political consciousness.
38 *Wonder*, verses 2–5, Ridler, p. 7.
39 A. Harvey, *The Direct Path: Creating a Journey to the Divine Through the World's
    Mystical Traditions*, Broadway Books, NY, 2000, p. 60.
40 As discussed in Chapter 2, Eckhart uses either *niht* or *nihil* for 'nothingness'.
    Creatures share nothingness, but divine nothingness is a positive figuration,
    pointing to the divine as beyond all being (therefore *niht*). As to is-ness (*Isticheit*)
    the term *wesen* ('being') is more common in Eckhart, as of course is *esse*
    ('existence').

41 In *God without Being* (trans. T. A. Carlson) Chicago University Press, Chicago, IL, 1991, p. 82.
42 McFague argues that the conceptual language of religion amounts to poetry that has become exhausted. The only possible theology, therefore, is metaphorical theology. Conceptual thought, which generates doctrine, retains value wherever it critiques the leading metaphors of a particular time and place. When metaphors cease to complement each other, writes McFague, they readily become idols. To counter an idolatry of the 'God the Father' metaphor, she proposes 'God as Friend' as a possible replacement. See S. McFague, *Metaphorical Theology: Models of God in Religious Language*, Fortress Press, Minneapolis, MN, 1982.
43 Schürmann, 2001, p. 219.
44 Ibid., p. 221.
45 Harvey, p. 110.
46 Drawing a contrast between mystics and activists, Harvey (2009) relates his experiences of both sides: 'Mystics, I saw, were mostly addicted to being, activists to doing. Both had profound narcissistic shadows that I recognized in myself. The mystic's shadow was a surreal dissociation from the body, the world, and the gruelling tasks of implementing justice. The activist's shadow lay in the messiah and martyr complexes that accompany the addiction to *doing*, with its vulnerability to burnout, rage, and despair'. Quotation from: A. Harvey, *The Hope: A Guide to Sacred Activism*, Hay House, Inc., Carlsbad, CA, p. 58.
47 *BgG* 4:18–20; trans. E. Easwaran, 1985, p. 87.
48 *Chāndogya Up.* 6:9–10; trans. E. Easwaran, 1995, p. 184f.
49 A summary of the *Vedas* might be: The *Vedas* acknowledge one ultimate truth, the supreme Spirit. This Spirit has innumerable immanent aspects, yet infinitely transcends all of them. As to Buddhism, see the Introduction to this book for three types of non-dualism recognized by Buddhist scholar/practitioner David Loy. Loy claims that Buddhist 'ungroundedness' amounts to being the source of spirituality. Our surrender to 'ungroundedness' discloses it to be formless and limitless. Hence Loy can adhere to a notion of transcendence, albeit one that would seem to exclude a Hindu or Judeo-Christian vision of inherent Ultimacy.
50 I am indebted, for some of these words, to Albert Nolan. When I was given a grant to study as an undergraduate at Cambridge, two special books came my way. These led me to look beyond the vitiated theism and the effete structures of parts of the anthrocentric and hierarchical church. Nolan's *Jesus Before Christianity: The Gospel of Liberation* (Darton, Longman and Todd, London, 1977) was one; the other was W. H. Vanstone's *Love's Endeavour, Love's Expense: The Response of Being to the Love of God* (Darton, Longman and Todd, London, 1977). These books also helped me to see past my disapproval of the narcissism of evangelists. Billy Graham ran a severely dualistic 'campaign' in Cambridge while I was there. True to his conditioning, he announced his disdain for theologians, including by implication those people who translated the (RSV) bible which he brandished.
51 Along these lines, a play of complementary energies was revered in Hinduism, some centuries before Judaism, Buddhism, Christianity and Islam first entered the imagination of human consciousness.
52 In my conditioning, the divine-as-triune provides a theopoetic foundation for intersubjective relations. Within 'God-self' the Spirit is regarded as the agent of a 'full' co-inhering or co-indwelling. Whatever one 'member' of the Godhead knows and

does, the 'others' know and do. One of the functions of the concept 'God the Son' is that it draws attention to the idea that the divine relates to that which is 'other', notably to *us*. NT passages which situate the notion of *perichoresis* in Christian theology include Jn 5:19–23, most of Jn 17 and most of 1 Cor. 2.

53 Traherne's near-contemporary Angelus Silesius (Johannes Scheffler) believed himself graced with non-dual wisdom rather than with the capacity to reason. Editions of his poems, particularly in German, are numerous. Scheffler was well-read in Eckhart; there is a sense in which he was the latter's versifier.

54 Traherne might have regarded traditional prayer, of the beseeching kind, as intellectually incoherent. We cannot know his true position; we might recognize ourselves as oscillating between unitive experience and dualistic experience, and as praying accordingly.

55 An aphorism from the teachings of Nisargadatta Maharaj (d.1981) has become well known in modern *Advaitin* circles. It runs as follows: 'When I see I am nothing, that is wisdom. When I see I am everything, that is love. My life is a movement between these two'. I am not implying that the traditions of Traherne and Nisargadatta are 'saying the same thing'. But, most curiously, Eckhart and Nisargadatta employ similar words, especially with respect to 'nothing' and 'everything'.

56 J. M. Clark & J. V. Skinner, ed. & trans., *Meister Eckhart: Selected Treatises and Sermons*, Collins/Fontana, London (1st edn Faber & Faber, 1958) 1963, p. 50. (This sermon is #39 in the critical German edition.)

57 In this connection, Merold Westphal writes: 'The bad news (to the false self) is that self-transcendence is self-denial. The good news (to the false self at the end of its tether) is that self-transcendence is self-discovery. Precisely as command, the voice of transcendence offers to the decentered self a triune gift – its own truest self in proper relation both to God and to neighbor'. Quotation from: M. Westphal, *Transcendence and Self-Transcendence: On God and the Soul*, Indiana University Press, Bloomington, IN, 2004, p. 226.

58 If I am correct here, the situation might be alleviated by greater emphasis on the essential interdependence of (all) phenomena. Cf. The analogy of Indra's net, in which any one jewel can be considered as empty because it only reflects all the other jewels. Contrariwise, any one jewel can be considered as full, because it contains all the other jewels. The main 'lesson' of Indra's net (to me) is that I had better keep waking up in order to experience the world non-dualistically.

59 See Chapter 4 regarding Weil and attention-giving.

60 Seldom used in Eckhart (as *Isticheit*) but of interest to me because of its implication of direct experience and/or Realization. Julian and Traherne do not use 'is-ness', as such, but can be taken to imply it. See Chapters 1 and 3.

61 For example, the putting forward of an ontological claim can be seen as a call (subtle or otherwise) for imaginative openness.

62 Cf. A remark by Stanislas Breton, '. . . the speculative principle of the *Logos* and the poetic principle of the *Mythos* are committed to each other in a creative conflict which unfolds in the free space of the *imaginaire*' (p. 141). Breton is quoted and referenced in Chapter 3 in connection with Phil. 2.

63 Ramana produced a loose translation in Tamil of a basic treatise on *Advaita* attributed to Śhaṅkara. The treatise is *The Crown Gem of Discrimination* (Skt. *Vivekachudamani*).

64 T. A. Forsthoefel, *Knowing Beyond Knowledge: Epistemologies of religious experience in classical and modern Advaita*, Motilal Banarsidass Publishers, Delhi, 2007, p. 142f.

65   Ibid., p. 179.

66   In Christian terms, Dorothy Lee could be commenting on Traherne's repeated use of 'Bliss', 'Delight' and 'Delightfull' when she writes: 'The rapture that draws God, as it were, out of heaven to earth also draws the believer out of an enclosed selfhood into the beauty and luminosity of God. Towards this rapture – the beauty of the life of God – Jesus leads his faltering disciples, as he ascends the mount of transfiguration. Here beauty is closely linked, not only to love and yearning, but also to pleasure, enjoyment and ecstasy, an experience that is as much sensuous as spirited'. Quotation from: D. Lee, *Transfiguration*, Continuum, London, p. 129. I do not imply that Lee is sympathetic to the *Upanishadic* language of the 'Self'.

67   Cf. Ramana Maharshi on this question: 'God's grace consists in the act that He shines in the heart of everyone as the Self. That power of grace does not exclude anyone, whether good or otherwise'. Quoted but not referenced, in: *Diary for 2010*, Sri Ramanasramam, Tiruvannamalai, Tamil Nadu.

68   I have not intended, in these reflections, to dismiss metaphysics *per se*. A. N. Whitehead points out that early Christians, given their contexts and their spiritual experiences, were obliged to tackle metaphysical issues. Principally, they had to attempt an adequate expression of a real immanence of God in the world. See Whitehead's *Adventures of Ideas*, The Free Press, NY, 1967 (or various much earlier editions).

69   See Jean-Luc Marion's *God without Being*, trans. T. A. Carlson, Chicago University Press, Chicago, IL, 1991.

70   To allude to the words of Karl Barth, an icon 'both unveils and veils' something of reality. I think Barth is advocating the view that God is not to be grasped; God is not cognitively understandable. That which is valuable must therefore be a relationship of dependency and trust.

71   This does not imply that there are two competing cosmologies, or that one or other of the two perspectives should be seen as static and unchanging.

72   In the language of *Vedānta*, and of Ramana Maharshi, this experience would be described as surrender to, or abidance in, Self-happiness (*Ātmā-sukhām*). It presupposes acceptance of the Self as the one Reality which 'works' from both within and without to bring about the transcendence of 'I-ness'.

73   The importance of truth as 'not truth unless lived out bodily' has been emphasized throughout the present study as a *sine qua non* of my three writers. It is truth understood to be literally 'experience-able' (*erfahrbar*).

74   Quotation from: S. Žižek & J. Milbank, *The Monstrosity of Christ: Paradox or Dialectic?* (C. Davis, ed.), The MIT Press, Cambridge, MA, 2009, p. 207.

75   Hence I can hypothesize that Traherne might have concurred with the general direction of twentieth-century process theology.

76   See Schürmann, p. xv.

77   R. J. Woods, *Eckhart's Way*, Veritas, Dublin [1986], 2009, p. 40; italics in the original.

78   *My Spirit, Goodnesse* and *Sister Spider* are quoted in Chapter 1.

79   Margoliouth, vol. 1, p. 26f.

80   *Centuries* 3:20, p. 122.

81   Like all other theologies, the one which might be called 'a relational theopoetic' is language-bound. But it rightly presumes to make reference to That which is not language-bound.

82   The quotation is from Ramana's short but principal work *Who Am I?* This is published in *The Collected Works of Sri Ramana Maharshi*, p. 43.

A Way Forward

1 Aspects of philosophy seem today to be following theology in a 'participatory turn'.
2 T. A. Forsthoefel, *Knowing Beyond Knowledge: Epistemologies of religious experience in classical and modern Advaita*, Motilal Banarsidass Publishers, Delhi, 2007.
3 Ridler, p. 14.
4 Different renderings of Ex. 3:14 ('I Am That I Am') were briefly mentioned in Chapter 2.
5 Jn 10:30, NRSV.
6 Eckhart uses the words *mit Eigenschaft* ('with attachment to self'). Thus he connotes an individual possessiveness which might generate the illusion of separate existence. To countermand *Eigenschaft*, Eckhart puts forward the interior activity of 'cutting loose', *abegescheidenheit*, which characterizes the letting-be or releasement of *Gelâzenheit*. There is no precise equation between the lesser or false self (of long tradition) and the ego (of modernist characterization). The contexts for the respective usages are incompatible. Nonetheless, 'ego' can serve, on the understanding that through mindfulness it can become an object of awareness.
7 Loy, p. 291.
8 A more recent exemplar of sub-continental *abheda bhakti*, namely, Mata Amritanandamayi (born 1953) likewise inculcates a union of the absolute level of truth and the relative or conventional level of truth.

Bibliography

'A monk of the west' (2004), *Christianity and the Doctrine of Non-Dualism*, trans. A. Moore, Jr. & M. M. Hansen, Hillsdale, NY: Sophia Perennis.

Abhishiktananda (1998), *Ascent to the Depth of the Heart*, ed. R. Panikkar, Delhi: ISPCK.

Backhouse, H. (ed.) (1966), *The Best of Meister Eckhart*, New York: Crossroad Publishing Company.

Balakier, J. J. (2010), *Thomas Traherne and the Felicities of the Mind*, New York: Cambria Press.

Barnhart, B. (2007), *The Future of Wisdom: Toward a Rebirth of Sapiential Christianity*, New York: Continuum.

Barratt, A. (2002), 'Julian of Norwich and the Holy Spirit, Our Good Lord', *Mystics Quarterly* 28, 2, pp. 78–84.

Barrett, C. K. (2nd edn, 1978), *The Gospel According to St John: An Introduction with Commentary and Notes on the Greek Text*, London: SPCK.

Bellette, A. F. (1968), *Form and Vision in Four Metaphysical Poets*, PhD thesis, Vancouver: University of British Columbia.

—. (1983), *Profitable Wonders: An Essay on Thomas Traherne*, unpublished manuscript.

Berthold, G. C. (ed. and trans.) (1985), *Maximus the Confessor: Selected Writings*, New York: Paulist Press.

Blevins, J. (ed.) (2007), *Re-Reading Traherne: A Collection of New Critical Essays*, Tempe, AZ: Arizona Centre for Medieval and Renaissance Studies.

Boesel, C. and Keller, C. (eds) (2010), *Apophatic Bodies: Negative Theology, Incarnation, and Relationality*, New York: Fordham University Press.

Bohm, D. (1983), *Wholeness and the Implicate Order*, London: Routledge & Kegan Paul.

Bourgeault, C. (2009), 'Centering Prayer and Attention of the Heart', *Crosscurrents* 59, 1, pp. 15–27.

Bradley, R. (1992), *Julian's Way: A Practical Commentary on Julian of Norwich*, London: Harper Collins.

Breton, S. (2002), *The Word and the Cross*, trans. J. Porter, New York: Fordham University Press.

Burrows, R. (1976), *Guidelines for Mystical Prayer*, London: Sheed and Ward.

—. (1978), *To Believe in Jesus*, London: Sheed and Ward.

Campbell, D. A. (2009), *The Deliverance of God: An Apocalyptic Rereading of Justification in Paul*, Grand Rapids, MI: Eerdmans Publishing.

Caputo, J. D. (2006), *The Weakness of God: A Theology of the Event*, Bloomington, IN: Indiana University Press.

Charlton, J. A. (2001), *Luminous Bodies*, Hobart, Tasmania: Montpelier Press.

—. (2007), *So Much Light*, Hobart, Tasmania: Pardalote Press.

Clark, J. M. and Skinner, J. V. (1958; 1963), *Meister Eckhart: Selected Treatises and Sermons*, London: Fontana/Collins.

Clements, A. L. (1969), *The Mystical Poetry of Thomas Traherne*, Cambridge, MA: Harvard University Press.

Cobb, J. B. (1999), *Transforming Christianity and the World: A Way Beyond Absolutism and Relativism*, New York: Orbis Books.

Colledge, E. and McGinn, B. (trans.) (1981), *Meister Eckhart: The Essential Sermons, Commentaries, Treatises and Defense*, New York: Paulist Press.

Colledge, E. and Walsh, J. (trans.) (1978), *Julian of Norwich: Showings*, Mahwah, NJ: Paulist Press.

Davies, O. (1991), *Meister Eckhart: Mystical Theologian*, London: SPCK.

—. (1994), *Meister Eckhart: Selected Writings*, London: Penguin.

Deane-Drummond, C. (2009), *Christ and Evolution: Wonder and Wisdom*, London: SCM Press.

Dearbon, K. (2002), 'The Crucified Christ as the Motherly God: The Theology of Julian of Norwich', *Scottish Journal of Theology* 55, 3, pp. 283–302.

de Caussade, J.-P. (1975), *Abandonment to Divine Providence*, New York: Image/Doubleday.

Demkovitch, M. (2005, 2006), *Introducing Meister Eckhart*, Saint Paul University: Novalis; Ligouri, MO: Ottowa & Ligouri Publications.

Donohue-White, P. (2005), 'Reading Divine Maternity in Julian of Norwich', *Spiritus* 5, pp. 19–36.

Easwaran, E. (trans.) (1985), *The Bhagavadgita*, London: Penguin/Arkana.

—. (trans.) (1995), *The Upanishads*, London: Penguin/Arkana.

Fiand, B. (2008), *Awe-Filled Wonder: The Interface of Science and Spirituality*, Mahwah, NJ: Paulist Press.

Forsthoefel, T. A. (2002; Indian edn 2007), *Knowing beyond Knowledge: Epistemologies of Religious Experience in Classical and Modern Advaita*, Delhi: Motilal Banarsidass Publishers.

Freeman, L. (1999), *Common Ground: Letters to a World Community of Meditators*, New York: Continuum.

Gadamer, H.-G. (1989: 2nd rev edn; this edition 2004), *Truth and Method*, New York: Continuum.

Godman, D. (ed.) (1985), *Be As You Are: The Teachings of Sri Ramana Maharshi*, London: Penguin/Arkana.

Hamilton, C. (2008), *The Freedom Paradox: Towards a Post-Secular Ethics*, Crows Nest, NSW: Allen & Unwin.

Hart, Mother Columba (trans. and intro.) (1980), *Hadewijch: The Complete Works*, Mahwah, NJ: Paulist Press.

Harvey, A. (2000), *The Direct Path: Creating a Journey to the Divine through the World's Mystical Traditions*, New York: Broadway Books.

—. (2009), *The Hope: A Guide to Sacred Activism*, Carlsbad, CA: Hay House, Inc.

Hick, J. and Knitter, P. F. (eds) (1987), *The Myth of Christian Uniqueness*, New York: Orbis Books.

Hopper, S. R. (1992), *The Way of Transfiguration: Religious Imagination as Theopoiesis*, R. M. Keiser & T. Stoneburner (eds), Louisville, KY: Westminster/John Knox Press.

Inge, D. (2009), *Wanting Like a God: Desire and Freedom in Thomas Traherne*, London: SCM Press.

Ingram, P. O. and Streng, F. J. (eds) (1986), *Buddhist-Christian Dialogue: Mutual Renewal and Transformation*, Honolulu: University of Hawaii Press.

Jantzen, G. M. (1987; reprinted with new Intro., 2005), *Julian of Norwich: Mystic and Theologian*, Eugene, OR: Wipf & Stock.

Kearney, R. (2001), *The God Who May Be*, Bloomington, IN: Indiana University Press.

Keel, H.-S. (2007), *Meister Eckhart: An Asian Perspective*, Leuven: Peeters Press.

Keller, C. (1986), *From a Broken Web: Separation, Sexism and Self*, Boston, MA: Beacon Press.

—. (2008), *On the Mystery: Discerning Divinity in Process*, Minneapolis, MN: Fortress Press.

Kelley, C. F. (1977; this edition 2009), *Meister Eckhart on Divine Knowledge*, Cobb, CA: Dharma Café Books.

Kershaw, A. (2005), *The Poetic of the Cosmic Christ in Thomas Traherne's The Kingdom of God*, unpublished PhD thesis, Perth: University of Western Australia.

Kierkegaard, S. (1958), *Journals 1834–1854*, trans. & ed. A. Dru, London: Fontana.

LaCugna, C. M. (1991), *God for Us: The Trinity and Christian Life*, San Francisco, CA: Harper Collins.

Lamm, J. A. (2005), 'Revelation as Exposure in Julian of Norwich's *Showings*', *Spiritus* 5, pp. 54–78.

Lanzetta, B. J. (1992), 'Three Categories of Nothingness in Eckhart', *The Journal of Religion* 72, 2, pp. 248–68.

Lee, D. (2004), *Transfiguration*, London: Continuum.

Llewelyn, R. (ed.) (1985), *Julian: Woman of our Day*, London: Darton, Longman and Todd.

Lomperis, L. and Stanbury, S. (eds) (1993), *Feminist Approaches to the Body in Medieval Literature*, Philadelphia, PA: University of Pennsylvania Press.

Lossky, V. (1957; 2005), *The Mystical Theology of the Eastern Church*, Cambridge: James Clark.

Love, H. (ed.) (1972), *Restoration Literature: Critical Approaches*, London: Methuen & Co.

Loy, D. (1988), *Nonduality: A Study in Comparative Philosophy*, New Haven, CT: Yale University Press.

Mahadevan, T. M. P. (2010), *Ramana Maharshi and his Philosophy of Existence*, Tiruvannamalai, Tamil Nadu: Sri Ramanasramam.

Malpas, J., Arnswald, U. and Kertscher, J. (eds) (2002), *Gadamer's Century: Essays in Honor of Hans-Georg Gadamer*, Cambridge, MA: The MIT Press.

Margoliouth, H. M. (ed.) (1958), *Thomas Traherne: Centuries, Poems, and Thanksgivings*, 2 vols, London: Oxford University Press.

Marion, J.-L. (1991), *God without Being*, trans. T. A. Carlson, Chicago, IL: Chicago University Press.

Martz, L. L. (revised edn 1962), *The Poetry of Meditation: A Study in English Religious Literature of the Seventeenth Century*, New Haven, CT: Yale University Press.

—. (1964), *The Paradise Within*, New Haven, CT: Yale University Press.

McFague, S. (1993), *The Body of God: An Ecological Theology*, Minneapolis, MN: Fortress Press.

—. (1997), *Super, Natural Christians: How We Should Love Nature*, Minneapolis, MN: Fortress Press.

McGinn, B. (ed.) (1986), in collaboration with F. Tobin and E. Borgstadt, *Meister Eckhart: Teacher and Preacher*, New York: Paulist Press.

—. (2001), *The Mystical Thought of Meister Eckhart*, New York: Crossroad Publishing Company.

—. (2008), 'Mystical Consciousness: A Modest Proposal', *Spiritus* 8, pp. 44–63.

Metz, J. B. (1998), *Poverty of Spirit*, New York: Paulist Press.

Miles, M. R. (2008), *Rereading Historical Theology*, Eugene, OR: Cascade Books.

Mitchell, D. W. (1991), *Spirituality and Emptiness: The Dynamics of Spiritual Life in Buddhism and Christianity*, New York: Paulist Press.

Moore, S. (1989), *Jesus the Liberator of Desire*, New York: Crossroad Publishing Company.

Nolan, A. (1977), *Jesus before Christianity: The Gospel of Liberation*, London: Darton, Longman and Todd.

Osborne, A. (1954), *Ramana Maharshi and the Path of Self-Knowledge*, London: Rider and Co.

—. (1987), *The Teachings of Ramana Maharshi*, London: Rider/Century Hutchinson.

—. (ed.) (1997), *The Collected Works of Ramana Maharshi*, York Beach, ME: Samuel Weiser.

Panikkar, R. (2004), *Christophany: The Fullness of Man*, New York: Orbis Books.

—. (2006), *The Experience of God: Icons of the Mystery*, Minneapolis, MN: Fortress Press.

—. (2010), *The Rhythm of Being*, New York: Orbis Books.

Paul, Sr, Mary (1976), *All Shall Be Well: Julian of Norwich and the Compassion of God*, Convent of the Incarnation, Fairacres, Oxford: SLG Press.

Pierce, B. J. (2005), *We Walk the Path Together: Learning from Thich Nhat Hanh and Meister Eckhart*, New York: Orbis Books.

Radler, C. (2006), 'Losing the Self: Detachment in Meister Eckhart and Its Significance for Buddhist-Christian Dialogue', *Buddhist-Christian Studies* 26, pp. 111–17.

Ramana Maharshi (2009), *The Collected Works*, Tiruvannamalai, Tamil Nadu: Sri Ramanasramam.

Reinhard, K. L. (2007), 'Joy to the Father, Bliss to the Son: Unity and the Motherhood Theology of Julian of Norwich', *Anglican Theological Review* 89, 4, pp. 629–45.

Ridler, A. (1966), *Thomas Traherne: Poems, Centuries and Three Thanksgivings*, London: Oxford University Press.

Rorem, P. (2008), 'Negative Theologies and the Cross', *Harvard Theological Review* 101, 3–4, pp. 451–64.

Rose, G. (1997), *Love's Work*, London: Vintage.

Ross, H. McG. (ed.) (1991), *The Gospel of Thomas*, London: Element Books.

Ross, J. (ed.) (2005 and thereafter), *The Works of Thomas Traherne*, a multivolume, definitive edition currently under progressive release, beginning with texts discovered relatively recently, Cambridge: D. S. Brewer.

Salter, K. W. (1964), *Thomas Traherne: Mystic and Poet*, London: Edward Arnold Ltd.

Schaab, G. L. (2007), *The Creative Suffering of the Triune God*, New York: Oxford University Press.

Schneider, L. C. (2008), *Beyond Monotheism: A Theology of Multiplicity*, London: Routledge.

Schürmann, R. (2001), *Wandering Joy: Meister Eckhart's Mystical Philosophy*, Great Barrington, MA: Lindisfarne Books.

Sherrard, P. (1992), *Human Image: World Image*, Ipswich: Golgonooza Press.

Sithamparanathan, J. (2008), *Ramana Maharshi's Philosophy of Existence and Modern Science*, Delhi: Motilal Banarsidass Publishers.

Smith, C. (1987), *The Way of Paradox: Spiritual Life as taught by Meister Eckhart*, London: Darton, Longman & Todd.

Smith, W. (2008), *Christian Gnosis: From Saint Paul to Meister Eckhart*, San Rafael, CA: Sophia Perennis.

Soelle, D. (2001), *The Silent Cry: Mysticism and Resistance*, Minneapolis, MN: Fortress Press.

Sri Sadhu Om (2008), *The Path of Sri Ramana (Part One)*, Tiruvannamalai, Tamil Nadu: Sri Ramana Kshetra.

Stewart, S. (1970), *The Expanded Voice: The Art of Thomas Traherne*, San Marino, CA: Henry E. Huntington Library and Art Gallery.

Stramara, D. F. (1998), 'Gregory of Nyssa's Terminology for Trinitarian Perichoresis', *Vigiliae Christianae* 52, 3, pp. 257–63.

Stuart, J. (2000), *Swami Abhishiktananda: His life told through his letters*, Delhi: ISPCK.

Tatakis, B. (1949; 2003), *Byzantine Philosophy*, trans. & intro. N. J. Moutafakis, Indianapolis, IN: Hackett Publishing Co.

Taylor, C. (1989), *Sources of the Self: the Making of the Modern Identity*, Cambridge, MA: Harvard University Press.

—. (1991), *The Ethics of Authenticity*, Cambridge, MA: Harvard University Press.

Teilhard (de Chardin), P. (1965), *Hymn of the Universe*, London: William Collins.

Thunberg, L. (1995; 2nd edn), *Microcosm and Mediator: The Theological Anthropology of Maximus the Confessor*, Chicago, IL: Open Court.

Turner, D. (1995), *The Darkness of God: Negativity in Christian Mysticism*, Cambridge: Cambridge University Press.

—. (2004), *Faith, Reason and the Existence of God*, Cambridge: Cambridge University Press.

Unno, T. (1998), *River of Fire, River of Water: An Introduction to the Pure Land Tradition of Shin Buddhism,* New York: Doubleday.

Vysheslavtsev, B. P. (2002), *The Eternal in Russian Philosophy*, Grand Rapids, MI: Eerdmans Publishing.

Walshe, M. O'C. (trans. and ed.) (1979, 1981, 1985), *Meister Eckhart: Sermons and Treatises*, 3 vols, London and Shaftesbury: Watkins/Element Books.

—. (2009), *The Complete Mystical Works of Meister Eckhart*, rev. edn, B. McGinn, London & New York: Crossroad Publishing Company.

Ward, Sr, Benedicta (trans.) (1973), *The Prayers and Meditations of Saint Anselm*, Harmondsworth: Penguin.

Weil, S. (1951; 1973), *Waiting for God,* trans. E Craufurd, New York: Harper & Row.

—. (1952; 1978), *The Need for Roots,* trans. A. Wills, London: Routledge & Kegan Paul.

Westphal, M. (2004), *Transcendence and Self-Transcendence: On God and the Soul*, Bloomington, IN: Indiana University Press.

Williams, R. (1979), *The Wound of Knowledge: Christian Spirituality from the New Testament to St John of the Cross*, London: Darton, Longman & Todd.

—. (2007), *Wrestling with Angels: Conversation in Modern Theology*, London: SCM Press.

Wolters, C. (trans.) (1966), *Julian of Norwich: Revelations of Divine Love*, Harmondsworth: Penguin.

Woods, R. J. (1986, 2009), *Eckhart's Way*, Dublin: Veritas Publications.

—. (2011), *Meister Eckhart: Master of Mystics*, London: Continuum.

Zimmermann, J. (2004), *Recovering Theological Hermeneutics: An Incarnational-Trinitarian Theory of Interpretation*, Grand Rapids, MI: Baker Academic.

Žižek, S. and Milbank, J. (2009; Davis, C. ed.), *The Monstrosity of Christ: Paradox or Dialectic?* Cambridge, MA: The MIT Press.

Index

balanced with immanence 4, 8, 37,
  63–4, 66, 77, 117, 126, 129–31, 138,
  143, 145, 155, 177n. 14, 179n. 49
Transgressive Saints (Charlton) 75–6, 80,
  172n. 29
Trinity 42, 61, 67, 78, 80, 83–5, 89, 105, 151,
  158n. 19, 168n. 6, 177n. 16
  perichoresis 2, 5, 39, 43, 71, 91, 103,
    112, 120, 129, 131, 134, 138, 145,
    155, 158n. 17
Truganini's Soliloquy (Charlton) 120,
  175n. 86
Turner, Denys 63, 156n. 4, 165n. 38

Unno, Taitetsu 158n. 22
Upanishads 25, 55, 63, 65–6, 136–7,
  157n. 11, 158n. 23, 160n. 35,
  167n. 90, 169n. 44, 171n. 26,
  181n. 66
Upanishads, Mahānārāyana,
  12:4 158n. 23
Upcher, Janet 114, 175n. 88

Vattimo, Gianni 111, 173n. 63, 175n. 85
Vaughan, Henry 18
Vedānta, Advaita,
  doctrine of self 15, 35, 59, 105, 148–51,
    153–4, 157nn. 9, 11, 170nn. 3, 49,
    175n. 84

inward focus 132, 136, 176n. 91
oneness with divine 53–5, 65, 72, 122,
  139, 141, 145, 153–4, 166n. 65,
  167n. 90, 170n. 7, 171n. 9, 174n. 70,
  181n. 72
Ramana Maharshi 3–4, 39, 51, 93,
  180n. 63
relation to Christianity 20, 74, 95–7,
  100, 117–20, 129–30, 180n. 55

Walking (Traherne) 90–1
Walking in Tamil Nadu (Charlton) 95
Wegman, Sheelagh 175n. 88
Weil, Simone 58, 80, 81, 100–2, 140,
  172n. 29, 180n. 59
Westphal, Merold 180n. 57
Whitehead, Alfred North 91, 155,
  181n. 68
Whitman, Walt 15
Williams, Charles 156n. 6
Williams, Rowan 102
Without images (Charlton) 55
Wonder (Traherne) 19, 35–7, 45, 64, 132–3
Woods, Richard 73, 144

Yellow-tailed Black Cockatoos
  (Charlton) 7

Zimmermann, Jens 176n. 8

CPSIA information can be obtained at www.ICGtesting.com
Printed in the USA
LVOW08s1019150514

385925LV00001B/38/P